PROPHETIC WORSHIP

Vivien Hibbert

ISBN 1-892976-03-X

Unless otherwise indicated, all Scripture quotations are from *Life Application Bible: New King James Version.* Copyright © 1988, 1989, 1990, 1991, 1993 by Tyndale House Publishers

Scripture quotations marked (KJV) are taken from the *King James Version.*

Scripture quotations marked (Amp.) are taken from *The Amplified Bible,* Copyright © 1965 by Zondervan Publishing House.

Scripture quotations marked (NASV) are taken from *New American Standard Version,* Copyright © 1969, 1962, 1963, 1968, 1971, 1972, 1973, 1975, 1977 by The Lockman Foundation.

Scripture quotations marked (NIV) are taken from the *New International Version,* Copyright © 1973, 1978, 1984 by International Bible Society.

Scripture quotations marked (Moffatt) are taken from *A New Translation of The Bible Containing the Old and New Testaments,* Copyright © 1922, 1924, 1925, 1926, 1935 by James Moffatt, Harper & Brothers Publishers, New York, NY.

Scripture quotations marked (NEB) are taken from the *New English Bible* © 1961,1970 by Oxford University Press and Cambridge University Press.

Scripture quotations marked (1912 Weymouth NT) are taken from the *1912 Weymouth New Testament.*

Printed in the United States by:
Morris Publishing • 3212 East Highway 30, Kearney, NE 68847
1-800-650-7888

CONTENTS

PART THREE:
Prophetic Worship—A New Exemplar

ACKNOWLEDGMENTS

I would like to thank the following family members and friends for all their input, assistance, encouragement and prayer over the past year as I have worked on this project. I feel that all have been partners in writing this book:

Stephen, Meghann and Chad—thank you for putting up with me when I needed silence. You guys are the greatest. I am proud of you three.

Rebecca, my assistant extraordinaire—you have been there for me, day and night, while writing this book. You have prepared meals, checked spelling, researched various subjects, edited, encouraged, prayed, and have supported me in every endeavor during this long and often painful process. God has enriched my life with yours. You are worthy of this title of greatness: *doulos*

Graham and Bev Wallace, my parents—you have given me the best gift that any parents can give their children. You gave yourselves to such an extent that I now hold excellent tools with which to succeed in life; I have hope for the future and a path of integrity to follow forever.

Pastor Olen, Syble, the elders and their wives, staff, Fine Arts Department and Shady Grove Church congregation in Grand Prairie, Texas—you have been my teachers as we have worshiped together. Your pursuit of God's presence has inspired me again and again. "Y'all" have a home in my heart forever. Thank you for the privilege of serving among you.

Charlotte Baker—I have always wanted to grow up and be like you. You are a faithful pioneer, prophet, and mentor to everyone in ministry. To me you are also a friend and mother. I run behind you with great joy.

Jo G.; David and Elaine; Brad and Julie; LaMar and Teresa; Steve and Mary G.; Mary Ann M.; Martha V.; Carl and Yvonne; Teresa and Linda; Renie and Lynn; Pat B.; Pat O.; Candy, Jean and Judy; David and Winona and all of the gracious friends who have prayed for and supported me as I have labored to write this book—I am forever grateful for your love and practical help. You have been a rich blessing to me; thank you all.

To my precious friends in Colombia, Curacao, Ireland, Norway, Singapore, Malaysia and all around the globe where we travel with this message—thank you for your love and prayers. You are so dear to me. Your nations live in our hearts.

Mitch Land—thank you for your editorial help. I appreciate the time you have taken to read this manuscript and offer suggestions. As always, you are a prince.

Mark Carruth, friend and editor—you are such a wealth of information, practical help and kindness. Like a box of treasure, I always marvel at the abundance of your knowledge, giftings, grace and friendship. Thank you for your help with this book.

FOREWORD

Olen Griffing

... "Worship God! For the testimony of Jesus
is the spirit of prophecy."
(Revelation 19:10b)

⬤

"Why," one might ask, "Do we need another book on worship?" However, in the case of this book, one might ask a totally different question: "Why wasn't it written sooner?" I sense God is desiring to bring a greater unity to the Body of Christ in the realm of worship. Even though I believe this book is in the perfect timing of God, I admit to having not a little concern that such a comprehensive treatment on worship had not been written.

In the season in which we live there are many ideas about worship. The reason for this is the great hunger which the Holy Spirit has divinely imparted to the people of God. Because of this hunger we either jump in over our heads where even angels fear to tread, or we get in just enough to get our feet wet. While maintaining a thoroughly Biblical perspective, the contents of this book will produce an assurance in your heart that extravagant worship is not "risky," but will be transforming and reviving to all.

The bottom line concerning worship is obedience to God. A life of obedience is the highest expression of worship. Though having said that, I emphatically believe what takes place in a sanctuary while His people are gathered is of greater importance than most believe. Worship is encountering God. Could it be that a sense of supernatural awe could be restored to the Church if through worship she pressed into God's presence? A "worship service" is simply His people gathered around His presence, worshiping in spirit and truth until they see or experience something which can only be explained as a God "thing."

A need has arisen which can only be satisfied by one on whom rests the anointing of God. Vivien Hibbert is one anointed with tremendous insight into the kind of worship which changes lives, churches and nations. I believe a mantle is upon her to proclaim the glorious truth about prophetic worship. She and her husband, Michael, have served together to bring fresh vision for worship to churches all over the world. She has pastored, so she has the understanding of a pastor's heart. While serving as worship director for the church I pastor, she truly brought Scriptural understanding of prophetic worship and a release of God's presence in our midst. It is her heart's desire to see the glory of the Lord cover the earth as the waters cover the seas.

If followed, the truths expressed in this book will help develop and keep worship life-changing and fresh for any congregation. I know of no other book as comprehensive as this concerning prophetic worship. Once you apprehend the heart of what God has shown Vivien, you will never again be satisfied with substituting a "song" service for a worship service.

Olen Griffing, Senior Pastor
Shady Grove Church
Grand Prairie, Texas

PREFACE

*The great search of the human heart is the search to discover the One
who is worthy of our worship.*
Sammy Tippit

≈

The prayer of all those who have helped with this project is that
this book will inspire worship in the hearts of every reader. Please
look beyond the words on these pages. My desire is to express the
heart of the Father as He longs for communion with His people.
May you see His face. May the weight of His glory constrain you
as you read these words. May something of eternity be opened to
you, and may your hunger for God be increased and even over-
whelm you.

> The (Holy) Spirit and the bride [the church, the true
> Christians] say, Come! And let him who is listening
> say, Come! And let every one come who is thirsty [who
> is painfully conscious of his need of those things by
> which the soul is refreshed, supported and strength-
> ened]; and whoever [earnestly] desires to do it, let him
> come and take and appropriate (drink) the Water of
> Life without cost. (Rev. 22:17 Amp)

Worship is the most fundamental activity of all mankind and
especially the church. It is born in the deepest longing of every
heart—the desire to know and be known. All true worship is a
delight to both God and man. It is God who initiates the call upon
the heart to arise to new places of intimacy and maturity in Him.
Because of this, He places within us a cry for more of Him. If the
Church is to minister life to all the earth, then this cry must
increase and be formed within us as our goal and chief end. The
longing for true communion in worship must become our life and
our breath. Worship is ultimately the key that unlocks our whole
lives before the Lord and provides a way of experiencing every
depth in Him.

At its very heart, worship is, and will always be, prophetic. Unfortunately, worship has not been taught or treated as prophetic in most of our churches, so few have glimpsed the glories or plumbed the depths of what God really intends for us as worshipers. Because of this lack, we have missed the very nature and essence of God's heart for us as we meet Him in church services and private devotion.

Worship is a greatly misunderstood word. Our experiences of praise and worship lie so far below their theological definitions that we tend to limit our practice of worship to the meager words expressed in the pages of our books and the words of our songs.

The word *worship* is often misunderstood, as is the word *revival*. Many churches post signs outside their buildings that inform the community of the dates of their next "revival." What they really mean is that special meetings are to be held at that location. Whether true revival occurs or not will depend on a sovereign act of God and the brokenness of His people.

This illustrates how many have reduced the meaning of *revival* to an event rather than an encounter with God. The same reduction has happened to the word *worship*. We may say that we have "worship services" on Sundays, but whether worship really takes place or not is a matter of debate.

To overcome this loss of meaning in the terms *revival* and *worship*, many writers are forced to add adjectives such as *true, real, genuine* or even *prophetic*. It would be the same as if I often said to you, "Let me give you some food," but all I ever gave you was a picture of food. If I wanted you to understand that there was really something to eat, I would have to indicate that the food on that particular occasion was "real."

I have tried to overcome such a loss of meaning with the title of this book. The term *prophetic worship* is really incorrect; all worship is prophetic by definition because it involves an encounter with the presence of God. It is not normal to have worship without an encounter with God. If God is not present it is impossible to worship. I have used the word *prophetic* as it is such an apt description of what takes place whenever we meet with the Lord. I am also trying to emphasize worship that is born in His presence rather than age-old traditions that have lost their significance. It is my conviction that people who give themselves to worship are also giving themselves to the spirit of prophecy. The reality of His presence and our communion with Him make worship prophetic. The problem with our definitions only arises when we stand back from His presence and refuse to commune with Him in the corporate worship setting. In that case, I would have to suggest that *true, real, genuine* or even *prophetic* worship is not taking place.

This book, *PROPHETIC WORSHIP*, is a call to every believer and artists of every sort to seriously consider the priority and possibilities of worship in their lives and ministries. Worship is the primary ministry of the angels; it is the only ministry that will continue for believers when they enter heaven; it is the ministry that causes the likeness of Christ to be formed in every heart, and it is the most noble of all earthly activities.

If major changes are not wrought in the core of our understanding and routine of worship, the only prospect we have as churches in these days is to reduce our spiritual expectations of worship and compensate by focusing on its musical presentation. But no matter how much practice we do or how many new songs we sing; no matter how many musical styles we incorporate or arts we include; no matter how many instruments we have in our band or what level of excellence we achieve, *we will not have worship unless we have God's presence.*

Take note of the plethora of skilled musicians and worship leaders in the Body of Christ today. Worship tapes are top sellers in Christian music stores. Exceptional new songs can be heard from every corner of the world and every denomination of the Church. Yet my questions to every musician and singer are these: *Where are we going in worship? Is it possible that there might be something more once the music has died down? Have we crafted the sight of God with our music so that the people can see and hear Him more clearly?* Let worship visit the arts, and the arts visit worship again. It is time for all the arts to return, both to the Church and to their place in worship. Let the Church experience genuine revival so that we might release prophetic artists to every nation, and have prophetic worship in every denomination.

In order for worship to resume its rightful place in our hearts and in the arts we must all make a serious commitment to becoming students of His presence. We must return to the simplicity of loving Jesus.

It is my desire that this book will point to Jesus and glorify Him. I have sought to make the motives of my heart pure. My desire is that every church and believer would be strengthened by reading this book. Ultimately, the truth of worship is found in Jesus Christ, Himself, not in the formats and traditions of our various denominations. Perhaps a new movement is being born in the Church, made up of believers of all denominations, nations, and generations—a zealous and worshiping people that arise from the north, south east, and west. These must be prophetic worshipers who hunger and thirst for the presence of God and who yield to His transforming work in their hearts.

Let us pray with Moses, the most dangerous prayer of the Bible:

. . . show me Your glory. (Ex. 33:18)

There are shelves of excellent books written on worship. I have no desire to rewrite these volumes or repeat the concepts that have already been penned. However, it is in humility that I seek to add some further thoughts to this vast subject. It is a subject that could never be fully explored, even after a thousand lifetimes.

I have already begun a second book on prophetic worship which will provide practical help for congregations, worship leaders, musicians, singers, dancers and other artists, explaining how to flow and participate in prophetic worship. It will be a much more practical guide for those desiring to train themselves and others in these truths.

I bless you as you read and enter into prophetic worship.

PART ONE

An Introduction to
PROPHETIC
WORSHIP

Chapter One

WHAT IS PROPHETIC WORSHIP?

Worship is the submission of all our nature to God.
It is the quickening of conscience by His holiness,
the nourishment of mind with His truth,
the purifying of imagination by His beauty,
the opening of the heart to His love,
the surrender of will to His purpose,
and all this gathered up in adoration,
the most selfless emotion of which our nature is capable
and, therefore, the chief remedy for that self-centeredness,
which is our original sin and the source of all actual sin.
William Temple

⚬⚬⚬

Worship is surely the most meaningful and delightful occupation of all humanity. God desires to be known by us and has made a way through our redemption for us to draw near to Him. It seems to me that humankind was made for worship. Every one of us will worship something or someone. Whatever we value the most and whatever captivates the deepest passions of our hearts will also earn our worship. All other occupations and activities on the earth only find their true meaning when they are experienced in the light of worship.

When we worship, we are loving the person of the Lord Jesus Christ—the One whom we meet as we praise Him and proclaim His excellencies.

Worship involves our deepest affections. When we consider the countless books and statements that have been written to define and refine worship, we come back to the same conclusion: Jesus must always remain the object and center of our worship.

> . . . For it is written, "you shall worship the LORD your God, and Him only you shall serve." (Matt. 4:10)

No matter what god a person may worship, our Lord far exceeds them all. He is excellent and far above any creature in heaven or earth. Every man, woman, and child is going to worship Him, either now, or when He returns—for He alone is worthy and is to be greatly praised.

> Therefore God also has highly exalted Him, and given Him a name which is above every name, that at the name of Jesus every knee should bow, of those in heaven, and of those on earth, and of those under the earth, and that every tongue should confess that Jesus Christ is Lord, to the glory of God the Father. (Phil. 2:9–11)

THE GOAL OF PROPHETIC WORSHIP

In the end, worship must be pleasing to God. We come before Him to minister to Him rather than have our own needs met; to wait on Him rather than include Him in our church program; to hear His voice rather than attend a religious concert; to abandon ourselves before Him rather than be part of a groomed or rehearsed program; to be changed by His glory rather than to have His seal of approval for our personal agendas. In the process of waiting on Him, ministering to Him and hearing His voice we do have our needs met, and His presence becomes a vital part of our church life and personal life.

In the end, worship must be pleasing
to God.

Because God's presence is real and powerful, it might be tempting for some of us (pastors included) to use worship and the presence of God as a means of achieving our own ends. Some seem to desire the presence of God only because it will attract more people to their churches.

We must never lose sight of our ultimate objective as Christians and as the Church: that the Lord might be glorified. This must become our chief goal—the object and purpose of our very lives and the reason for every breath. As Tom Schwanda has said:

> In other words, worship is an end. It is not primarily a tool for evangelizing or attracting visitors or for recruiting teachers for Sunday school or advisors for the youth group. Neither is it intended to motivate or manipulate people into increasing contributions to the church. Nor is it a means to challenge people to become more involved in social justice or any other legitimate dimension of the church. . . . Things which are ends in themselves move us far more profoundly than things which are simply means to other ends.[1]

THE PREMISE OF PROPHETIC WORSHIP

Throughout this book, I want to explore the idea that *worship is, by definition, prophetic in nature.* This is the premise and underlying theme of every chapter. I believe that worship is prophetic by definition because all true worship flows from the presence and self-revelation of God. When God reveals Himself to man, worship will always be the result. Worship is not possible until God reveals Himself, but once He has revealed Himself, it is impossible for man *not* to worship Him. This thought may be repeated several times throughout the text, but it is a fundamental and pivotal concept of prophetic worship.

. . . worship is a natural response to an awareness of God's presence.[2] (Judson Cornwall)

. . . worship is the human response to divine revelation, set in a dialogue pattern.[3] (Ralph P. Martin)

Prophetic worship involves God's initial revelation of Himself through His Son, His Word, His creation, and His people; and the response of the worshipers, God's prophetic people.

The term *prophetic worship* is something of a misnomer, as true worship always has been and always will be *prophetic.* No matter what style or form it takes, worship "in spirit and in truth" (Jn. 4:24) is worship that is alive with the thoughts and voice of God.

In a wider sense God's voice and will encompass the essence of the term *prophetic*.

Prophetic worship is worship that goes beyond the realm of our songs, prayers, or readings and allows God to make Himself known in the midst of our forms. Paul spoke to the Philippians about the priority in his life of knowing Christ more and more. Worship is one of the most significant occupations of the soul that causes us to know Him.

> Yet indeed I also count all things loss for the excellence of the knowledge of Christ Jesus my Lord . . . (Phil. 3:8)

Prophetic worship allows God to have His way among us and "uncover" Himself before us through our songs, prayers, and worship forms. It is worship where we wait long enough in His presence to become aware of the conversation He desires to have with us. He longs to hear our voice, and He requires us to listen for His voice as He sings and speaks to us. Surely, this is what the Lord has intended for us all on a regular basis. Prophetic worship is to be experienced by all people—of all denominations, cultures, and generations—for it is the voice and heart of God, imparted to His people everywhere. Prophetic worship, then, is really an extended and explanatory name for worship itself.

PROPHETIC WORSHIP AND THE REVELATION OF GOD

In the first chapter of his letter to the Ephesians, Paul prayed that we would all gain a spirit of wisdom and revelation in order that we would know Him and His work in our hearts in greater measure.

> [For I always pray] the God of our Lord Jesus Christ, the Father of Glory, that He may grant you a spirit of wisdom and revelation—of insight into mysteries and secrets—in the [deep and intimate] knowledge of Him, by having the eyes of your heart flooded with light, so that you can know and understand the hope to which He has called you and how rich is His glorious inheritance in the saints—His set-apart ones. (Eph. 1:17–18, see also through verse 23)

It is this "spirit of wisdom and revelation" that is so important in worship. In His presence, the ". . . eyes of our hearts are flooded with light. . . " so that we might know Him and the ". . . riches of the glory of His inheritance" (KJV). True prophetic worship is inseparable from revelation. God desires to reveal Himself day by day to His people in the midst of worship:

True prophetic worship is inseparable from revelation.

Worship leader and writer John Stevenson stresses the importance of prophetic worship among the entire congregation:

> I believe there should never be a time that we come together for worship that we don't end at a place where God can begin to move prophetically amongst His people. This is not just for worship leaders or musicians; God is wanting to move through His entire body this way.[4]

By writing about prophetic worship, I am not pushing some new doctrine. This is an attempt on my part to broaden the Church's understanding and experience of worship. The people of God have limited the scope and meaning of *worship* by using this term to describe their particular Sunday service. True worship is so much more than this. Worship in both the Old and New Testaments holds a vast meaning and consequence for believers—beginning with our personal relationship with God and ending with our place in eternity, where we will continue to behold Him forever as we offer unending adoration.

Pastor, author, and worship leader Bob Sorge defines prophetic worship this way:

> Prophetic worship is, quite simply, walking and talking with the Lord. . . . Worship is an exchange—it is two-way communication.[5]

PROPHETIC WORSHIP AND PROPHECY

We must remember that the overwhelming majority of Biblical prophecy does not involve the predicting of the future. It is primarily concerned with confronting a backslidden people with God's claim on their lives for righteousness and their future hope in Him. (When I use the term "prophetic," I am using it in its widest sense where God's voice, will, and character are made known to His people.)

In the New Testament, one of the main purposes for prophecy is not to tell of future events, but to edify the church:

> But he who prophesies speaks edification and exhortation and comfort to men. . . he who prophesies edifies the church. (Cor. 14:3–4)

Many wonder how prophecy and worship are related. In fact, they are very closely related. Prophecy is really the mind of God permeating the mind of man. Praise and worship produce the most natural atmosphere for entrance into the prophetic realm and to receive His mind, heart, and attributes. Bob Sorge concurs:

> Praise and worship are natural complements to the functioning of the gifts of the Spirit (see 1 Corinthians 12:4–11), particularly prophecy. Both relate to and interact with the prophetic ministry.[6]

While I plan to examine the connections between prophecy, music, and worship in my next book, I would like to point out that in 1 Chron. 25:1–7, we find David's chief musicians and leaders of worship—Asaph, Heman and Jeduthun—listed as prophets and seers in Israel. They, their sons and daughters prophesied with various instruments and were trained to be skillful in the prophetic song.

The primary Hebrew root word for *prophecy*, used on this and many other occasions, is *naba* (Strong's # 5012) meaning *to prophesy, to speak or sing by inspiration, to boil up, to pour out words with emotion*. A secondary meaning is *to chant, to sing sacred songs, to praise God while under divine influence*.

Sorge's definition of "moving prophetically" in worship is:

> . . . to move with an awareness of the desire and leading of the Holy Spirit moment by moment, to discern the direction of the Spirit, and to lead God's people into a fuller participation of that.[7]

A key scripture in understanding the link between prophecy and worship is Revelation 19:10. In this passage, John was taken into heaven by a vision and was somehow in the presence of an angel. He was so overwhelmed by the magnificent sight of the heavenly being that he prostrated himself before the angel. John either felt that the angel was God or represented God, or he was beside himself with excitement over the glorious sight. In response, the angel told John not to worship him:

> . . . do not do that! Worship God! For the testimony of Jesus is the spirit of prophecy. (Rev. 19:10) (See also Col. 2:18)

Here are some other translations of Rev. 19:10b that aid in clarifying the meaning of this verse:

> . . . worship God: for the testimony of Jesus is the spirit of prophecy. (KJV, NIV, NASB)

> . . . worship God! For the substance (essence) of the truth revealed by Jesus is the spirit of all prophecy—the vital breath, the inspiration of all inspired preaching and interpretation of the divine will and purpose [including both mine and yours]. (Amp.)

> . . . it is God you must worship, for the testimony of Jesus is the Spirit that inspires prophecy. (NEB)

> . . . worship God. Testimony to Jesus is the spirit which underlies Prophecy. (1912 Weymouth NT)

In other words, we could say that prophecy loosely covers these meanings:

- Whenever we testify of Him or make Him known in the earth we are participating in the *spirit of prophecy*.

- When the person, office, grace, obedience, sufferings, and death of Christ, and the glory following are made known, this is the *spirit of prophecy*.

- When the character, life and work of the Father, Son or Holy Spirit are revealed in any setting—individual or corporate—this is the *spirit of prophecy*.

- The *spirit of prophecy* is not a form of speaking or expression but a divine quickening. It is the life, will, and voice of God expressed in and through His people.

- The *spirit of prophecy* is the unction of the Holy Spirit in a given situation.

- The *spirit of prophecy* is the life and breath of God in our meetings.

We might also say that all the work of the Holy Spirit is accomplished through the *prophetic anointing*. The primary work of the Holy Spirit in the earth is to uncover the character, nature, will, and purposes of the Father, and Christ His Son, to us all. The prophetic anointing is not the same as a prophetic word that is given to an individual or a group; it is the life and breath of the Holy Spirit in the midst of His people. The prophetic anointing keeps every aspect of our worship from being a dead form and opens our hearts to the voice and image of God that the Holy Spirit wants to reveal to us at any particular time.

Prophecy is the life and breath of the Holy Spirit in the midst of His people.

If we can imagine the very life and breath of God upon every aspect of our worship service or liturgy—every song, prayer, reading, vocal gift of the Spirit, the preaching, and offerings—the character of God can be known in any, or every part of the service. Therefore, we might say that the whole service has a sense of the prophetic anointing. What that means in a practical way is that we "meet God" there and will forever be changed. Bob Sorge makes this insightful statement concerning prophecy and the prophetic anointing:

> . . . when we testify of Jesus, the prophetic spirit rests upon us; and when we prophesy, we should testify of Jesus.[8]

The foundational purpose of all prophecy is to build up the Body of Christ. The focus of all prophetic truth is Jesus Christ and His continuing work in the earth (Luke 24:25–27). He completely radiated the glory of God, which the earlier prophets reflected only in part. Prophecy can be delivered as an inspired utterance, song or action, or whenever we speak with divine authority and uncover the thoughts, plans, character, and nature of God. In *Nelson's New Illustrated Dictionary* there is an excellent statement concerning the way God uses His people to express His will:

The full panorama of God's will takes many forms; it may be expressed through people, events, and objects.[9]

FIVE TYPES OF PROPHECY

According to Pastor Robert Morris five types of prophecy are found in Scripture:[10]

1. *The spirit of prophecy* (Rev. 19:10)—During corporate worship or private devotion, the word of the Lord may come forth in an audible manner. Everyone may hear the voice and direction of God and participate in speaking or singing the prophetic word. The word may be for the whole body or for personal edification.

2. *The manifestation of prophecy* (1 Cor. 12:7)—God can use any person at any time to manifest His prophetic word. This is a word to an individual or to the congregation. The manifestation of prophecy is one of the gifts of the Spirit for edifying the Body. We do not own these gifts; the Holy Spirit manifests them through whomever he chooses. Everyone may participate in this ministry.

3. *The motivational gift of prophecy* (Rom. 12:6–7)—This is one of the motivational gifts mentioned in this passage. The purposes of prophecy, as a motivational gift, are to reveal the motives of man and help bring people into conformity with God. Only some have this ministry.

4. *The ministry gift of prophecy* (1 Cor. 13:2)—God has given this gift to certain individuals who use the gift of prophecy to edify the Body. Only some have this ministry.

5. *The office of the prophet* (Eph. 4:11–12)—Not everyone who prophesies is a "prophet." The main purpose of a prophet is to equip the saints for the work of the ministry. Only a few people have this ministry and can truly be called "prophets". The office of the prophet is in the process of being restored to the Church in these days.

We tend to limit our services to the same singing, prayers, and readings that we have participated in for decades—even centuries. I believe that our eyes and ears need to be opened to the prophetic anointing that is nascent in every service, liturgy or worship framework of all churches. The prophetic realm opens all our senses to behold Christ. Paul invites every believer to experience the presence of the Lord in such a way that we see Him and all His glory with the eyes of our heart or understanding (Eph. 1:18).

A CALL TO PROPHETIC WORSHIP

Prophetic worship must become the norm for every congregation. Sometimes we take our age-old traditions too seriously. If we could return to the simplicity of loving Jesus and welcoming His manifest presence among us, we would experience prophetic worship regularly. Many churches continue carrying the weight of dead traditions, thinking so highly of them that they do not even realize their meetings lack the manifest presence of God. We all should confess our need of Him and take time to learn from the Holy Spirit. In order for this to happen, great changes must take place in the Church.

> If we could return to the simplicity of loving Jesus and welcoming His manifest presence among us, we would experience prophetic worship regularly.

Robert E. Webber has been on the forefront of the worship renewal movement for over two decades as a speaker, author, and teacher. He has been a professor of Theology at Wheaton College since 1968 and is currently involved in the development of a school for pastors and other church leaders, The Institute for Worship Studies. He is the editor of *The Complete Library of Christian Worship*, a comprehensive seven-volume set. Webber's writings and those of numerous other authors are included in these volumes. They are insightful and beneficial for Christians from all traditions and are often quoted in this book.

Webber has some very helpful comments to make concerning the changes that need to take place among us. First of all, he calls for an understanding of our past—the valuable traditions of the Church—and an honest evaluation of our present worship:

I find American evangelicalism to be secularized in its attitude toward history. There is a disdain for the past, a sense
that anything from the past is worn out, meaningless, and
irrelevant. . . . it is all relegated to tradition and dismissed as
form. At the same time, no critical examination is directed
toward present distortions which have been elevated without
thought to a sacred position. Evangelicals who want to
reform their worship must therefore abandon their disdain of
the historical, and return to a critical examination of the
worship of the church in every period of history.[11]

THE IMPORTANCE OF WORSHIP

It is impossible to exaggerate the importance of worship. Pastor
and writer A. W. Tozer writes candidly to the church of our lack
and need of the presence of God. No other writer has expressed so
profoundly our urgent need for the presence of God—manifested
in worship—to be restored to preeminence within the Church:

The world is perishing for lack of the knowledge of God, and
the church is famishing for want of His presence.[12]

Tozer's writings resound with the priority of worship. He
believes that ". . . the whole work of God in redemption is to undo
the tragic effects of [sin]"—which wrenched us loose from the
presence of God—"our right and proper dwelling place, our first
estate. . . "[13] Tozer considers conscious communion with God—living in the presence of God as Adam and Eve did—to be the "central fact of Christianity. At the heart of the Christian message is
God Himself waiting for His redeemed children to push in to conscious awareness of His presence."[14]

Jesus emphasized the priority of worship when He reiterated the
first commandment:

And you shall love the LORD your God with all your heart,
with all your soul, with all your mind, and with all your
strength. (Mark 12:30)

Consider these two statements that stress the importance of worship:

Worship is the supreme and only indispensable activity of the Christian Church. It alone will endure . . . into heaven, when all other activities of the Church will have passed away. [15] (William Nicholls)

[Worship] is intimately linked with all the major emphases of biblical theology such as creation, sin, covenant, redemption, the people of God, and the future hope. Far from being a peripheral subject, it has to do with the fundamental question of how we can be in a right relationship with God and please him in all that we do. [16] (David Peterson)

As William Nicholls says above, *"worship is the supreme and only indispensable activity of the Christian Church."* I have heard some say that since we will be worshiping for all eternity, we need not worship so much now. Instead, we should be winning souls to Christ. Although evangelism is of great significance to the Church, I believe that worship is even more so. The greatest evangelists will be those who have met God face to face and who love His presence more than anything else.

The greatest evangelists will be those who have met God face to face and who love His presence more than anything else.

We could also say that because worship is the only earthly activity that will continue throughout eternity, we must begin now—for even eternity will not grant us the time to declare all His praises and behold all the depths of His glory(!). No other occupation but worship can provide us with the preparation needed to stand before Him and make entrance to His holy place. ✎

Chapter Two

WHAT IS THE DIFFERENCE BETWEEN PRAISE AND WORSHIP?

*Praise is an expression of faith that results
in our declaration of what God has done,
what He is doing, and what He is going to do.*

*Worship is ultimately a relationship of love
in which we focus on and respond to God.*[1]
Tom Schwanda

≈

S ome have suggested that by defining praise and worship, we will confine our expression of worship. Rather, I believe that by fully understanding praise and worship we release greater depths of their expression within our lives. Worship, in particular, involves the vast encounter that we have with the Lord on a daily basis. It encompasses every area of the communion between God and His people.

It is a difficult, yet necessary task to define praise and worship. Some may be intimidated by definitions, as definitions may seem to "box us in" or confine our thinking. We can be especially wary of definitions when it comes to our personal relationship and experience with God. Yet, I believe our worship experience can be enhanced by definitions that lead to a deeper understanding.

Simply put, praise is the preoccupation with and declaration of God's acts; worship is our reverent devotion and response to His very presence. While worship is more difficult to define, it includes the communion and fellowship with God that fills every part of our lives.

> There is one thing we do on earth that we will contin-
> ue to do in heaven. That is to praise and worship God.
> That is why we view life on earth, for those who love
> Jesus, as choir practice for heaven. To say that praise
> and worship is the most important category of music
> today is an understatement. In light of that, there is no
> more important activity of the human heart than to
> praise and worship God.[2] (Michael Coleman)

Simply put, praise is the preoccupation
with and declaration of God's acts;
worship is our reverent devotion and
response to His very presence.

DEFINING PRAISE

One of the best Biblical definitions of praise is found in Hebrews 13:15. The writer to the Hebrews sums up the key elements of praise in this one verse:

> Therefore by Him let us continually offer the sacrifice
> of praise to God, that is, the fruit of our lips, giving
> thanks to His name.

> Through Him therefore let us constantly and at all
> times offer up to God a sacrifice of praise, which is the
> fruit of lips that thankfully acknowledge and confess
> and glorify His name. (Amp.)

This verse teaches us several things about praise:

- Praise is born in Him.

- Praise needs to exude from us constantly and at all times.

- Praise is directed to God.

- Praise is a sacrifice.

- Praise involves our lips—it is difficult to praise Him without some form of outward expression.

- Praise is like fruit—it has purpose, it grows, it nourishes, and is capable of reproducing itself.

- Praise includes giving thanks and glory to God.

- Praise is preoccupied with His name.

When we praise God, there must be
faith intermingled with the praises.

THE NATURE OF PRAISE

1. Praise requires faith

The only Biblical definition of faith is found in Hebrews 11:1. This precious gift of God is essential whenever we come before the Lord in praise.

> But without faith it is impossible to please Him, for he who comes to God must believe that He is, and that He is a rewarder of those who diligently seek Him. (Heb. 11:6)

The Greek word for "comes" in this passage is *proserchomai* (Strong's #4334). This word means *to come near, visit or worship.* The word "seek" is the Greek word *ekzeteo* (Strong's #1567), which means *to search out, investigate, crave, demand, worship, require, seek after carefully and diligently.*

There is clearly an implication in this scripture concerning those who come to God to worship Him. We are instructed that we must first approach Him by faith and that He rewards us with His presence. Some would use this scripture in the sense that they would try to please God by believing "hard enough" so that they might *get* something from Him. Quite the opposite is true. The essence of faith here is that we please Him by *giving* ourselves to Him in faith-filled praises. His reward is for those who earnestly seek to

worship Him. In other words, this is more a scripture about entering His presence through praise and faith than it is about getting
blessings from God. When we praise God, there must be faith
intermingled with the praises. This is pleasing to the Lord.

Whenever we praise God, we are exercising faith by believing in
His existence and continuing work in our lives through every situation and circumstance. Every time we lift our hearts in praise, we
must accept God's. . .

Person	His character and nature—He desires to reveal Himself to us.
Presence	His omnipresence—He is everywhere and always with us.
Promises	He is faithful to meet us in the midst of our praises.
Power	He is omnipotent—all-powerful; nothing is too difficult for God.
Perfection	It is impossible for God to make a mistake with our lives.

> Praise . . . acknowledges the sovereignty of God in all
> our circumstances.[3] (Paul Sarchet-Waller)

2. Praise requires sacrifice

> Therefore by Him let us continually offer the sacrifice
> of praise to God, that is, the fruit of our lips, giving
> thanks to His name. (Heb. 13:15)

Since the beginning of time, God has called mankind to the
principle of sacrifice. We no longer offer blood sacrifices to the
Lord, but "spiritual sacrifices," or sacrifices from the heart. The
sacrifice of praise is one of the seven spiritual sacrifices that are to
be offered to the Lord by every Christian as we minister before the
Lord as a holy and royal priesthood (1 Pet. 2:5):

- The sacrifice of joy: Ps. 27:6
- The sacrifice of a broken spirit: Ps. 51:16–17
- The sacrifice of righteousness: Ps. 4:5; 51:19
- The sacrifice of thanksgiving: Ps. 107:22; 116:17

- The sacrifice of praise: Jer. 17:26; 33:11; Hos.14:2; Heb.13:15
- The sacrifice of our bodies, a living sacrifice: Rom.12:1
- The sacrifice of doing good/fellowship/unity (koinoia): Heb. 13:16

The Old Testament priests were called to draw near to the Lord and minister to Him (Ez. 44:15). As New Testament priests, we are to use these seven sacrifices for that same purpose: to draw near to the Lord and minister to Him. Now, our ministry to God is less of an event; it is a lifestyle. These seven sacrifices encompass every area and every day of our lives.

Our ministry to God is less of an event; it is a lifestyle.

Ralph Martin offers an excellent statement on sacrifice. He shows us that every worshiper is actively involved in the act of sacrifice.

> The theological code word for man's offering to God is *"sacrifice."* The worshiper is not a passive, motionless recipient, but an active participant, called upon to "make an offering."[4]

As we offer sacrifices to the Lord, we must be aware of this fundamental principle: No matter how excellently we sing, how often we attend church, or how much we place in the offering, our sacrifice cannot be "perfected" by our efforts, nor can we influence God to grant our requests or perform in a prescribed manner. His grace has made a way for our full acceptance before His throne and His sovereignty.

There are three aspects of the praise sacrifice that deserve careful examination:

a) The sacrifice of praise is costly—The implication in the word "sacrifice" is that there is a cost involved. We must become like David who would not offer a sacrifice to the Lord that had cost him nothing:

> ". . . I will surely buy it from you for a price; I will not
> offer burnt offerings to the LORD my God with that
> which costs me nothing." (2 Sam. 24:24)

Sometimes it is more difficult and costly to praise the Lord than
to wallow in our own needs and sorrows. We are to praise God
even through difficulties when we may not have any special "feelings" to praise the Lord. We are to live a life of praise and thank-
fulness to Him at all times. Whatever our situation, it is a Biblical
principle that the sacrifice of praise should be regularly and
unselfishly offered to the Lord.

   b) The sacrifice of praise is pure—The concept of sacrifice in the
Old Testament is crucial to our understanding of worship. The
sacrifice was to be set apart from its ordinary usage and consecrated to God. The Old Testament priests would examine the sacrifices before they were offered. They were told numerous times
not to offer blemished or unclean sacrifices to the Lord (for example, Lev. 22:21; Deut. 15:21). In the New Testament, Jesus became
the perfect and unblemished sacrifice that was offered to the
Father on our behalf (1 Pet. 1:19).

   In the same manner, we must examine our hearts and make sure
that the things we are singing and saying to the Lord when we
praise Him represent the full intent and purpose of our hearts. The
sacrifice of praise is not just praising God when we do not feel like
it. It must also include the sincere offering of our hearts.

   From Rom. 12:1, we know that we are to make an offering of
our whole bodies ("all your members and faculties," Amp.) as a
living sacrifice to the Lord. It is hard to imagine that such an offering can be pure and without blemish, as every one of us struggles
with issues of holiness. But the Lord's master plan is in place. He
will have His glorious Bride presented to Himself without spot,
wrinkle or blemish. Praise and worship ultimately bring us to the
place of laying self down before the Lord, and embracing the miracle of holy exchange—more of Him for less of self. Purity is born
here.

> . . . that He might present it to Himself a glorious
> church, not having spot, or wrinkle, or any such thing;
> but that it should be holy and without blemish. (Eph.
> 5:27)

   c) The sacrifice of praise is vocal—Unless we have some kind of
physical disability, it is not enough to think thoughts of praise that

never give voice to ardent expressions of thanks and exaltation
before the Lord. The sacrifice of praise must be spoken or sung—
it must come from our lips. The writer of Hebrews refers to this
sacrifice as the "fruit of our lips." In order for there to be fruit,
there must be a tree or some other source of life. Our lives and
relationship with the Lord should be the source of a continuous
flow of praise that is heard from our lips. Some say there is no such
thing as "silent" and "private" Christianity.

> . . . praise involves the use of words audibly expressed.
> Silent prayer is not a Hebrew practice. . .[5] (Ralph P.
> Martin)

Eli thought that Hannah was drunk because she prayed without
being heard (1 Sam. 1:12–14). Reticence to praise the Lord ardent-
ly and vocally may be the fruit of a weak relationship with Him.
However, genuine and vital faith will be evident to all because the
fruit of praise will abound in our lives.

UNDERSTANDING THE SACRIFICE OF PRAISE

The key to understanding the sacrifice of praise is to grasp the
concept that praise must become an integral part of our daily lives.
This is the central issue of Christian existence. When we come into
the presence of God, our focus should not be upon the things we
can *get* from the Lord, but on the offerings we have to *give* to Him.

> Give to the LORD the glory *due* His name; bring an
> offering, and come into His courts. (Ps. 96:8)

Our primary purpose in praise is to proclaim and show the marvelous excellencies and perfections of God (1 Pet. 2:9, Amp.,
NASV). We rehearse the things He has done throughout the ages;
we admire and boast about His present acts of greatness as He
moves among His people; and we triumph in the certain victories
and wonders of the days to come.

The *Life Application Bible* makes this statement concerning the
basis of praise:

> The basis of praise is declaring God's character and
> attributes in the presence of others. When we recognize
> and affirm His goodness we are holding up His perfect
> moral nature for all to see.[6]

Paul punctuated his epistles with thanksgiving and spontaneous outbursts of praise (2 Cor. 9:15; 11:31). Many of his letters began or ended with such praises (Rom. 16:27; 1 Cor. 1:4; 2 Cor. 1:3; Eph. 1:3–14; Col. 1:3; 2 Tim. 1:3; 1 Pet. 1:3). Praise should also permeate our everyday speech and influence our thoughts, day and night.

DEFINING WORSHIP

Webster's Dictionary defines worship as:

> . . . reverence for God, a sacred personage, or a sacred object. A formal ceremonious expression of worship. Adoring reverence or regard.[7]

The Oxford English Dictionary defines worship as:

> . . . to honour or revere as a supernatural being or power, or as a holy thing, to regard or approach with veneration or devotion, or that attitude expressed in particular actions.[8]

Judson Cornwall captures the essence of worship so succinctly:

> Worship is one person responding in his or her spirit to the one true God. . . .[9]

Sally Morgenthaler focuses on the aspect of relationship and response between the Lord and His people in the context of worship:

> Worship is two-way communication between believers and God, a dialogue of response involving both actions and speech. God reveals His presence; our need for intimacy with God is met, and we respond in thanksgiving and praise. God speaks through the Word; we are convicted and repent. God extends mercy through Jesus Christ; we respond with adoration. In other words, real worship provides opportunities for God and God's people to express their love for each other. It is not just a room full of people thinking inspired thoughts. Nor is it human beings speaking and acting as if God were incapable of reply. In real worship, we carry an exchange of love with the God who is present, the God

who speaks to us in the now, who has done and is doing marvelous things. And it is supernatural exchange—this interaction between the God of Scripture and God's people—that is the primary difference between public Christian event and Christian worship.[10]

True Christian worship does not originate from the outside. It originates from the innermost part of our being. It springs forth from the heart that has been touched, prevailed upon and conquered by God Himself. As Sally Morgenthaler states, worship is inseparable from the exchange of love and communication with God that we all experience when we encounter His presence.

Worship must infiltrate every area of our lives. It must become the reason for our existence, the basis for every belief system we hold dear, and the center of our world view. The Church's ultimate mission on earth is to minister praise and worship to God and to summon all people to partake of the triumph of His kingdom here and in the world to come.

> . . . true worship consciously sets God at the center of all life, celebrates his gifts in creation and providence, but reserves an unshared place for what he has done in the redemption of the world through our Lord Jesus Christ.[11]   (Ralph P. Martin)

THE ORIGIN AND USE OF THE WORD *WORSHIP*

The English word *worship* comes from the Anglo-Saxon word, *weorthscipe,* or *weordhscipe,* which was later changed to *worthship,* and then *worship.* It is a word that denotes the worthiness of the one receiving special honor or devotion. It means "to attribute worth" to someone or something. The word is still used in this manner in Commonwealth countries, where the Mayor is referred to as "His Worship, the Mayor." Used in this manner, *worship* refers to the respect and dignity that is given to a person of honorable office.

In all our study and definitions of worship, we must never lose sight of the primary reason for worshiping the Lord: *He is worthy above all things in heaven and earth to receive praise and adoration.* Everything within us cries out for relationship and communion with God, but we must not use that relationship to try to "soft-en" God as He works to perfect us in His presence. Our focus must always be upon Him. His eternal purpose is that we might become like Him and commune with Him forever.

**His eternal purpose is that we might
become like Him and commune
with Him forever.**

> Because of the fallen nature of man, worship has become distorted. It has become a means of covering up the dirt on the conscience of man rather than the expression of pure adoration and reverence for the Creator.[12] (Sammy Tippit)

We might join the Psalmist and the Apostle Paul in their spontaneous and overwhelming bursts of adoration:

> Great is the Lord, and highly (greatly, NKJV; most worthy, NIV) to be praised, and His greatness is [so vast and deep as to be] unsearchable. (Ps. 145:3, Amp.)

> Oh, the depth of the riches both of the wisdom and knowledge of God! How unsearchable are His judgments and His ways past finding out! (Rom. 11:33)

> (See also: Job 5:9; Pss. 48:1; 96:4)

So many people reduce the meaning of the word "worship" to a Sunday service, which might be termed "The Worship Service," or to their own particular denominational expressions. David Peterson, a lecturer at Moore Theological College in Sydney, Australia, indicates the difficulty we experience with language as we try to define worship:

> The problem for translation and for theology is that the English word "worship" is generally used too narrowly.[13]

There are angels whose full created purpose is to stand and bow before the throne of God and cry aloud His attributes. After thousands, even millions, of years, the worthiness of our King will not

be fully declared. Even eternity will not afford these angels the time
needed to adequately proclaim His excellencies. All of this, and yet
these heavenly beings know nothing of being redeemed. How then
can we, who are sons and daughters of God, remain silent in the
presence of His Majesty, the King of Kings and Lord of Lords? We
must not allow the angels to confess His magnificence with more
vigor and passion than we who are His children, His Bride, and
His servants. It is this relationship and intimacy with the Lord that
I want us to focus on as we explore various aspects of praise and
worship.

There are many definitions of worship in use around the world.
It is difficult to capture the awe and wonder of our intimacy and
reverence for God in any single definition.

> If we studied the terms used for "worship" in other lan-
> guages, we would get a much more comprehensive pic-
> ture. For instance, the German term *Gottesdienst*
> means "God's service {to us} and our service to God."
> The French term *le culte* and the Italian *il culto* both
> indicate a "lifelong engagement. . . a relationship of
> giving and receiving." [14]   (Sally Morgenthaler)

Once we have established the priority of worship in our lives we
can then turn our attention to the way we express our worship. I
intend to cover many and different forms of worship more fully in
a later book. I believe that Gerrit Gustafson's comments suffice for
now as an overview of the relationship between our heart for worship, and our expression of worship:

> The physical expression of worship is not inferior to the
> spiritual expression of worship. It is the vehicle of spir-
> itual worship. The physical act of lifting hands, for
> instance, is a token of the spiritual disposition of ado-
> ration and surrender. Dancing is the demonstration of
> great joy and gladness. [15]

THE DIFFERENCE BETWEEN PRAISE AND WORSHIP

There is a difference between praise and worship. Some are
reluctant to concede this—possibly because they fear that over-
analysis and definition will inhibit true expressions of praise and

worship. This fear might be justified if we spent more time evalu-
ating and judging our services than simply worshiping the Lord.
While we must never stop learning about worship and maturing as
ministers in God's presence, such self-critiques will rarely be prof-
itable. Evangelist and author Sammy Tippet says this of our constant analysis of our praise and worship:

> I have discovered that Christians in the western world
> are often divided over the method of worship rather
> than the essence of worship. . . we must never forget
> that the end of true worship, then, is not the method.
> The objective of true worship is the glory of Jesus.[16]

Ernest Gentile believes that praise and worship are synonymous
terms:

> . . . with praise emphasizing the public acclamation of
> God, and worship emphasizing intimate, personal,
> devotional communication.[17]

English author Paul Sarchet-Waller makes it very clear that the
purpose for defining the differences between praise and worship is
not to give any of us a choice—both are essential in the life of a
believer:

> The object is to give the believer a clear concept of
> praise and worship from the scripture that will lead to
> a greater expression of both praise and worship.[18]

Likewise, Bob Sorge feels that there is a clear difference between
praise and worship:

> It is not uncommon to hear references to "praise and
> worship" as though they were identical entities, or at
> least combined to form one complete whole. Praise and
> worship are mutually cooperative activities and are fre-
> quently very similar in the way they are outwardly
> expressed, but they are not one and the same. Each has
> its own nature and purpose.[19]

Terry Law, writer and speaker on praise and worship, makes
this comment:

> Many Christians find themselves using the words
> thanksgiving, praise, and worship interchangeably.

However, we must be aware of the fact that there are different meanings for the words. Thanksgiving is distinct from praise which is distinct from worship.[20]

While I do not wish to get into a debate on this subject, I do believe it is important to understand the differences between praise and worship, though our definitions and terminology often bog us down. Too often, we end up concentrating on what we are doing (in our expressions of praise and worship) rather than on perceiving and understanding what the Lord is doing (in communion with us). It is the Lord who initiates this fellowship with us, the Holy Spirit who draws us into the attitude of praise. While our involvement and actions in praise and worship are important, we must also be aware of what the Lord is doing and respond to His pursuit of our hearts. It is He who inhabits our praises and invites us into intimate and continual communion with Him.

David Peterson makes this point clear:

Acceptable worship does not start with human intuition or inventiveness, but with the action of God. The earliest books of the Bible emphasize God's initiative in revealing his character and will to his people, rescuing them from other lords in order to serve him exclusively, and establishing the pattern of response by which their relationship with him could be maintained.[21]

The difference between praise and worship, then, does not rely on what style or tempo of song we are singing (some simplistic explanations of praise and worship incorrectly point out that praise constitutes the fast songs, and worship the slow songs), what praise book or hymnal we are singing from, or what posture we are in; it is dependent on what the Lord is doing. When we praise Him, we heave our songs and words before Him as a sacrifice—as the Old Testament priests did with their burnt offerings. The Lord is in a place of receiving our praise, much as a king would receive a gift or a father would receive his children.

When we praise God, we describe Him and declare his acts. At times, the Holy Spirit may even draw prophetic praises from us, where we praise Him for things that He is yet to do and wonders we have not yet experienced. Worship, on the other hand, cannot take place unless the Lord draws near to us and manifests Himself to us. As we praise, we draw near to God. Worship results when

God draws near to us. He uses our praises as a vehicle to draw
near to His children:

> But You are holy, O You who dwell in [the holy place
> where] the praises of Israel [are offered]. (Ps. 22:3
> Amp.)

As we praise, we draw near to God. Worship results when God draws near to us.

When God inhabits our praises or is enthroned upon our praises, He manifests, reveals, or "uncovers" Himself before us. We
catch a glimpse of Him in a way that reveals layers of His character that we may never have seen before. For example, we already
know that He is our Father. But there may come a time in the midst
of praise, when we are extolling Him as our Father or singing a
song concerning His Father-heart, that He speaks to us again of
His Fathering.

Like an onion that has many layers, so the Lord has endless
realms of His glory to make known to us. If we were to spend
every moment for a thousand years receiving wave after wave of
the knowledge of His Father-heart, we would scarcely have peeled
back the first layer of this particular revelation of God. In fact,
there is not enough time in all eternity to complete the uncovering
of this or any revelation of God's character. The depths of the
knowledge of God are everlasting. Man will never uncover all of
God—nor would we so desire.

> A comprehended God is no God at all.[22] (Gerhard
> Tersteegen)

Esteemed Christian author and leader Judson Cornwall emphasizes this same point in many of his writings on praise and worship:

> Fundamentally, worship is a person responding to a
> person, so we can't worship until we get a glimpse of
> God. We can praise out of our memory circuits, but we
> must worship out of a present relationship; that is, we
> must be in God's presence to worship. True worship

will not begin to flow until we get a good glimpse of Christ Jesus.[23]

Where there is an awareness of Christ's presence and position, there is an automatic response of worship. . . for we were created to worship.[24]

Praise is an expression of faith that results in our declaration of what God has done, what He is doing, and what He is going to do. Worship is the most natural response to God's manifest presence. When we praise God, we are responding to His acts; when we worship, we are responding to His manifest presence—His person. Praise and thanksgiving are the gates of entrance into the very courts of His majesty. Worship is our response and communion with God once we find ourselves before His manifest Presence.

The sight of Him will take our very breath away.

LaMar Boschman also concurs that there is a difference between praise and worship:

> Praise is an act of faith. It is extolling the Lord despite how we feel and the circumstances that exist. On the other hand, praise involves sacrifice. Worship does not. We do not worship in faith. We worship out of the attitudes and feelings in our hearts. We love when we worship. We cannot love in faith.[25]

It is because of our faith that the Lord inhabits our praise—He has always responded to acts of faith in His people. This is no less true of praise. When we enter His presence—by faith, through the gates of righteousness, thanksgiving, and praise (Pss. 100:4; 118:19; Is. 60:18)—we are assured that He will respond and make Himself known to us.

Once He has inhabited our praises, we will not be able to keep ourselves from worshiping. The sight of Him will take our very breath away—every glimpse, every whisper, and every sense of His wondrous presence. True worship will ruin us forever, and we will

never be the same again. We will have little heart for the unin-
spired, inflexible, and mundane moments of traditionalism that
exist in every denomination.

LaMar Boschman points out that whenever we find worship in
Scripture, it is usually as a result of an individual being captivated
by the sight of God.[26] Worship always follows a revelation of His
character—or His glory—to His people. This revelation might take
place as He invades the words of our songs and hymns with His
precious presence, or He might cause us to "see" or "know" Him
in our hearts. It is not a seeing with our natural eyes as Moses did,
or a knowing with our minds, but a revelation of His thoughts,
words, character and attributes deep within our spirits. Such a
sight will change us forever and will draw the sweetest and deepest adoration from our being.

> . . . the depth of our worship is always propor-
> tional to the extent of our revelation of God . . .[27]
> (Judson Cornwall)

THE LORD DESIRES TO REVEAL HIMSELF

Revelation of God in corporate worship or in our personal communion with Him should occur regularly. It should not be a "hit
or miss" experience, but a consistent part of daily Christian life.
We must come to worship with expectancy and repentance flood-
ing our hearts. Who knows what wonders He might unveil to you
today?

Revelation of God in corporate worship
or in our personal communion with
Him should occur regularly.

Although we must not wait until we feel perfect and holy before
we approach God, we endeavor to enter His presence with clean
hands and hearts, with eager anticipation of His glory. We make
preparation in our worship ministries for the awesome presence of
God in our midst. Surely His nearness and divine manifestation
await every hungering heart. He is patiently waiting for us to ". . . enter
into His gates with thanksgiving, and into his courts with praise"

(Ps. 100:4) so that He might respond to our longings with His secrets.

Our only other choice is for churches to prepare for "business as usual" in their worship services. For most, that means a few hymns or songs, prayers, an offering, a sermon, and the benediction. If God is not allowed to unveil Himself in our midst, we might find comfort in the perpetual routine of worship rituals, but we will fail to fulfill our potential as ministers of the glory of the Lord—a potential that can only be realized by those for whom prophetic worship is the norm.

Table 1 contains a summary of what I consider to be the major differences between praise and worship:

Table 1

Major Differences Between Praise and Worship

Praise	Worship
God dwells in our praises.	God reveals Himself in worship.
Praise is a sacrifice requiring faith.	Worship is a response requiring the sight of God.
In praise, we declare His acts: What He has done, is doing, and will do.	In worship, we commune with Him in intimacy.
Praise brings us to the presence of God.	Worship responds to the presence of God.
We praise God for what He has done.	We worship God for who He is.
We praise God as we come before Him with thanksgiving.	We worship God when He comes before us by revelation.
We praise God from afar.	We worship God face to face.
Praise involves the remembrance of God.	Worship involves a present glimpse of God.
Praise is increased through faith.	Worship is increased through relationship and revelation of God.

Chapter Three

THE FOUNDATION OF WORSHIP

*. . . true worship is that exercise of the human spirit
that confronts us with the mystery and marvel of God
in whose presence the most appropriate and salutary
response is adoring love.*
Ralph P. Martin

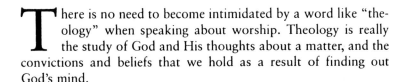

There is no need to become intimidated by a word like "theology" when speaking about worship. Theology is really the study of God and His thoughts about a matter, and the convictions and beliefs that we hold as a result of finding out God's mind.

> A first principle of Christian theology is that God alone can speak His own word about Himself. Consequently the first and continuing task of Christian theology is to listen to and then reflect upon what it hears. When this is faithfully done, Christian theology is the reflective and obedient response of the church to the Word that God speaks about Himself in Jesus Christ.[1] (J. Daane)

These few pages are by no means a comprehensive theology of worship. But I have attempted to gather some sound observations that will lay for us a foundation for deeper communion with God in worship.

God's relationship with us cannot fail to affect the way we respond to Him.

THEOLOGY AFFECTS OUR RELATIONSHIP WITH GOD

God's relationship with us cannot fail to affect the way we respond to Him. Each of us has a different view or experience of the Lord that ultimately results in different worship experiences. Our theology of worship will be formed out of our relationship with and view of God. We might even say that all our theology is affected by our worship and all our worship is affected by our theology. In the end, it is our hunger for God that becomes a primary shaper of our worship theology.

If worship is one of the foundations of our Christian life and our relationship with God, then our understanding or theology of worship remains as one of the most significant areas of our faith to consider.

Webber calls theology "a reflective discipline."[2] We are bound to model or reflect our theology as we worship, since our worship expressions and experiences are shaped by our theology. We must have both: good theology and good worship—they go hand in hand. You can never have one without the other. While worship expresses the heart's love for God, theology expresses the mind's love for God. Both are needed for us to respond to Him fully as worshipers.

THE RELATIONSHIP BETWEEN WORSHIP AND THEOLOGY

Consider the following observations of the relationship between worship and theology:

> Worship is integrally related to both theology and ethics.[3] (Halbrooks)

> Our way of worship is inseparable from our way of believing.[4] (Henry Jauhianinen)

LaMar Boschman, internationally known teacher and leader of worship, has remarked on the relationship between worship and theology:

> If our worship has good theology and our theology has good worship, from the beginning of the service to the end it is a worship experience.[5]

Our relationship with God in worship will ultimately flow out
of our definition and theology of worship. Theology has its roots
in worship; it arises out of our experience with God. Theology is
one of the forms worship takes, as correct theology and worship
are both expressions of love for God. We must give time and detail
to the grasp of each.

It is important, therefore, that we not only develop our understanding of worship, but also our theology of worship. Without
this foundation we are prone to allow our experience of worship
to fit our inaccurate grasp of true Biblical worship. Sally
Morgenthaler indicates this in her book, *Worship Evangelism:*

> Christian worship is not anything and everything we
> want it to be. Worship has Biblical parameters with
> which we need to acquaint ourselves. Until we do, we
> will continue to offer worship substitutes.[6]

Henry Jauhianinen stresses the need for greater theological discussion of the true nature of worship:

> A serious defect of Pentecostal and Charismatic wor-
> ship is the lack of intense, in-depth biblical and theo-
> logical reflection upon the nature of worship. As a
> result, worship tends to be a means to an end, whether
> that be church growth, personal fulfillment, or the
> defeat of God's enemies. Worship tends to become a
> utility or self-absorbing "experience." Worship style is
> adjusted frequently to meet consumer appetites.
> Pragmatism wins over theology; that which attracts
> and holds a crowd is seen as that which God endorses.[7]

Some Christians nearly gag at the mention of the word "theology." We have been taught to trust in the experiences that we have
as believers rather than the perceived theological absolutes of anti-
quated intellectuals. Those who persist in theological debate are
often thought of as outdated and inflexible in their views. Others
feel that theology should only be debated when it comes to the
foundational doctrines of the Church; issues such as worship
should remain as a practical encounter with God rather than a
holy debate. In other words, worship is private—no one else's business.

Further understanding should bring us to the conclusion that the purpose of theology is not to explain or defend our statements of faith or our worship expressions, but to express clearly what we believe and hold dear.

The purpose of theology is not to explain or defend our statements of faith, or our worship expressions, but to express clearly what we believe and hold dear.

There are at least four benefits to studying and organizing our beliefs into a personal theology of praise and worship:

1. Our theology can enhance our worship experience: Our understanding and expressions of worship can only be enhanced by Biblical study and theological deliberation on the true nature and essence of worship. If we understand both *what* we are doing and *why* we do it, we will most likely gain greater meaning and purpose from our experience of worship. Experience, in turn, gives life to what we already know. Spiritual depth and growth will be a natural result of this process.

2. Our theology of worship can deepen our relationship with God: Any theology of worship should bring us into a greater knowledge of God Himself. Worship presupposes and further examines the majesty, sovereignty, and transcendence of God. When we have a sound Biblical and theological foundation for worship, our understanding of God's attributes will be expanded, and our worship experience enriched.

3. Our theology of worship will affect how we worship God through the Word: Theology will bring us to God's Word for the sake of truth and accuracy. Those who rely on the Word will find their worship enlivened by Scripture. Whenever the Word of God stands at the center of our worship, its truth increases our love for God. He is found in His Word again and again. Often He will respond to us through His Word and by His Spirit during our worship.

4. Our theology of worship can improve our relationship with other believers: By defining and understanding worship theology, we should be able to come to a greater degree of unity within the Body. People who have different views and beliefs about God will ultimately have different worship experiences. New churches are often formed when those with a similar worship theology gather to meet with each other. If we could all ask the Holy Spirit to unfold the Lord's definition and expectations of praise and worship, greater unity would ensue.

It is crucial that we discover how to be pleasing to the Lord. My goal is not that we should all come to the same experience of worship, but that every church would experience the presence of God in a dynamic and prophetic manner. This is true Biblical worship.

> If we could all ask the Holy Spirit to unfold the Lord's definition and expectation of praise and worship, greater unity would ensue.

THE RELATIONSHIP OF THEOLOGY AND FORM IN WORSHIP

It is possible to worship in a manner that is not pleasing to the Lord (see the example of Cain and Abel in Gen. 4:3–7). Just because we call what we do in our church "praise and worship" does not mean that we are automatically correct in our theology, attitude or expression of worship. Surely every theologian from every denomination is confident that his or her group has the correct definition of how the Lord desires to be worshiped—thus implying that all other denominations are somewhat askew in their worship expressions. But it is not our understanding of worship or our forms of worship that produce true worship. It is the simplicity of our desire and response to the Lord in our hearts. Devotional writer Richard Foster says this of our forms of worship:

> Forms and rituals do not produce worship, nor does the disuse of forms and rituals. We can use all the right techniques and methods, we can have the best possible liturgy, but we have not worshiped the Lord until Spirit

> touches spirit. . . . Singing, praying, praising all may
> lead to worship, but worship is more than any of them.
> Our spirit must be ignited by the divine fire.[8]

Bible teacher and author Kevin Conner also stresses that our forms of worship are not to be considered the worship itself. He argues that we have constructed various forms of worship to suit us because we do not truly know how to worship God:

> Of himself, man does not know how to worship God,
> yet he longs to worship. It is for this reason that man
> designs forms of worship or some sort of program for
> religious services and then asks God to bless his pro-
> gram. Also, because man does not know how God
> desires to be worshiped, he develops a variety of forms.
> People generally congregate to the particular form that
> suits their tastes, their spiritual disposition and which
> does not offend their mentality.[9]

Forms, then, are not the central issue of our worship; it is the heart. The forms or expressions of worship from all our church traditions are merely the vehicles by which our hearts ascend to the Father and His voice is heard in our spirits. For this reason we must all reject any semblance of spiritual elitism that assumes "my way of worship is the only right way to worship." If true worship is a matter of the heart and not dependent upon outward forms, then we must find it in our hearts to remain open—always a student of His presence, His Word, and His work among mankind.

Each of us has drawn boundaries as to how far he thinks he should go in the expression of his love for God. Some want to sing with only the accompaniment of an organ or piano. They believe that all other instruments do not belong in church and have drawn a line in their hearts at this place of musical expression. Others do not want instruments in church at all. Still others like a variety of instruments in their worship, and some like to see the congregation dancing, clapping or lifting their hands to the Lord. In some churches people bow or kneel before the Lord. Other congregations allow banners and streamers to be lifted in praise processions and in celebration before the King. Which line is correct theologically? How far does God allow us to go? Are we wrong for setting limits and drawing lines for God on this matter?

I believe it *is* wrong to establish boundaries within which to worship. Our patterns for "correct worship" are the Biblical examples of worship, including the worship in heaven. If we study the worship that takes place around the throne of God, we might be surprised at the things the Lord allows in His presence. Our goal should be pleasing Him, not keeping traditions and meeting standards. When worship flows freely from our spirits and is based on Biblical principles, I feel there is no limit to the way we are able to abandon ourselves in the presence of the Lord. (Not that we would be ridiculous and strange just for the sake of it, but that we would give our all to Him without regard to man-made rules, customs and practices.)

Paul warns us not to put men's ideas and traditions above the Lord's expectations of us in worship, and the Lord is quite clear in His statements on worship throughout the Bible. I am sure it would benefit each of us to review what the Bible has to say on these issues and renew our commitment to make pleasing God our first priority in worship rather than satisfying personal preferences or traditions.

> Beware lest anyone cheat you through philosophy and empty deceit, according to the tradition of men, according to the basic principles of the world, and not according to Christ. (Col. 2:8)

JESUS: OUR EXAMPLE OF A WORSHIPER

Surely Jesus is our best example of a worshiper (Jn. 13:15). He knew how the Father desired to be worshiped, and worshiped Him almost all the time. From His conception, birth, and throughout His life, Jesus was a man surrounded by worship, prayer and devotion. People regularly came into His presence with worship and praise (Matt. 21:15-16; Mk. 14:3-9; Lu. 17:15-16; 18:38-43; 19:37-40; Lk. 7:37); teachings on praise and worship found their way into many of His sermons and conversations (Matt. 5:12; Lu. 6:23; 15:5-6, 9, 22-32; Jn. 4:5-42); at His crucifixion there is mention of His heart of praise (Ps. 22); and worship was the first thing the disciples did after the resurrection (Lu. 24:50-53). Jesus is still singing praise today in the midst of the Church (Heb.

2:11–12). The Spirit of God now dwells in every believer to bring us into continuous praise and worship of the Father.[10]

> Therefore by Him let us continually offer the sacrifice of praise to God, that is, the fruit of our lips, giving thanks to His name. (Heb. 13:15)

> And because you are sons, God has sent forth the Spirit of His Son into your hearts, crying out, "Abba, Father!" (Gal. 4:6)

No matter how many chapters are written on the definition and theology of praise and worship, there will be no true worship unless an individual gives himself or herself to God in utter abandon. As Foster puts it:

> . . . we learn to worship by worshiping.[11]

Faith in Jesus should ultimately birth worship in our hearts and cause His love to reach into every far corner of our hearts. He draws us to adore and to imitate the God who first loved us.

Faith in Jesus should birth worship in our hearts.

Several writers have adeptly described and defined worship for us:

> Christianity, as John Wesley describes it, is the method of worshiping God which has been revealed to us by Jesus Christ. . . . In its most general sense, worship is adoration, the loving contemplation of God's holiness.[12] (Mark Horst)

> . . . worship is. . . a breaking into the Shekinah of God, or better yet, being invaded by the Shekinah[13] of God.[14] (Richard Foster)

> Wonder is the basis of worship.[15] (Thomas Carlyle)

> It would be *very* difficult to draw the line between holy wonder and *true worship*. . . . Let your soul lose itself

in holy wonder which will lead you to grateful worship.
. . [16] (Charles H. Spurgeon)

If your understanding cannot comprehend Him, let
your affection overtake Him.[17] (Charles H. Spurgeon)

WHAT IS CHRISTIAN WORSHIP?

My quest is not to define Charismatic or Pentecostal worship,
but to answer the question: "What is Christian worship?"
Jauhianinen focused on this question in his article *A
Pentecostal/Charismatic Manifesto* (published in *The Complete
Library of Christian Worship*, Volume Two):

> This is not a call to a bland eclecticism, nor a denial of
> so called Pentecostal or Charismatic distinctives. It is a
> call to join other evangelicals in recovering from his-
> torical amnesia and regaining a sense of continuity with
> the worshiping church through the ages, thus enriching
> our present experience.[18]

Gerrit Gustafson has described five principles of Christian worship that I believe are worthy of note:

1. *The Activation of the Priesthood* (1 Pet. 2:5)—the intervening
presence of the Holy Spirit activates the priestly functions of worshipers.

2. *Spirit, Soul, and Body* (Mark 12:30)—worship involves the
whole person—spirit, soul, and body

3. *Entering His Presence* (Psalm 100:2, 4)—the act of worship is a
progression into the manifest presence of God.

4. *Praise and Power* (2 Chron. 20:22)—worship creates an atmosphere where God's power is revealed.

5. *Beyond the Song* (Heb. 13:15–16)—worship is more. than
singing—it is serving.[19]

I deeply desire that these five principles of worship be understood and applied by Christians of all denominations. Just as the

theology of salvation applies to all true Christians, so should our understanding of worship. Our worship is "Christian" before it is Pentecostal, Charismatic, Baptist, Lutheran, Presbyterian or any other denomination. Certain expressions of worship tend to take place in the Pentecostal–Charismatic context, but they are in no way owned by this branch of the Body of Christ. If churches from any tradition base their worship expressions on sound Biblical theology, those same worship experiences should make sense to all of us and lead us into intimate and satisfying fellowship with God.

God alone must define the true nature and character of worship, as worship is directed toward Him, inspired by Him, made real because of Him, and fulfilling only as we meet with Him. This is the greatest fulfillment for any Christian—to stand before God and commune with Him through prayer, praise, and worship.

Gregory Wilde lists the following points as being central to Charismatic worship theology:

1. The Word of God, prayer, and personal devotion.
2. Openness to the prompting and moving of the Holy Spirit both in oneself and in others . . .
3. Evangelism and personal holiness.
4. The power and authority of Christ and His name in intercession, whether in prayer, healing, exorcisms, evangelism, or general Christian concern.[20]

Our definition and theology of worship
must bring us to a preoccupation with
God and His attributes.

Finally, our definition and theology of worship must bring us to a preoccupation with God and His attributes. Unfortunately, some people use the worship experience to become consumed with the things He can do for them or the experiences He can give them. Worship must be about God—not us, or it will become corrupted. We must not become absorbed with the things God can do for us or what we are supposed to be doing for God. True worship will lead us to absolute and all-consuming adoration of His loveliness.

Our goal as worshipers is to adore God for His own sake. It is He, alone, who is worthy of all worship.

UNDERSTANDING THE PRESENCE OF GOD

Throughout this book we will be examining the presence of God. Three aspects of His presence need to be understood in any discussion of praise and worship:

1. His abiding presence—The Lord will never leave us nor forsake us (Heb. 13:5). He has promised to abide with us forever. The Holy Spirit lives in us, and there is never a moment when He is not with us. We abide in Him and He, in us. Without His abiding presence, we are unable to do anything.

> And I will pray the Father, and He will give you another Helper, that He may abide with you forever—the Spirit of truth, whom the world cannot receive, because it neither sees Him nor knows Him; but you know Him, for He dwells with you and will be in you. I will not leave you orphans; I will come to you. (John 14:16–18)

> (See also: Pss. 61:4, 7; 91:1; Jn. 15:4; 15:5–10; 1 Jn. 2:28; 3:6, 24)

True worship will lead us to absolute and all-consuming adoration of His loveliness.

God's abiding presence causes us to have intimacy with Him in worship. He is very near and easily found by those who would seek Him:

> Seek the Lord while He may be found, call upon Him while He is near. (Is. 55:6)

2. His omnipresence—He is everywhere at all times. God is the only One in heaven or upon earth who is able to be present in all places at all times. He is also the only One who is omnipotent and omniscient. Although the terms *omnipresent* and *omnipresence* are not found in Scripture, *the idea* of God's omnipresence is presupposed and found throughout. The omnipresence, omnipotence, and omniscience of God are all related—He is God who is present

everywhere, all-powerful and all-knowing (see: Deut. 4:39; Prov.
15:3; Jer. 23:23–24; Amos 9:2).

David knew that he could not escape the presence and gaze of
God when he cried:

> Where can I go from Your Spirit? Or where can I flee
> from Your presence? (Ps. 139:7; see vs. 6–16)

For the worshiper, God's omnipresence makes worship much
simpler. We do not have to rely upon a particular location, building, liturgy or format in order to worship Him. Our hearts are His
tabernacle—wherever we go we are able to draw near to Him.

> . . . the omnipresence of God. . . guarantees that the
> actual nearness of God and a real communion with
> Him may be enjoyed everywhere, even apart from the
> places hallowed for such purposes by a specific gra-
> cious self-manifestation.[21] (G.W. Bromiley)

3. *His manifest presence*—God is especially present at certain
times and places. "Manifest" describes God's revelation of Himself
or His will and purpose—He makes Himself known to us in our
hearts and minds. The *abiding* presence and omnipresence of God
are a continuous fact, but His *manifest* presence is an act of God
toward His people that takes place in a certain moment of time.

> You are God who does wonders; You have declared
> Your strength among the peoples. (Ps. 77:14)

> (See also: Ps. 90:16; Ez 28:25; Jn. 17:6; 1 Cor. 12:7;
> Col. 1:26)

When we worship God, we are completely dependent upon
Him to manifest Himself to us—it is a work of grace in response
to our hunger. True and prophetic worship is not possible unless
His presence is made manifest. My desire is that we would all
come to know His manifest presence in our churches.

David knew that he could never get away from the (omni) presence of the Lord (Ps. 139:7). He was speaking of God's manifest
presence when he entreated the Lord:

> Do not cast me away from Your presence, and do not
> take Your Holy Spirit from me. (Ps. 51:11)

Imagine a room full of people. If I might say to them that there is a doctor in the room, everyone would look around to see who it is. Though the doctor is present in the room, no one yet knows who he is. But if the doctor began to administer medication to sick people in the room, he would then be *manifesting* or revealing himself through his actions.

The presence of the Lord is very much like that. When we gather for worship, we know that God is present with us because He abides with us at all times. But at certain moments in the service, the Lord may choose to speak to an individual or to the whole church through songs, prayers, gifts of the Spirit, preaching, body ministry, fellowship, and so forth. I believe God is always wanting to manifest Himself to His people. We must give Him room to do so in our services and look and listen for His self-revelation.

> ". . . For where two or three are gathered together in My name, I am there in the midst of them." (Matt. 18:20)

I wholeheartedly agree with Tozer as he describes the process of encountering the presence of God (and the difference between His omnipresence and manifest presence).

> The Presence and the manifestation of the Presence are not the same. There can be the one without the other. God is here when we are wholly unaware of it. He is manifest only when and as we are aware of His presence. On our part, there must be surrender to the Spirit of God, for His work is to show us the Father and the Son.[22]

Two conditions must be met in order to encounter the presence of God: our hearts have to be filled with an attitude of surrender and receptivity, and we must wait for the Lord to move within us by a sovereign revelation of His person. Let us be sure to do our part: to give our hearts with all earnestness to seek His face, and relinquish self so that our hearts become a holy sanctuary fit for the Almighty.

The manifest presence of God is revealed when His abiding presence is known. In other words, those who have made their hearts a sanctuary for His presence and live as if God is with them are the ones who are likely to experience His manifest presence.

Jesus manifested the power of God because God was with Him (Jn. 3:2; Acts 10:38). When Martha questioned Jesus concerning raising Lazarus from the dead, Jesus said to her, "Did I not say to you that if you would believe you would see the glory of God?" (Jn. 11:40). We need to expect God to manifest Himself to us because He is with us, just like He was with Jesus, and because we believe in Him, just as Martha was instructed to believe.

Judson Cornwall explains the rabbinical understanding of the manifest presence of God:

> The rabbis chose to speak of God's manifested presence on the earth as the *shekinah*. This is not a Biblical word, but it is consistently used in the Jewish Targums—rabbinical commentaries on the Old Testament—to designate "the divine presence" or "the divine manifestation." . . . *shekinah* means "to dwell." The rabbis used this word to avoid any localization of God. They consistently conceived of God as being omnipresent, but they fully recognized a sense in which God revealed His presence among His people, and they referred to this as the *shekinah*.[23]

God desires to manifest Himself to everyone—He has no favorites. His desire is towards all mankind. He requires broken and repentant hearts in order to manifest His glory.

God desires to manifest Himself to everyone—He has no favorites.

> And I heard a loud voice from heaven saying, "Behold, the tabernacle of God is with men, and He will dwell with them, and they shall be His people. God Himself will [personally—Amp.] be with them and be their God." (Rev 21:3)

Gregory Wilde gives us an excellent summary for understanding the place of worship and of God's presence within Charismatic theology:

> For the charismatic, the idea that the Lord inhabits the praises of his people says much. This is because for those who truly are charismatic all of life has become

Eucharist; all of life has become a praise response to God's initiative of love. The gathered praises of God's people voiced on Sunday mornings are only symptomatic of a lifelong reality of praise, for by the power of the Holy Spirit every day has become the Lord's day, every day a day of death and resurrection. Charismatic communities can be thought of as "epicletic communities"[24] for the lives of people have become instruments for constantly calling upon the Holy Spirit to come and transform into new creation everything that the believer is, says, does, and touches. . . . True theology is the Church's word about God, which responds to and is controlled by the word that God Himself has spoken in His self-revelation.[25]

Chapter Four

UNDERSTANDING THE ANCIENT WORDS FOR PRAISE AND WORSHIP

Worship is . . . the acknowledgment and celebration
of God's utter perfection. Enjoyment of God begins
with the privilege of discovering Him.[1]
Andrew Wilson-Dickson

≈

The ancient Hebrew and Greek words for *praise* and *worship* are so essential to understanding the Biblical conception of praise and worship that they deserve an entire chapter to themselves. I am not presenting these words and their meanings so that we might become overly introspective, intensely analyzing our practice of praise and worship in every detail. However, serious study can be helpful if we are seeking to discover what the Holy Spirit really intended as He inspired the writing of Scripture and carefully phrased the original text. David Peterson describes the proper perspective from which to approach this study:

> The biblical words for worship do not represent discrete concepts but are part of a whole mosaic of thought about the way to relate to God.[2]

Ernest Gentile has uncovered this remarkable fact: *more than fifty different words* are used in the Hebrew Scriptures to denote *praise*. Not all these words have been translated "praise," yet they all describe the action of praising God.[3]

I have studied these ancient words in depth over the past twenty years and gleaned insight from many sources. However, in this book I intend only to briefly outline the most significant of these Hebrew and Greek words*. The definitions presented here are either paraphrased from my research or taken directly from *Strong's Exhaustive Concordance, Theological Wordbook of the Old Testament,* or *An Expository Dictionary of New Testament Words.* I have included the numbers and phonetic pronunciations from *Strong's Exhaustive Concordance* as an aid to further study.

ANCIENT HEBREW WORDS FOR PRAISE

Seven key Hebrew words for "praise" describe the various aspects of Biblical expressions of praise.** These words are presented here in a specific order, beginning with the quietest proclamation and ending with the most exuberant or seemingly extreme expressions of praise.

> The important thing to notice about all these verbs for praise in the Old Testament is that they are words of sound. Praise in the Old Testament always is accompanied with sound. It is vocal, it is public, and it is excited.[4] (Terry Law)

a. *barak* (baw-rak'), Strong's #1288

- To kneel, bless, praise, salute
- To remember joyfully—He is the source of all your blessing[5]

---

* Ernest Gentile has outlined the meanings of these Hebrew words very thoroughly in his book, *Worship God,* which I heartily recommend for those who desire to do further study on this subject. Also, Richard Leonard has covered the Old and New Testament words for worship quite comprehensively in Volume One, Chapter Two, of *The Complete Library of Christian Worship.*

** Very few Biblical references to praise indicate silence of any sort, and most praise is expected to be in the company of others.

In the King James Version *barak* was translated as "praise" only twice: in Judges 5:2 and Psalm 72:12–15. However, in more recent translations *barak* has been translated as "praise" up to seventy times.

b. *yadah* (yaw-daw'), Strong's #3034100

- To confess with outstretched hands

- To revere or worship with raised hands

Yadah incorporates the Hebrew word *yad*—which means "hand"—implying the stretching out or holding out of the hands, and possibly the pointing, throwing, casting, extending or shooting out of the hands. The name *Judah*—meaning "praise"—also comes from this root word. We know that Jesus descended from the tribe of Judah (Heb. 7:14).

- Expressing one's public declaration of God's attributes or His works—an active rather than passive praise

Second Chronicles, Chapter 20 provides a powerful example: a heart filled with praise, combined with the outward expression of lifting the hands, brought victory in battle. (See also Pss. 9:1; 28:7; 43:4; 111:1; 138:1)

> Lift up your hands in the sanctuary, and bless the LORD. (Ps. 134:2)

c. *towdah* (to-daw'), Strong's #8426

- To offer a thanks

- To offer the sacrifice of praise in faith for what God is going to do

Towdah is a noun (derived from *yadah*, meaning *the extending of one's hands*) and implies the outward display of the faith we find in our hearts. (See also Pss 50:23; 69:30; 107:22; Is. 51:3)

d. *zamar* (zaw-meer'), Strong's #2158, from #2167

- Literally "to touch the strings"

- To make melody

- Instrumental and sung praises—making music in praise
  to God

Found more than forty times in the Hebrew Scriptures, *zamar* is
a key word for *praise* as well as being a musical term. This word
is used exclusively in poetry, most often in the Book of Psalms.
While it is always used in reference to instrumental music, singing
may or may not be involved. The Greek Bible translates this word
as *psallo: to sing hymns.* (See also Pss. 47:7; 57:7; 68:4; 144:9;
147:7; 149:3)

e. *shabach* (shaw-bakh'), Strong's #7623

- To commend or laud

- To shout or address in a loud tone

- To give glory or triumph in praise

"O praise (shout or speak loudly) all ye nations; praise (triumph
and address loudly) Him all ye people"(Ps. 117:1, Amp.). Note the
call for all nations and people to *shabach* the Lord. While this
expression of praise is clearly demonstrative and loud, we might
also note that *no allowance is made for any nation or people to
excuse themselves from this injunction to shout to the Lord,*
whether due to national pride or personal preferences. (See also
Pss. 35:27; 63:3; 145:4; 147:12; Dan. 2:23; 4:34, 37)

f. *halal* (haw-lal'), Strong's #1984

- To make noise

- To shine, give light; make glorious

- To make a clear and brilliant tone or sound

- To rave, celebrate, boast, to be clamorously foolish

This is the most commonly translated word for praise, used
approximately 121 times in the Old Testament. *Halal* was considered an essential ingredient in public worship, according to the
Theological Wordbook of the Old Testament, and it comes from
the imperative "Hallelujah!" (combining *halal* and *Jah,* an abbre-
viated form of *Yahweh*—the name of God), meaning: "Praise the
LORD!" (Ps. 150).

(See also 1 Chron. 16:4, 36; 23:5, 30; 25:3; 29:13; 2 Chron. 5:13; 7:6; 8:14; 20:19, 21; 30:21; 31:2; Ezra 3:10–11; Neh. 5:13; 12:24; Pss. 22:23, 26; 34:2; 35:18; 44:8; 56:4; 63:5; 69:30, 34; 74:21; 84:4; 99:3; 105:3; 107:32; 109:30; 111:1; 119:30, 164, 175; 145:2; 148:1–7; 149:3; 150:1–6; Prov. 31:28, 31; Jer. 20:13; 31:7; Joel 2:26)

> The grand climax of the entire book of Psalms, chapter 150, uses halal in every verse, beginning and ending this glorious worship manifesto with a resounding hallelujah.[6] (Ernest Gentile)

g. *tehillah* (teh-hil-law'), Strong's #8416.

- To sing, celebrate with song
- To laud, sing 'hallals'
- Extravagant praise
- High praise

The noun *tehillah* is a derivative of *halal* The plural, *tehillim*, is the Hebrew name for the Book of Psalms. The Bible cites more than 300 commands to sing praises to the Lord.

HOW THE WORD *TEHILLAH* RELATES TO PROPHETIC WORSHIP

The word *tehillah* is not the word translated most frequently as "praise," nor does it indicate the loudest expression of praise, but it does have a most unusual characteristic. I have noticed that every time *tehillah* is used in Scripture, something special seems to be occurring in the praise. It is almost as if the Lord has responded to the praise that has been offered by faith and is now inhabiting or manifesting Himself in the midst of the praise.

This attribute of *tehillah* shows a link to the prophetic characteristic of worship. When the other Hebrew words for praise are used, they indicate the one who praises is lifting his praise by faith to the Lord. When we praise (*tehillah*) the Lord, He begins the very process of His inhabiting (see the paragraph on Ps. 22:3 below).

Consider each of the following occasions where *tehillah* was translated as *praise*. Though these situations were very different, the reality of the presence of God was made quite noticeable through supernatural events:

Exodus 15:11, ". . . glorious in holiness, fearful in *praises*. . . ." After the Israelites crossed the Red Sea, the revelation of God to His people was that He is awesome and to be feared or revered in the midst of praise *(tehillah)*. This shows that there has been more involved in the praise setting than just man's exaltation. Clearly, God has "shown" Himself in the midst of the praise.

2 Chronicles 20:22, " . . . when they began to sing and *to praise*, the LORD set ambushes against the people of Amon, Moab, and Mount Seir, who had come against Judah. . . . " Other words for praise—*yadah* and *halal*—were used to describe the types of praise that were offered to the Lord prior to verse 22. From this, we know that this army of singers went forth with their hands lifted in praise to God and their mouths filled with boisterous exaltation.

But the Hebrew word for *praise* changes to *tehillah* in verse 22. I suggest it was at this point—when the singers were praising the Lord with all their hearts—that the Lord descended in the midst of their praises and defeated the enemy. Perhaps we need to be reminded that the enemy is not afraid of noise—he is capable of making plenty of noise himself. He is, however, afraid of the sound that comes from a people who have the manifest presence of God in their midst. Praise of this sort will be like a two-edged sword (as described in Psalm 149:6—another instance of *tehillah* praise). When God's presence fills our praises, Satan will be utterly defeated every time (!).

Psalm 22:3, " . . . You are . . . enthroned in the *praises* of Israel." The indication here is that He sits in the midst of our praise as a king would sit upon a throne. We experience His kingship as He inhabits our praise (see also Ps. 114:2). While the presence of God is not necessarily manifested in all forms of praise, the verses that use *tehillah* seem to indicate that His divinity and kingship are being made known in these instances. God is the King of heaven and earth—with or without our praises.

Psalm 33:1 (KJV), " . . . *praise* is comely for the upright." The very faces of God's people are made supernaturally beautiful as we encounter Him in the *tehillah* praises. (See also Ps. 147:1.)

Psalm 33 describes praise as an act of beauty. When God's people praise Him rightly, it is something beautiful they do. They bring beauty to him . . . Praise is an act of beauty to God![7] (Allen)

Psalm 34:1, " . . . His *praise* shall continually be in my mouth." Such *tehillah* praise accompanied by the presence of the Father makes continuous exaltation a delight. True worshipers are quick to praise the Lord and find communion with God only a breath away. *Rejoice in the Lord always* . . . (Phil. 4:4). (See also Ps. 35:28.)

Psalm 40:3, "He has put a new song in my mouth—*Praise* to our God; Many will see it and fear, And will trust in the LORD." The *tehillah* song of praise is able to be seen(!). This song is not like any other. It is more than mere music. The *tehillah* song contains the very sight of God. When He inhabits our praises, we need to look out for the manifestation of His presence—the sight of God displaying Himself in the earth. If we wait on God for the prophetic song, the rest of this promise will come to pass—"many will see it and fear" (revere, worship) and will put their trust in the Lord. The greatest days of evangelism are ahead for the worshiping church that sings songs that are not only heard, but seen.

Psalm 65:1, "*Praise* is awaiting You, O God . . . " and "To You belongs silence [the submissive wonder of reverence which bursts forth into praise] . . . " (Amp.). In this instance the *tehillah* praise is born out of silence. When God makes His presence known to us, we do not need to be talking all the time. Learn to wait upon God for His appearing in your soul. Allow wonder and awe to grip you to the core at the very sight of Him.

Psalm 71:14, " . . . I will *praise* You yet more and more.". This *tehillah* praise creates a hunger for more and more of God's presence. The more of Him that we see and know, the more we will desire—He is irresistible!

Psalm 100:4, " . . . enter His gates with thanksgiving, and His courts with *praise* . . . " I believe that this *tehillah* praise is the doorway between praise and worship. The six previous types of praise we have studied must be lifted to the Lord in faith, but *tehillah* praise makes possible true worship, which requires the presence of the Lord. We are ushered in to His very courts through this praise. Please note that this verse is not giving us a formula with which to manipulate God, so no set time restraints should be applied in advance for this journey into His presence.

Psalm 106:2, " . . . Who can declare all His *praise*?" Such is the sight of Him in the midst of our *tehillah* praise that it becomes impossible to unfold all His wonders and declare all the praise that is due Him.

Isaiah 42:10, " . . . Sing to the LORD a new song, and His *praise* from the ends of the earth . . . " The Amplified Bible says that this song of praise is a song that has never been heard before in the heathen world(!). No matter how creative or talented the composers, musicians, and singers, there is no way that any one of them will be able to match the aesthetic beauty of the new song of *tehillah* praise that is arising from all the nations of the earth. One sound of heaven, touched by the glory of God, will surpass every other musical endeavor yet attempted on this earth.

One sound of heaven, touched by the glory of God, will surpass every other musical endeavor yet attempted on this earth.

Isaiah 60:18, " . . . But you shall call your walls Salvation, and your gates *Praise*." Salvation provides the protective wall around God's people; *tehillah* praise is the gate to the very habitation of the Lord. "Lift up your heads, O you gates! . . . And the King of glory shall come in." (Ps. 24:7)

Isaiah 61:3, " . . . the garment of *praise* for the spirit of heaviness . . . " Any who mourn in Zion (the place of the presence of the Lord) are offered three things: a diadem of beauty (see Amp.); the oil of joy, and a garment of *tehillah* praise. What a garment! What provision! This one is clothed in praises that are filled with the supernatural presence of the Lord. We are to wear *tehillah* as a garment.

This verse then describes the three-fold purpose for such favor:

- That we might be called oaks of righteousness [lofty, strong and magnificent, distinguished for uprightness, Amp.]

- That we might be planted by the Lord

- That He might be glorified [for the display of His splendor, NIV]

Isaiah 61:11, "So the LORD GOD will cause righteousness and *praise* to spring forth before all the nations." (See also Is. 62:7; Hab. 3:3; Zeph. 3:19–20) *Tehillah* praise and worship bring us face to face with the Lord. It is here that we are changed into His likeness, from glory to glory. Because of this, the Church is urged to become ministers of His glory in all the earth. All nations will see and know the power and grace of God as the Church fulfills her priestly ministry of standing before the King and giving Him honor and praise.

Isaiah 43:21, "This people I have formed for Myself; they shall declare My *praise*." It is interesting to note that righteousness and praise are linked in God's eternal plan for the earth. It is no good for us to grow solely as a praising people, we must also grow strong in righteousness. Only then will the nations be able to see the glory of the Lord upon us, for we will grow in beauty and favor like a garden of beautiful blossoms in the spring time.

> Now thanks be to God who always leads us in triumph
> in Christ, and through us diffuses the fragrance of His
> knowledge in every place. (2 Cor. 2:14)

(Other verses where *tehillah* is used: Deut. 10:21; 1 Chron. 16:35; Neh. 9:5; 12:46; Pss . 9:14; 22:25; 47:6–7; 48:10; 51:15; 71:6, 8, 14; 79:13; 102:21; 109:1; 111:10; 119:171; 145:21; 149:1; Is. 42:8, 10, 12; 48:9; 60:6; Jer. 13:11; 17:14; 33:9; 51:41.)

ANCIENT HEBREW WORDS FOR "WORSHIP"

There appears to be just one primary word in Hebrew for the worship of God: *shachah**. Other Hebrew words for worship are used only when referring to the worship of idols. *Shachah* draws its meaning from the actions of our bodies as we worship the Lord. The ancient Hebrews found no better way to define worship than to describe the process of positioning our bodies to show our total humility before Him:

---

* The spiritual state of true worship is really indescribable by words alone, though the richness of worship and devotion to God is revealed from Genesis to Revelation.

shachah (shaw-khaw'), Strong's #7812

- To depress, i.e. to prostrate, bow down flat, do reverence, worship.

- To humbly beseech.

The verb *shachah* is used one hundred and seventy times in the Hebrew Bible.

> The literal meaning of the verbal root is the act of falling down and groveling or even wallowing on the ground before royalty (2 Sam. 14:22; 1 Kings 1:16) or deity (Exod. 34:8; 2 Sam. 12:20; 2 Kings 19:37). Whether in the context of doing obeisance to the King or worshiping a deity, the basic idea conveyed is unworthiness and humility. The word pictures an inferior being in the presence of a superior being.[8]

The spiritual state of true worship is really indescribable by words alone, though the richness of worship and devotion to God is revealed from Genesis to Revelation.

Additional Hebrew words have been used in the context of worship, translated variously as:

> *darash* (daw-rash'), Strong's #1875
> —To seek or inquire (Ezra. 4:2; 6:21; Pss. 24:6; 69:32;Is. 11:10)

> *abad* (aw-bad'), Strong's # 5647
> —To serve (Ex. 3:12; Is. 19:21, 23)

> *sharath* (shaw-rath') Strong's # 8334
> —To minister (Deut. 10:8; 18:5–7; Ps. 103:21; Jer. 33:21–22; Ez. 44:12)

A familiar concept in the Old Testament when speaking about worship is *the fear of God.* Closely associated with this concept are words such as *awe, respect, worship,* and *veneration.* The fear of God is not just an attitude of the heart, but a lifestyle to be diligently pursued. The Hebrew word used in this context is:

yare (yaw-ray'), Strong's # 3372

Yare is used over three hundred times in its various forms, meaning:

- To fear
- To revere
- To dread
- To frighten
- To stand in awe

We can learn so much about the fear of the Lord by studying those passages where the Lord is instructing us on walking in His fear. As you read the following verses, consider how the fear of the Lord stands as a foundation for worship:

> Ex. 14:31 "Thus Israel saw the great work which the LORD had done in Egypt; so the people feared the LORD, and believed the LORD and His servant Moses."

> Deut. 31:12–13 "Gather the people together, men and women and little ones, and the stranger . . . that they may learn to fear the LORD your God . . . and that their children . . . learn to fear the LORD your God . . . "

> Ps. 19:9 "The fear of the LORD is clean, enduring forever . . . "

> Ps. 25:14 "The secret of the LORD is with those who fear Him."

> Ps. 31:19 "How great is Your goodness, which You have laid up for those who fear You."

> Ps. 33:18 "Behold, the eye of the LORD is on those who fear Him . . . "

Ps. 34:7,9 "The angel of the LORD encamps around all those who fear Him; and delivers them. . . . there is no want to those who fear Him."

Ps. 34:11 "..I will teach you the fear of the LORD."

Ps. 86:11 " . . . unite my heart to fear Your name."

Ps. 96:4 "For the LORD is great and greatly to be praised; He is to be feared above all gods." and "Let all the earth fear the LORD . . . " Ps. 33:8

Ps. 103:11, 13, 17 "For as the heavens are high above the earth, so great is His mercy toward those who fear Him . . . the LORD pities those who fear Him . . . the mercy of the LORD is . . . on those who fear Him."

Ps. 111:10 "The fear of the LORD is the beginning of wisdom . . . " (Also Prov. 1:7; 9:10; 15:33)

Ps. 112:1 " . . . blessed is the man who fears the LORD . . . "

Ps. 147:11 "The LORD takes pleasure in those who fear Him, in those who hope in His mercy."

Prov. 3:7 " . . . Fear the LORD and depart from evil." and "The fear of the LORD is to hate evil." (Also Prov. 8:13; 16:6)

Prov. 10:27 "The fear of the LORD prolongs days . . . "

Prov. 14:27 "The fear of the LORD is a fountain of life . . . " Prov. 19:23

Prov. 22:4 "By humility and the fear of the LORD are riches and honor and life."

Mal. 3:16 "Then those who feared the LORD spoke to one another, and the LORD listened and heard them; so a book of remembrance was written before Him for those who fear the LORD and who meditate on His name."

How often the Lord links the concept of loving and revering Him with obedience (Jn. 14:23)! My favorite verse on the fear of the Lord is Ecclesiastes 12:13. These are possibly some of the last words of the wisest man who ever lived. In translating this verse, the Amplified version includes some helpful insights concerning the fear of the Lord. I have deliberately laid out the verse so that each thought can be separated and meditated on independently. Each line has great significance for worshipers:

> All has been heard. The end of the matter is,
> fear God—
> know that He is,
> revere and worship Him—
> and keep His commandments;
> for this is the whole of man
> [the full original purpose of creation,
> the object of God's providence,
> the root of character,
> the foundation of all happiness,
> the adjustment to all inharmonious
> circumstances and conditions under the sun],
> and the whole duty for every man.

It is crucial that every Christian regains a holy fear and reverence for the Lord, a respect for His Word and an esteem for His presence, that prevails over every other priority and interest in our lives.

Notice the three components of the fear of God outlined here:

1. The knowledge of God and understanding of His character: "know that He is"

2. Worship: "revere and worship Him"

3. Obedience: "keep His commandments"

Lack of reverence for God and an incorrect fear of God have weakened the modern Church. It is crucial that every Christian regains a holy fear and reverence for the Lord, a respect for His Word and an esteem for His presence, that prevails over every other priority and interest in our lives.

> To fear God is to stand in awe of Him; to be afraid of God is to run away from Him.[9] (Simcox)

> Holy fear is a loving anxiety to please God.[10] (Hall)

NEW TESTAMENT GREEK WORDS FOR PRAISE AND WORSHIP

As in the Old Testament, New Testament writers found it is easier to describe what one *does* in praise and worship rather than the inner feelings of the heart.

PRAISE:

a. *ainos* (ah'ee-nos), Strong's #136, from #134

- Praise of God

  (Matt. 21:16; Lu. 2:13, 20; 18:43; 19:37; 24:53; Acts 2:47; 3:8–9)

b. *epainos* (ep'-ahee-nos), Strong's #1868, from #1909 and #134

- To laud and commend

  (Rom. 2:29; 13:3; 1 Cor. 4:5; 11:2, 17, 22; 2 Cor. 8:18; Eph. 1:6, 12, 14; Phil. 1:11; 4:8; 1 Pet. 1:7; 2:14)

c. *humneo* (hoom-neh'-o), Strong's #5214, from #5215

- To sing and celebrate in song
- A song or hymn of praise

(Heb. 2:12)

d. *doxa* (dox'-ah) Strong's #1391

- To glory, honor or esteem
- Dignity

(Lu. 14:10; Jn. 9:24; 12:43; 1 Pet. 4:11)

e. *eulogeo* (yoo-log-eh'-o), Strong's #2127, from #2095 and #3056

- To speak well of
- To bless or pronounce blessing or benediction upon
- To Thank

(Lu. 1:64)

f. *eusebeo* (yoo-seb-eh'-o), Strong's #2151, from #2152

- To be reverential or pious towards God
- To respect

(Acts 17:23)

g. *arete* (ar-et'-ay), Strong's #703, from #730

- Excellence
- Praise

(1 Pet. 2:9)

WORSHIP:

a. *therapeuo* (ther-ap-yoo'-o), Strong's #2323, from #2324

- To wait upon
- To attend to, or serve

- To cure or heal

(Acts 17:25)

It is interesting to note the link between worship and healing. When we worship with *therapeuo*, we come face to face with the God whose name and character is " . . . the LORD who heals . . . " (Ex. 15:26). Of course the Lord is not the One who is in need of healing—*we are*. He is perfect. When we worship Him, all of His goodness and virtue are poured back upon us and we are the ones who are healed, changed, and made whole.

The best place for physical, emotional
and spiritual healing is in the midst of
worship—right in the presence
of the Lord.

Matthew and Mark describe occasions when some approached Jesus for help and healing by worshiping Him (Matt. 8:2; 9:18; 15:25; Mark 5:6). These did not make their requests known to the Lord until they had first drawn near to Him with worship in their hearts. The best place for physical, emotional and spiritual healing is in the midst of worship—right in the presence of the Lord.

b. *ethelothreskeia* (eth-el-oth-race-ki'-ah), Strong's *#1479,* from *#2309, #2356*

- Religious observance, sanctimony

(Col. 2:18)

c. *latreuo* (lat-ryoo'-o), Strong's *#3000*

- To worship publicly
- To minister to God
- To serve—sometimes through the devout and upright life

(Acts 7:42; 24:14; Rom. 1:9; Phil. 3:3; Heb. 10:2)

Worship is more than singing—it is serving. Wholehearted worship will cause us to be wholehearted in our service within the community.

d. *proskuneo* (pros-koo-neh'-o), Strong's #4352, from #4314

From pros (meaning "toward") and kuneo (meaning "to kiss"). This word is used over fifty times in the New Testament and is the word most commonly translated as worship.

- To kiss the hand; to kiss—like a dog licking his master's hand; to kiss toward

- To fawn or crouch to

- To prostrate oneself in homage

- To do reverence, worship

   (Matt. 2:2, 8; 4:9–10; Lu. 4:7; John 4:20–24; 12:20; Acts. 7:43; 8:27; 24:11; 1 Cor. 14:25; Heb. 11:21, as well as the entire book of Revelation, use this word for *worship*.)

e. *sebomai* (seb'-om-ahee), Strong's #4576

- To venerate, to awe

   (Matt. 15:9; Mark 7:7; Acts 16:14; 18:7, 13, 19:27)

Three ideas sum up the Hebrew and Greek words used for praise and worship in Scripture:

- Adoration expressed through visible acts of reverence

- An inner attitude of humility and self abasement

- Adoration through service and sacrifice with no thought of reward

The New Testament is filled with a constant attitude of thanksgiving, praise, and worship—particularly surrounding the life of Jesus:

- At the conception of Jesus (Lu. 1:46–55)

- At the birth of Jesus (Matt. 2:1–12; Lu. 2:13–14, 17, 20, 38)

- At the dedication of Jesus (Lu. 2:28–32)

- During the life and teaching of Jesus (Matt. 5:11-12; 6:9–10; Matt. 21:15-16; Matt. 26:26–27; Mk. 14:22–25; Lu. 6:23; 10:17–21; 15:5-6, 9, 22–32; 17:15-16; 18:38, 43; 19:37-40; 24:50–51; John 4:5-42; 6:11, 23; 11:41)

- After the resurrection of Jesus (Matt. 28:9, 17; Luke 24:50-53; Jn. 20:20, 28)

- In the present ministry of Jesus (Psalm 22:25; Heb 2:11-12)

The first thing that the disciples did after Jesus ascended into heaven was to worship. They did not go and seek their former employment after Jesus ascended. They went to the temple and the upper room and continued waiting upon the Lord in prayer, praise, and the blessing of God (Lu. 24:52–53; Acts 1:14). On the day of Pentecost, when the believers were all filled with the Holy Spirit, they began to speak in tongues. Devout men from every nation heard the Christians praising God in their own language, and three thousand of them were saved (Acts 2:11, 41). Likewise, when the Gentiles received the Holy Spirit they also praised God in tongues (Acts 10:46). Believers today are called to this same life of continuous praise, through the example of the early Church and through the teachings of the Apostles:

Acts 2:46–47; 3:8–9; 4:24; 7:55–56; 8:39; 9:31; 10:1-2, 36; 11:18; 13:2; 16:14, 25, 34; 18:7, 13; 24:11, 14; Rom. 5:2-3, 11; 8:28; 12:1; 15:9, 17; 16:27; 1 Cor. 6:20; 10:31; 14:25; 15:57; 2 Cor. 2:14; 3:18; 9:12–13; 10:17; Gal. 1:5, 24; 6:14; Eph. 1:3–6, 12, 14, 16; 3:14, 21; 4:6; 5:4, 18–20; Phil. 1:11; 2:9–11; 3:3; 4:4, 6; Col. 2:7; 3:16; 4:2; 1 Thess. 2:13; 5:16, 18; 1 Tim. 2:8; 6:15–16; Heb. 1:6; 2:9–12; 10:19–22; 12:28; 13:15; 1 Pet. 2:5, 9; 4:16; Jude 24–25

The book of Revelation is filled with worship. It is a glorious revelation of the exalted Christ and the atmosphere of continuous worship in heaven. The throne of God is central to this book (it is mentioned thirty-two times), suggesting that an understanding of authority is a key to true worship. Richard Leonard calls this book, ". . .the supreme worship book of the New Testament." [11] What a fitting way to conclude the written Word of God. Genesis begins with our awesome Creator walking with man, face to face in intimacy with Him. Revelation concludes the story of redemption, with man again restored for all eternity to the place of worship and intimacy.

Part Two

II Corinthians 3:18

The Scriptural Pattern for Prophetic Worship

Worship is extravagant love and extreme submission.

Charlotte Baker

∾

The truth, and practice, of worship is simple enough that even the youngest child can experience its wonder. Yet, so much study is required to fully explore its length, breadth, depth, and height. What a vast and endless journey the Lord has us on as we seek to know Him more fully and intimately!

In an attempt to simplify and encapsulate the concepts of prophetic worship, I have outlined what I believe is the Scriptural pattern for worship, based on seven key points taken from 2 Corinthians 3:18. I have been fascinated with this verse my entire Christian life, as it bridges the philosophical and intellectual aspects of our faith in God with His unlimited invitation to a personal and intimate encounter.

This pivotal passage is a summary of the essential theological elements of prophetic worship:

> But we all, with unveiled face, beholding as in a mirror
> the glory of the Lord, are being transformed into the
> same image from glory to glory, just as by the Spirit of
> the Lord. (2 Cor. 3:18)

It is interesting to note that the word "glory" is mentioned three times in this one verse. Whenever a concept is uncovered in Scripture with three layers such as this, it signifies the following:

- This is the completion of a matter. The number *three* connotes divine perfection and completeness.

- Somewhere here, there is a principle that will uncover something of God's glory to us.

Herbert Lockyer adds these insights concerning the number three:

> Three. . . is a prominent number that indicates what is real, perfect, substantial, complete, and divine. . . . It also suggests the resurrection.[1]

> Pythagoras calls three the perfect number, expressive of beginning, middle, and end, and therefore a symbol of Deity.[2]

The seven key principles of prophetic worship drawn from this passage are these:

1. *But we all*—worship is all-inclusive.

2. *With unveiled face.*—worship requires transparency.

3. *Beholding as in a mirror*—worship is prophetic.

4. *The glory of the Lord*—worship is transcendent.

5. *Are being transformed into the same image*—worship is transforming.

6. *From glory to glory*—worship is eternal.

7. *Just as by the Spirit of the Lord*—worship is initiated by the Holy Spirit.

We will examine each of these principles in greater depth in the chapters that follow.

Chapter Five

WORSHIP IS FOR EVERYONE
"But We All. . . "

God is an unutterable sigh, planted in the depths of the soul.
Jean Paul Richter

≈

*B*ut we all—In contrast to the time when only chosen leaders like Moses could come before the face of the Lord*, we are all beckoned into the very presence of God to commune with Him as a friend.

So the LORD spoke to Moses face to face, as a man speaks to his friend. And he would return to the camp, but his servant Joshua the son of Nun, a young man, did not depart from the tabernacle. (Exod. 33:11)

Moses was the only one who spoke face to face with God in Exodus 33. But as New Testament believers, all of us are now invited to such an encounter. According to the first three words of 2 Corinthians 3:18 there are no restrictions based on age, intelligence, or the length of time one has been a Christian. The call here is to all who would know Him. Profound and intimate worship is available to everyone.

This is a universal "we." No one is exempt from Paul's revelatory command, "But we all. . . . " It is as if the Lord has made the most momentous and profound aspect of Christianity—worship

---

* all the others—apart from Joshua—stayed in their tents (Ex. 33:10–11)

and the sight of God—available to even the weakest one of us. No props, degrees, callings, or special talents are needed; only hungry hearts and thirsty souls.

As Christians, we stand in contrast to those who are under the Old Covenant and must still veil any reflection of the glory of God. But any Christian—of any persuasion—only needs to turn his heart toward the Lord, and the sight of Him will be his.

Every Christian is able to draw near to the Lord. Consider the following truths that grant each of us access to the very throne of God:

- The death of Jesus—He has made a way for us through the veil of His flesh (His blood)—Eph. 2:13; Heb. 10:19–20

- Repentance—Heb. 10:22

- The washing of pure water (the Word of God)—Heb. 10:22

As related in Acts 17:23, Paul found some in Athens who were worshiping an "unknown God." He told them it was our Jesus whom they were worshiping.

I believe it is rare to be able to worship God when we do not even know His name, as His name is so much entwined in the revelation of His person. Yet, God—being so gracious and so desirous that all men would worship Him—gave these idol worshipers the slightest glimpse of Himself. The veil was beginning to lift from their eyes even as Paul was being prepared for ministry.

Likewise, we are all welcome in the place of devotion: the saved and the sinner, the rich and the poor, the young and the old, the wise and the inane, the humble and the arrogant, the strong and the weak. Let everyone be invited to the courts of the King!

WE ALL HAVE A PART

But we all—It would be hard to overemphasize the part that we all have to play in worship. Worship was never intended to be the prerogative of just a few leaders or "spiritual" people. The Bible clearly indicates that worship is the universal occupation of all creatures:

> Let everything that has breath praise the LORD. Praise
> the LORD! (Ps. 150:6)

Worship is foundational to all Christian experience. This is true
for all people of every nation and generation on the earth. Worship
will always be relevant in every setting and activity of our lives.
Michael Marshall expresses the same thought in this way:

> Nothing in the human experience lies outside the scope
> of true Christian worship.[1]

We are all welcome in the place of
devotion: the saved and the sinner, the
rich and the poor, the young and the
old, the wise and the inane, the humble
and the arrogant, the strong and
the weak. Let everyone be invited
to the courts of the King!

WE ALL MUST WORSHIP IN UNITY

But we all—In 2 Corinthians 3:18, Paul calls us all to worship,
regardless of our denomination, generation, culture, or preferences. I believe the Lord has a huge amount to say to us on the subject of worship and is not particularly concerned with our individual preconceptions, preferences or inhibitions. He is calling all of
us to receive *His* understanding of the intimate communion with
Him that we call "worship."

There can be little debate that the Lord intends for us all to
become passionate and exuberant in our worship from time to
time. The Word is full of directives such as these:

> Oh, clap your hands, all you peoples! Shout to God
> with the voice of triumph! (Ps. 47:1)

> All the ends of the world shall remember and turn unto
> the LORD, and all the families of the nations shall wor-
> ship before You. (Ps. 22:27)

(See also Pss. 22:29; 45:17; 66:4; 67:3. 5; 79:13; 86:9; 96:9; 98:4; 106:48; 117:1; 145:10, 21; Isa. 42:10; Isa. 66:23; Rom. 15:11; Rev. 15:4)

Not only are all peoples and nations called to worship, we are all called to a life of untiring and consistent praise:

I will bless the LORD at all times: his praise *shall* continually *be* in my mouth. (Ps. 34:1) (See also Ps. 35:28; Ps. 44:8; Ps. 71:8)

No exception is made in Scripture for shy people to settle back with a different style of worship that might be more reserved, or for people of a particular denomination or culture to be exempt from continuous, expressive, heart-felt praise and worship.

When Paul called us all to transparent and life-changing encounters with the Lord in worship, I am sure he had no idea that the Church at the end of the age would be wrought with such diversity (and controversy) in matters of worship form, preference, and style. That fact, however, does not diminish the universal summons to appear before the face of God and respond to His awesome presence with impassioned and genuine devotion.

I am not saying that those who minister to the Lord quietly are incorrect in their expression. There are definitely times for that and occasions for a great variety of styles and expressions of devotion before the Lord. The Biblical injunction to praise God has more to do with the heart than it does with the outward expression. Therefore, it would be wrong to insist on a simplistic interpretation of these scriptures. It is important to note, however, that the Word stresses repeated, exuberant, and public expressions of praise that are born from passionate and sincere hearts.

Webber says this of our worship:

Passive worship cannot be justified on the grounds of Scripture, theology, or history.[2]

When Paul calls us all to worship in this passage, he is not suggesting the whole congregation "give it a try." Nor is he attempting to combat passivity among those who would prefer not to sing. Rather, he is reinforcing the call to unity within corporate worship. The Lord is blessed by our unity as much as He is by our songs and words of adoration. During praise and worship, we need to come to a place of unity in heart, mind, and voice.

That you may with one mind and one mouth glorify the
God and Father of our Lord Jesus Christ. (Rom. 15:6)

WE ALL MUST CHOOSE TO WORSHIP

But we all—In order for us to be consistent in our devotional
lives, we need to bring our will into subjection. Ritual is always
easier than revelation. True worship costs us our time, energy and
emotions. We must learn, like David, to say, "I will." David
instructed himself more than one hundred times to praise and worship the Lord. For example:

> But as for me, I will come into Your house in the mul-
> titude of Your mercy; In fear of You I will worship
> toward Your holy temple. (Ps. 5:7)

> I will praise *You*, O LORD, with my whole heart; I will
> tell of all Your marvelous works. I will be glad and
> rejoice in You; I will sing praise to Your name, O Most
> High. (Ps. 9:1–2)

The Lord is a Gentleman. He has given us a free will which He
honors in worship as in every other part of our lives. We are not
robots, who worship because we are commanded to, but friends
who embrace intimacy with Him by choice. Worship is forever a
choice. You will find, time and again, that He responds to our
choices with His delightful presence. As James puts it:

> Draw near God and He will draw near to you . . .
> (James 4:8)

Graham Kendrick, a worship leader and author from England,
writes:

> Sometimes worship starts because it is felt sponta-
> neously in the heart, sometimes it is an act of the will.
> Either way, God is equally worthy of our worship, and
> it is his worthiness that is the important thing, not our
> fickle and unreliable feelings. . . . The will to worship is
> our part, while God's part is to supply the fire that
> ignites it within us.[3]

We are drawn by God, but still we must choose to be part of this holy and intimate communion. ❧

Chapter Six

WORSHIP IS THE PLACE FOR TRANSPARENCY
"... with unveiled face"

Worship is the occupation of the heart,
not with its needs or even its blessings,
but with God Himself.
Judson Cornwall

≋

W *ith unveiled face*—The Lord desires to call to the very deepest parts of our hearts and reveal His glory and His secrets there (Ps. 42:7; Ps. 92:5; Dan. 2:22; 1 Cor. 2:10). Only when we come with honesty, transparency, and holy expectancy will we see the desire of our hearts fulfilled in His presence. The secrets of His Person and His Word can only come to those whose faces are uncovered.

REMOVING THE VEIL TO BEHOLD HIS GLORY

Unfortunately, every one of us has a veil of some sort over our hearts. Sin and hurts have caused us to hide ourselves from one another and from God. There are two ways we can become unveiled: either we remove the veil by our own honesty and pursuit of transparency, or the Lord—the great "Render of Veils" (Matt. 27:51)—will tear it for us if we ask Him sincerely. The Word of God, personal prayer, and worship do the best work of rending the veil, plowing our hearts and making us ready for His glory.

Charles Spurgeon speaks of the mysteries that are uncovered to us through prayer and anchored in our hearts through our own reasoning:

> Thoughts and reasonings are like the steel wedges which give a hold upon truth. But prayer is the lever which forces open the iron chest of sacred mystery. Then, we may get the treasure hidden within.[1]

Worship uncovers our faces and allows the awesome and unfathomable mysteries of God to be dropped upon our hearts

---

Worship uncovers our faces and allows the awesome and unfathomable mysteries of God to be dropped upon our hearts.

There are three kinds of people the Lord opens His treasures to:

- *Those who fear (worship) Him*—"The secret [of the sweet, satisfying companionship] of the Lord have they who fear—revere and worship—Him, and He will show them His covenant, and reveal to them its [deep, inner] meaning." (Ps. 25:14, Amp.)

- *The righteous*—". . . His confidential communion and secret counsel are with the uncompromisingly righteous—those who are upright and in right standing with Him." (Prov. 3:32b, Amp.)

- *His prophets*—"Surely the LORD GOD does nothing, unless He reveals His secret to His servants the prophets." (Amos 3:7) (See also Dan. 2:19)

I would like to suggest that righteous, prophetic worshipers—with faces and hearts unveiled before God in transparency and expectation—are candidates to receive the secrets of the Lord.

THE COST OF TRUE WORSHIP

. . . *with unveiled face*—True worship is probably the most exposing and costly act that we can ever engage in as humans. For us to really worship God, we must be willing for all of self to be exposed and laid out before Him. We never know what area of our lives His Hand of love might touch in our worship time. When we worship the Lord, there can be no place for the covering of our faces. When He died, Christ rent the veil that stood between us and the Father (Matt. 27:51; Mark 15:38; Luke 23:45). We must allow the full meaning of that to affect our worship and remain transparent before the Lord. All pretense must be gone from us as we come into the Holy of Holies to worship Him.

Sometimes when I am worshiping the Lord, I catch myself "wandering" somewhere else, or thinking about other things. I have to remind myself to "Look at Jesus!" It is only with an unveiled face that we can look Him in the eye.

. . . *with unveiled face*—The unveiling of our faces includes the unveiling of our minds and thoughts. Every one of us has areas of our lives that are "blind spots"—often called "strongholds of the mind." It is almost as if we were blinded to certain weaknesses in our lives, being either unable to see them or to think correctly about them.

For example, some Christians are gripped with fears, conquered by sins, or struggle with a distorted self-image. Even godly men and women may be unaware of certain areas in their lives that cause pain to the Lord, to themselves, or to their brothers and sisters. Everyone around them might see their problem areas very clearly, but they remain either unaware of them or ignorant of how deeply rooted they are.

Paul spoke of the war that goes on in our minds and bodies:

> But I see another law in my members, warring against
> the law of my mind, and bringing me into captivity to
> the law of sin which is in my members. (Rom. 7:23)

This is certainly a war we are expected to win. Through worship, we are to set our gaze upon Him who has already won the victory over sin and death on our behalf. If we continue on our own way, and refuse to allow the Lord to woo us into His likeness, it is possible to become given over to a reprobate mind (Rom. 1:28).

Only as we cry out to the Lord for His unveiling of our faces and minds are we enabled to see Him, see the grave state of our hearts, and be changed in His presence. Worship is the place for this work. Jesus commanded us to:

> ". . . love the LORD thy God with all thy heart, and with all thy soul, and with all thy mind." (Matt. 22:37; Mark 12:30)

We are not able to fully love the Lord with our minds until the veil is lifted from us. Then we can yield our minds to His thoughts (Is. 55:8–9). Without this process, we will remain at war with God and not even realize it.

> Because the carnal mind is enmity against God; for it is not subject to the law of God, nor indeed can be. (Rom. 8:7)

The following scriptures reveal Paul's emphasis on the process of transformation that needs to take place in our minds:

> And be not conformed to this world: but be ye transformed by the renewing of your mind. . . . (Rom. 12:2 KJV)

> And be constantly renewed in the spirit of your mind . . . (Eph. 4:23, Amp.)

> Let this mind be in you which was also in Christ Jesus. . . . (Phil. 2:5)

Again, Peter shows us that it is through prophetic worship and the revelation of Jesus that our minds are changed:

> So brace up your minds; be sober—circumspect [morally alert]; set your hope wholly and unchangeably on the grace (divine favor) that is coming to you when Jesus Christ, the Messiah, is revealed. (1 Pet. 1:13, Amp.)

Tozer speaks of this veil of flesh that remains in our hearts and hinders intimate worship:

> A veil not taken away as the first veil was, but which remains there still shutting out the light and hiding the face of God from us. It is the veil of our fleshly, fallen nature living on, unjudged within us, uncrucified and unrepudiated. It is the close-woven veil of the self-life

which we have never truly acknowledged, of which we have been secretly ashamed, and which for these reasons we have never brought to the judgment of the cross. It is not too mysterious, this opaque veil, nor is it hard to identify. We have but to look into our own hearts and we shall see it there, sewn and patched and repaired it may be, but there nevertheless, an enemy to our lives and an effective block to our spiritual progress.[2]

As we come before the Lord in worship and unveil our faces and minds, He is able to shine the light of His truth on any matter of significance within us. This truth is costly, for we then must choose: either to agree with God—embracing His likeness in exchange for our inadequacies and unworthiness—or to return to darkness.

Brace yourself. Worship is an adventure of the soul. He takes us to the depths of self so that we might become transparent before Him in the beholding of His glory—our eternal hope.

THE WORK OF UNVEILING

. . . with unveiled face—There is a degree of unveiling that we must do ourselves, but the greatest work of unveiling is done by Him—the Render of all veils. Every unveiling is largely a work of His grace.

When I see this phrase, I am reminded of a bride and groom standing before an altar. One of the greatest moments of any wedding ceremony is when the groom lifts the veil off the face of his bride, and kisses her. Our Bridegroom has come to unveil the Christian and cause our hearts to become more and more transparent before Him. Our worship is the kiss of devotion that we give to our true love—Jesus Christ.

The Song of Solomon begins with the Shulamite woman asking her Beloved for a kiss:

> Let him kiss me with the kisses of his mouth—For your love is better than wine. (Song of Sol. 1:2)

As we kiss the Lord, we need to be reminded of the following points:[3]

- We can only kiss one person at a time. Worshipers only have eyes for Him.

- When we kiss we have to stop talking. There are times in worship when we need to stop talking, and commune with Him from the inner sanctuary of our hearts.

- A kiss is a face to face encounter. Worship is all the more delightful because it, too, involves a face to face encounter.

Our worship is the kiss of devotion that we give to our true love—Jesus Christ

---

Other kisses of worship between the Lord and His people are found in Luke 7:38,45, and Luke 15:20.

Hosea 2:14–23 speaks prophetically of the Lord alluring His love, the Church, into the wilderness. Here is where He desires to meet with us, bringing changes to our lives and betrothing us to Him forever. In the wilderness, He. . .

- Turns our desert into a vineyard—v. 15
- Turns our valleys into doors of hope and opportunity—v. 15
- Turns our sorrows into songs—v. 15
- Turns our hearts which worship false gods (Baals) into hearts which cry "My Husband"—vs. 16–17
- Turns our broken promises into a fresh covenant born in righteousness, justice, lovingkindness, mercy and faithfulness—vs. 19–20

How the Lord delights in his people! He is the one who draws us, cleanses us, and restores us to right standing with Him.

> Who is this coming out of the wilderness like pillars of smoke, perfumed with myrrh and frankincense, with all the merchant's fragrant powders? (Song of Sol. 3:6)

> Who is this coming up from the wilderness, leaning upon her beloved? (Song of Sol. 8:5)

Worship is the place of our encounters with God, time and again. When He ravishes our hearts in the wilderness, we become as a pillar of smoke or a city conquered; we smell like Him—the fragrances of his victories—as we lean upon Him with utter dependence, every devotion centered in Him. Hear His voice as He calls for us to draw near:

> "O my dove, in the clefts of the rock, in the secret places of the cliff, let me see your face, let me hear your voice; for your voice is sweet, and your face is lovely." (Song of Sol. 2:14)

JESUS RENT THE VEIL ON CALVARY

. . . *with unveiled face*—As Christians, we are able to approach the Lord with every man-made veil and hindrance between us removed because of Calvary. These passages reveal the confidence that adorns the Church as we are invited to come to His very throne with boldness:

> Let us therefore come boldly to the throne of grace. . . (Heb. 4:16)

> Therefore, brethren, having boldness to enter the Holiest by the blood of Jesus, by a new and living way which He consecrated for us, through the veil, that is, His flesh, . . . let us draw near with a true heart in full assurance of faith, having our hearts sprinkled from an evil conscience and our bodies washed with pure water. (Heb. 10:19–20, 22)

> (See also Eph. 2:13)

We now have access to the Father through Christ—His humanity being the only veil that stands between us and the Father. As He was being "wounded for our transgressions and bruised for our iniquities" (Is. 53:5), the veil in the temple was rent from top to bottom as a sign that Christ had given us access to God. How He longs to reveal Himself to every believer!

In Exodus 33:18, Moses uttered the most dangerous and yet most wonderful prayer in the Bible: "Please, show me Your glory." In His answer, the Lord told Moses that no man could see His face and stay alive (v. 20). God's plan was to hide Moses in the cleft of the rock (Christ) and place His hand over the cleft as He passed in front of Moses and spoke His names. Moses was then permitted to see His back each time God passed by. The implication here is that the fullness of the glory of God is manifested in His face and in the utterance of His names. He has revealed Himself in and through His names.

No man has ever been able to look upon the face of God, as His glory is too much for human flesh to bear. Moses would have been killed had he seen the full glory of God's face. Jacob was amazed that he was not consumed when he saw the face of God (Gen.32:30).

To this day, flesh will be consumed in His presence. When we see Him as He is, flesh will melt away, and we will be like Him— a spirit (1 Jn. 3:2). In truth, only a spiritual body could survive being with Him for eternity.

As we approach the Lord today, we still need to be hidden to see His glory. For now, God "hides" Himself from His people so that only smaller, more bearable glimpses of His glory are commonly seen. His hand covers and protects us, as it protected Moses, from the full impact of His glory.

The blood of Jesus acts as a veil to hide us and make us able to stand in the presence of His Shekinah glory. Through prayer and worship, He has provided a hiding place for us so that His nature and name might be made known to us.

Consider each of these five hiding places of God; they are like secret entrances into His holy place:

- The secret place of darkness (Job 20:26; Ps. 18:11; Is. 45:3)

- The secret place of His tabernacle (Ps. 27:5)

- The secret place of His presence (Ps. 31:20)

- The secret place of thunder (Ps. 81:7)

- The secret place of the stairs (cliff, mountain), (Song of Sol. 2:14)

As always, His secrets are not for the purpose of keeping things from us, but that we would become aware of even greater unfoldings of His glory.

When Moses came down from the mountain of God, he had to veil his face because it was made so bright—from the sight of the back of God and the glory that shone around Him—that the Hebrews could not bear to look at him. When he returned to talk with God, he removed the veil (Ex. 34:29–35).

> Just as Moses removed the veil when he "went in before the Lord to speak with Him" (Ex. 34:34), so now any man who turns to the Lord finds the veil lifted from his heart.[4] (Abingdon)

According to Paul, Jews today still have a veil on their hearts, but, like any of us, they will find the veil lifted when they turn to the Lord (2 Cor. 3:16).

Press into God with all your heart. Seek
His face and allow the glory of the
Lord, His beauty and character, to
shine like a light from your face
for everyone to see

THE FATHER SEEKS THREE KINDS OF PEOPLE

. . . with unveiled face—As we come before the face of God in worship, we will often be drawn by the Holy Spirit into the place of intercession. Worship and intercession are so closely related. God's transparent people must be an interceding people.

The Father only seeks three kinds of people:

- The lost (Ez. 43:12, Lu. 15:11–32, 19:10)
- Worshipers (Jn. 4:23)
- Intercessors (Is. 59:16, Ez. 22:30)

These three remain inextricably linked forever in the place of worship.

WE SEEK HIS FACE

. . . with unveiled face—As we remove the veil from our faces, we are more able to receive the blessing that comes from the face of God (see also Ps. 119:135; Ps. 67:1):

> The LORD make His face shine upon you, and be gracious to you. (Num. 6:25)

It is His face, or presence, that we seek. The Hebrew word for *the face of God—peniyel* (Strong's, #6439), which comes from *panah* (Strong's, #6437)—is the same as the Hebrew word for *the presence of God*. To come into the presence of God is the same as coming before His face. When we seek His face, we are seeking His presence. Note the intensity with which the Psalmist instructs us to seek the face of God:

> You have said, Seek you My face—inquire for and require My presence [as your vital need]. My heart says to You, Your face [Your presence], Lord, will I seek, inquire for and require [of necessity and on the authority of Your Word]. (Ps. 27:8, Amp.)

> Seek, inquire of and for the Lord, and crave Him and His strength [His might and inflexibility to temptation, seek and require His face and His presence continually] evermore. (Ps. 105:4, Amp.)

Press into God with all your heart. Seek His face and allow the glory of the Lord, His beauty and His character to shine like a light from your face for everyone to see. ❧

Chapter Seven

WORSHIP IS PROPHETIC
" . . . beholding as in a mirror"

. . . to behold Him is to love Him, and to love Him is to worship Him.
Judson Cornwall

≫

*B*eholding as in a mirror—one of the key words, here, is "beholding." It is because of the beholding that worship is prophetic. There is a sight to see whenever we unveil our faces and worship. The sight is that of the glory of God. Again, this sight is for every worshiper of every denomination, generation, and nation on earth. It makes worship alive, full of meaning and completely delightful rather than a ritual to be performed weekly. The greatest hope of every believer is to see God, and the greatest worship comes from the things we have seen and experienced of Him ourselves.

GAZING UPON GOD

The yearning heart of the worshiper is described in these verses as the Psalmist lifts His eyes to the Lord to feast upon the sight of His mercy:

> Unto You I lift up my eyes, O You who dwell in the heavens. Behold, as the eyes of servants look to the hand of their masters, as the eyes of a maid to the hand of her mistress, so our eyes look to the LORD our God, until He has mercy on us. (Ps. 123:1–2)

The true worshiper has every opportunity to gaze upon God—not during a few select moments of life, but whenever our hearts would desire to meet with Him. The inward eye of the spirit needs only to focus upon His presence, and every longing of our hearts will be satisfied. May our longing for the sight of God match that of Charles Spurgeon, who wrote:

> We will never want any joy beyond that of seeing Him.[1]

As I have stated again and again in this book, true worship is dependent upon our sight of or encounter with God. The sight of Him should not just be our desire, but our goal for every moment with the Lord. Judson Cornwall also emphasizes this point:

> Thanksgiving and praise are often responses to Christ's deeds, but worship is always based on his person. Fundamentally, worship is a person responding to a person, so we can't worship until we get a glimpse of God. . . we must be in God's presence to worship. True worship will not begin to flow until we get a good glimpse of Christ Jesus.[2]

David clothed himself in the righteousness of God. Because of this, he was able to look upon the face of the Lord just as Moses did. Although we do not need to wait until we are perfect, worshipers under the New Covenant must also be clothed in righteousness as we draw near to the Lord. It is entirely a work of His grace; there is nothing we can do to earn His approval. When we behold the Lord we will cry out with this prayer of David, who desired to wake, morning by morning, with more and more of God's likeness upon his life:

> As for me, I will see Your face in righteousness; I shall
> be satisfied when I awake in Your likeness. (Ps. 17:15)

There is an important spiritual principle revealed in our text (2 Cor 3:18): *we become like the God we look upon and worship.* This makes worship far more than a duty to be performed; it is a holy exchange of life and devotion between the Lord and His people.

David made his desire to see God an urgent request—one that was even commanded by God in His Word:

One thing have I asked of the Lord, that will I seek after, inquire for and [insistently] require, that I may dwell in the house of the Lord [in His presence] all the days of my life, **to behold and gaze upon the beauty [the sweet attractiveness and the delightful loveliness] of the Lord,** and to meditate, consider and inquire in His temple. . . You have said, Seek you My face— inquire for and require My presence [as your vital need]. My heart says to You, Your face [Your presence], Lord, will I seek, inquire for and require [of necessity and on the authority of Your Word]. (Ps. 27:4, 8, Amp.)

It is because of the beholding that worship is prophetic.

Because of the overwhelming sight of God, anyone who desires to see His glory must first be hidden in the Rock:

- Moses was hidden in a rock
  (Ex. 33:21–22)

- David was hidden in a rock
  (Ps. 27:5)

- Jesus was hidden in a rock
  (Matt. 27:60–28:2)

Now we have this same opportunity: to become worshipers who behold the face of God. Because of His great grace, Christ— the Rock (Rom. 9:33; 1 Cor. 10:4)—has made a way for us to be hidden in Him:

For you died, and your life is hidden with Christ in God. (Col. 3:3)

What a magnificent plan! He died and rose again so that He might live in us and His glory would be revealed:

Christ within and among you the hope of [realizing] the glory. (Col. 1:27b, Amp.)

Many Christians accept Christ as their Savior, but do not avail themselves of the second part of this great mystery: that we must also die (to self) and live as ones who are hidden in Him.

. . . beholding as in a mirror—In his book, *All the 3s of the Bible*,[3] Herbert Lockyer comments on the passage in Hebrews 9:24–28 where there are three aspects of the Lord's appearing. For easier reference, I have organized Lockyer's thoughts into a table along with Vine's Greek definitions (Table 2).

It is obvious that the Lord is not passive on the issue of appearing before His people. The sight of Him in our past, present and future should change us forever. All believers need to look for Him at every opportunity.

TABLE 2

THREE ASPECTS OF THE LORD'S APPEARING

Heb. 9:26 The past appearing	Heb. 9:24 The present appearing	Heb. 9:28 The prospective appearing
"...He has appeared to put away sin..."	"...now to appear in the presence of God for us..."	"...He will appear a second time..."
phaneroo[4]—Gk. for *appear*: to be manifested or revealed in one's true character as opposed to one who might appear in a false guise or without disclosure of what he truly is	**emphanizo**—Gk. for *appear*: "to shine in," used literally of physical manifestation (Matt. 27:53; Jn. 14:22) or metaphorically of the spiritual experience of Christ by believers who abide in His love (Jn. 14:21)	**optomai**—Gk. for *appear*: "to see." The English word optical comes from this word
This appearing is past and permanent	This appearing is present and progressive	This appearing is prospective and perfect
We have salvation from the penalty of sin	We have salvation from the power of sin	We have salvation from the entire presence of sin
Looking back, we see Jesus dying for us	Looking up, we see Jesus pleading for us	Looking forward, we see Jesus returning for us

Note Vine's commentary on the Greek word, *emphanizo*. This word indicates that Christ manifests Himself "by the Holy Spirit in the spiritual experience of believers *who abide in His love*." Vine takes this from John 14:21 where Jesus said that He would manifest (disclose and give intimate knowledge of) Himself to those who love Him. Above all else, worshipers must be those who love Him.

Allow the Lord to reveal Himself in every aspect of your life in Him. As Lockyer has said, this beholding of God is not only *present*, but it is *progressive* in its revelation. The sight of His glory awaits us all!

. . . *beholding as in a mirror*—Worship always includes some aspect of beholding God. When we are focused on Him, our eyes turn away from ourselves and focus on the only One who is worthy of worship. Worship is only possible when we see Him as He really is and surrender our hearts to Him in humility, abandon, and adoration. We waste every moment in His presence while we are thinking about ourselves, our needs or our surroundings.

As we stand in the light of God, more and more of His glory and holiness are revealed to us—". . . in Your light we see light" (Ps. 36:9).

All created beings look for Him when they worship, and become consumed with the sight of Him in all His glory and splendor. The Book of Revelation is filled with John's descriptions of the heavenly beings who crowd around the throne of God to adore Him. The worship in heaven is made possible because of the sight of God. How much more should our focus be upon Him. He is worthy beyond all measure to receive praise and worship from every fiber of our being.

THE MIRROR

. . . *beholding as in a mirror*—When we look into a natural mirror, we see our own reflection. But when we look into *this* mirror, it is like no other. We see the face of God in all His glory looking back at us, and we are changed into His likeness as we behold Him. The only way that this supernatural beholding can work is if we have the abiding presence of God within us. For Believers, Christ and all His glory dwell within us: ". . . Christ in you the hope of glory" (Col. 1:27). This is the essence of prophetic worship.

The image in a mirror is extremely accurate. It is not like a painting that may show an enhanced or idealized image, depending upon the whim and skill of the painter. The very nature of a mirror conveys an exact image to the one looking. The degree of the beholding, then, must depend upon the unveiling. Only to the degree that we unveil ourselves, or allow ourselves to be unveiled by Christ, will we see accurately in the mirror.

The Greek word for *mirror* that is used in this passage is *katoptrizomai*—(Strong's #2734) from *kata*, "against," and *opomai*, "I look." It means "to mirror oneself," "to see reflected," "looking into a mirror" or "discerning by reflected light."

> Mirrors in antiquity consisted of a metal surface, made usually of copper, silver, gold, electrum, or, especially in Palestine during the postexilic period, of bronze.[5] (Danker)

Because the ancient mirror was made of metal, it was liable to rust or tarnish and needed regular attention to be kept bright. Likewise, we must read the Word of God and minister before Him in worship on a regular basis so that our vision of Him will remain clear and sharp.

I believe the mirror in 2 Corinthians 3:18 represents the Word and presence of God. When we stand in the light of these, that same light is strangely reflected, in and through our lives. Bible Commentator Adam Clark expresses this same thought in reference to the Gospel:

> Now as mirrors, among the Jews, Greeks, and Romans, were made of highly polished metal, it would often happen, especially in strong light, that the face would be greatly illuminated by this strongly reflected light; and to this circumstance the apostle seems here to allude. So, by earnestly contemplating the Gospel of Jesus, and believing on Him who is its Author, the soul becomes illuminated with His divine splendor, for this sacred mirror reflects back on the believing soul the image of Him whose perfections it exhibits; and thus we see the glorious form after which our minds are to be fashioned; and by believing and receiving the influ-

ence of His Spirit, . . . our form is changed. . . into the same image, which we behold there; and this image of God, lost by our fall, and now recovered and restored by Jesus Christ: for the shining of the face of God upon us, i.e. approbation, through Christ, is the cause of our transformation into the Divine image.[6]

> Whenever we look into the Word of
> God with open hearts and unveiled
> faces, there is the potential for us to
> behold aspects of Christ that we
> have never seen before.

Whenever we look into the Word of God with open hearts and unveiled faces, there is the potential for us to behold aspects of Christ that we have never seen before. He is there as a jewel on every page. True worshipers are those who love and crave the Word of God. Tippit speaks of beholding the Lord through His Word and the mystery of finding Him there:

> Anytime and anywhere people have discovered the truth of the Scriptures, it has resulted in a great awakening of their hearts to worship the Lord Jesus . . . Something dynamic happens when the Bible is opened. Lives are changed. Christ is exalted. And worship flows from the hearts of God's people. The miracle that transpires in the hearts of people is inexplicable.[7]

We usually look into a mirror as we clothe, beautify, and perfect ourselves. So also, as we look into this mirror, let us be clothed, made beautiful, and perfected as we look upon Christ. Let us adorn ourselves with His glorious attire: the beauty of His character and the perfection of His holiness.

LOOKING FOR HIS COUNTENANCE

. . . *beholding as in a mirror*—In 2 Corinthians 3:7–16, Paul contrasts the plight of the Hebrews, who were not able to look upon the glory that shone from Moses' face, with this invitation to us all to look into the glorious face of God. Moses was the mediator of the Old Covenant, which was to be done away with. Paul argues that if this Old Covenant—which passed away—was delivered with such glory and splendor, how much more glory is there for us to see who peer into the resplendent face of Christ.

> But if the ministry of death, written and engraved on stones, was glorious, so that the children of Israel could not look steadily at the face of Moses because of the glory of his countenance, which glory was passing away, how will the ministry of the Spirit not be more glorious? For if the ministry of condemnation had glory, the ministry of righteousness exceeds much more in glory. (2 Cor. 3:7–9)

Whenever hungry people saw Jesus, they were "greatly amazed, and running to Him, greeted Him" (Mk. 9:15). Jesus was more glorious than Moses—who had to veil his face after he had been with God—yet the multitude were never blinded or repelled by His glory.

> The glory of the law repels, but the greater glory of Jesus attracts.[8] (Spurgeon)

Sinners were never put off by the light of grace and truth that shone from the face of Jesus. The touch of His hand, the gaze of His eye and the sound of His voice only served to heal broken and desperate seekers. That same sight is still at hand for the saved and unsaved alike. We must continue to run to the light of His glory and behold Him again and again. The Church must become the beacon of grace, truth, and glory that men so desperately thirst for in this day.

. . . *beholding as in a mirror*—We are to worship as *a prophetic people*, not merely as a people who believe in prophecy. Prophetic people look for the Lord at every opportunity.

Dr. David Blomgren speaks of a corporate "prophetic unction which brings a dimension of Divine quickening into our worship. . . . The prophetic spirit coming and permeating the worship atmosphere is a witness of the presence of Jesus being manifest in the service."[9]

There must come a sense of destiny upon God's people in these days. We live in a time of great privilege and blessing. Surely, we *shall* witness the glory of God cover the earth as the waters cover the sea.

We are to worship as a prophetic people, not merely as a people who believe in prophecy.

. . . *beholding as in a mirror*—The Holy Spirit uses a great variety and multitude of means to make Christ "visible" to us in praise and worship. Each of these causes us to "see" Him more clearly and to embrace His likeness more fully. Some of the tools the Holy Spirit uses to draw us to Himself in worship include:

- The Word of God—(Ex. 24:7; Neh. 8:1–12; Ps. 119:162; Matt. 3:1–3; Mk. 1:14; Acts 4:4, 31; 10:44; 24:14; Rom. 10:15, 17; 1 Cor. 1:17, 23; Col. 3:16; 1 Tim. 4:13; Heb. 4:12; 1 Jn. 2:14; 5:7; Rev. 1:3)
  —The preached word of God
  —The written Word of God
  —The prophesied word of God

- The service (liturgy), communion and the body ministry or fellowship that follows—
  (Acts 2:42–47; 4:32–35; 20:7, 11; 1 Cor. 10:16; 11:23–26; 14:26)

- All nine gifts of the Holy Spirit—
  (1 Cor. 12:8–10)

  —Three help us think the thoughts of God: knowledge, discerning of spirits, wisdom
  —Three help us speak like God: prophecy, tongues, interpretation of tongues
  —Three help us do the acts of God: faith, miracles, healing

- The songs we sing—(Acts 16:25–26; 1 Cor. 14:15; Eph. 5:19; Col. 3:16; Jas. 5:13)
  —Psalms: the "Old Testament" Psalms were the hymnal of the early Church. Other New Testament psalms were also written.

—Hymns: songs of praise and worship that are composed by man. They usually contain the truths of the New Covenant.

—Spiritual songs: a song (mostly spontaneous) that has been inspired by the Holy Spirit. Spiritual songs may be sung in our native tongue, or in an unknown tongue. The spiritual song may be sung by one or two people so that everyone can hear (some call this, the "prophetic song"), or by the whole congregation at once.

- Silence—(Ps. 65:1 Amp.; Hab. 2:20; Acts 11:18; Rev 8:1)

- Prayer—(Ps. 141:2; Matt. 6:9–13; Lu. 3:21; 11:2–4; Acts 4:31; 16:25; 1 Cor. 14:15; Jas. 5:13, 16; 1 Pet. 3:12; Jude 20)

- Acts or services of dedication and repentance—(2 Chron. 7:1–11; Lu. 15:10; Acts 2:38; 3:19; 2 Cor. 7:10–11)
  —Altar calls
  —Special public prayer such as healing prayer

- Other symbolic events:
  —Baptism, Matt. 3:13–17; Mk. 1:9–11;
     Lu. 3:21–22; Jn. 1:31–34; Acts 2:38; 19:5
  —Laying on of hands, Acts 8:17; 19:6
  —Processions, 1 Chron. 13:5–8; Ps. 68:24–27; Matt. 21:1–9; Mk. 11:1–10; Jn. 12:12–15; Rev. 14:1–4; 19:11–14

- Other art forms, such as:
  —Instrumental music played to inspire or
     prophesy: 1 Chron, 25:1–6
  —Dance: 2 Sam. 6:14; Ps. 149:3; 150:4
  —Mime/drama/storytelling/poetry:
     Ez. 37:1–15; Psalms and other poetry books:
     Lu. 15

—The arts that beautify the house of God and reveal
His nature there: Ex. 25:8–9; 35:4–19, 35:30–39

When music is ministered as part of the prophetic "uncovering"
of the Lord in a given setting, it is almost as if there is a "sound
within the sound." This is not a sound that is heard with the ear
but an anointing that is only perceived in the heart.

Other art forms may also become involved in the prophetic
ministry of the Lord—and can become so unified that the dancers
dance what the musicians play, the singers sing what the dancers
dance, and so forth. Music and the other arts also have the ability
to present symbols for ideas and feelings that lie above and beyond
them. The ultimate significance of all this is that the sight and
sound of God are made known more fully in the service.

Prophetic worship is dependent upon
music that contains a
"sound within the sound."

I believe that more and more art forms are about to be restored
within the worship context of the Church. For example, I once witnessed a painter paint a beautiful mural on the inside wall of a
church during worship.[10] I have watched dramatic sculptor, Tracy
Sugg, create prophetic sculpture during worship, molding images
that draw the heart to worship Him, again and again.

The purpose of incorporating such graphic arts into worship is
to craft, more completely and more excellently, a vision of God
before His people. When we are able to "see" and "hear" God in
or through a work of art, we can truthfully deem that work to be
prophetic. As with Michelangelo, the work of truly great and
prophetic artists will last forever. 🖎

Chapter Eight

WORSHIP IS TRANSCENDENT
"... the glory of the Lord"

Worship is eternally and inseparably linked to the glory of God.

≈

*T*he glory of the Lord—What a sight! According to this scripture, we are privileged to behold the very glory of God whenever we worship. In fact, the chief goal of worship is to bring mankind into contact with the glory of the Lord.

The Lord is known in Scripture as *The Lord (or God) of Glory* (Pss. 24:8, 10; 29:3; Acts 7:2; 1 Cor. 2:8; Eph. 1:17; Jas. 2:1). He is also called the *Father of glory* (Eph. 1:17). Judson Cornwall points out that He cannot be God without His glory.[1]

I would venture to say that the main subject of the whole Bible is the glory of the Lord. The entire book is centered around our glorious God who, in His infinite wisdom, has created a universe that is in the process of being formed into the likeness of His glory.

> For of Him and through Him and to Him *are* all things,
> to whom *be* glory forever. Amen. (Rom. 11:36)

The *International Standard Bible Encyclopedia* includes the following statement on the glory of the Lord:

> *Glory of God.*—In the ultimate sense, no subject is more important than this.[2]

Throughout the Word, we are being called to the transforming process that works in us because of the glory: if we would behold Him and worship Him, we would be changed and conformed into His glorious image. This is probably why worship is such a key issue for every individual. It is the grace and mercy of God that has always provided a way for mankind to draw near to Him. He is the one who has taken the initiative in making Himself known.

. . . *the glory of the Lord*—The plan of God is simple, yet so profound and powerful. He has created a people who would worship Him of their own free will. In the context of worship, God's people will behold His glory, become changed into the likeness of that glory and serve as ministers of His glory in all the earth. We must understand that to see God's glory is to see the King whose beauty outshines all imaginable loveliness. To look into the face of God is to look at the sight of pure love, holiness and every degree of His most excellent graces.

> The chief goal of worship is to bring mankind into contact with the glory of the Lord.

Adam Clarke comments on the sight of His glory and the change that is woven into the lives of those who see Him:

> As clearly as we can see our own natural face in a mirror, [we also see] the glorious promises and privileges of the Gospel of Christ; and while we contemplate, we anticipate them by desire and hope, and apprehend them by faith, and are changed from the glory there represented to the enjoyment of the thing which is represented, even the glorious image—righteousness and true holiness—of the glory of the God of glory.[3]

. . . *the glory of the Lord*—In the Hebrew, the primary word for glory is *kabod* (kaw-bode', Strong's #3519), meaning: *weight, splendor, glorious, copious, heavy.*

It is almost as if the glory of God, when encountered, is like a sublime heaviness that rests upon the soul. His weight is not a burden or imposition of any kind. Every thought of Him and every layer of the knowledge of His glorious character is the joy, nourishment, delight and full satisfaction of every man.

> . . . for the biblical worshiper, God is not an idea; he is a compelling reality encountered at the deepest level of being.[4] (Richard Leonard)

Every church and every believer must make room for God to presence Himself within them. We must allow the weight of His glory to rest upon every area of our lives until His virtue permeates every thought, every breath and every desire of our hearts.

Every thought of Him and every layer of
the knowledge of His glorious character
is the joy, nourishment, delight and full
satisfaction of every man.

THE GLORY OF GOD FILLS OUR SENSES

... *the glory of the Lord*—The glory of the Lord is more than a supernatural manifestation that will be seen in the earth during the last days (Hab. 2:14). I believe that the glory of God is also His nature and character revealed to us in some way through our spiritual and natural senses—sight, sound, touch, taste and smell. Through these, God has made a way for us to know Him more deeply.

To see or know the glory of God really means that we are seeing or knowing another layer of His essence or nature. There is no sight as lovely as Him in all the earth. He desires to draw nearer to us than our very breath and uses every means available to make Himself known to us. By filling the universe with His presence, He has demonstrated His intention to communicate with us at every moment of every day.

> He is delightful to every sense, to the eye most fair, to the ear most gracious, to the spiritual nostril most sweet. The excellencies of Jesus are all most precious, comparable to the rarest spices . . . all sweetness meet in Jesus, and are poured forth wherever he is present.[5] (Charles Spurgeon)

In Exodus 33:18–23 and 34:5–7, Moses prayed the most dangerous, yet delightful, prayer in the whole Bible when he asked God if he could see His glory. God's response to Moses' request was very interesting. It shows us two important ways we can experience the glory of God:

1. *Seeing the glory of God*—God said to Moses that no one could see His face and stay alive. (That is why Moses' prayer was so dangerous.) We must assume that the sight of God's glory some- how involves the sight of His face. (Other scriptures that refer to seeing the glory of God: Ex. 16:7; Pss. 63:2; 97:6; Is. 35:2; 40:5; 62:2; Is. 66:18; Matt. 24:30; Mark 13:26; Luke 21:27; John 11:40.) I believe we see His glory in all creation, in His Word, in the smile of a child and in the kindness of a friend. All believers are invited to behold the sight of His glory (or radiance) every day. "Blessed are the pure in heart, for they shall see God" (Matt. 5:8).

The sight of His glory may also include supernatural manifesta- tions such as healings, miracles, a visible cloud of glory in the room or other unusual effects. On one occasion, during worship at Shady Grove Church, some ceiling lights fell out of their sockets and the lights all surged on and off as if they were unable to con- tain the power and the glory of God (!). That day, great miracles of deliverance took place in the presence of God.

2. *Hearing the glory of God*—The Lord allowed Moses to be hidden in the cleft of a rock while He walked back and forth before Moses, declaring His name. Moses was not permitted to see the face of God on this occasion, but he saw the back of God and heard His voice as the Lord spoke of His name and attributes. Moses also heard God's voice out of the burning bush. At the sound of His name ("I Am"—Ex. 3:4–14), Moses was changed forever.

There are layers of glory that He desires to reveal to us through the sound of His name and every time He speaks to us.

When we sing of the Lord and declare His name and mysteries, we are meant to partake of the wonders we are singing about. Jesus desires that we hear His voice: "My sheep hear my voice. . . " (John 10:27) for "The words that I speak to you are spirit, and they are life" (John 6:63).

We must tune our ears to hear His voice, for we are worshipers, and our very food is to hear His voice. There are layers of glory that He desires to reveal to us through the sound of His name and every time He speaks to us.

Our other three senses are also able to receive revelations of God's glory (but we must remember that, although our five senses are able to physically see, hear, smell, taste, and touch the glory and essence of God, sometimes He reveals Himself to our inner spiritual eyes and ears):

3. *Tasting the glory of God*—The Lord invites us to taste and see that He is good (Ps. 34:8). His words taste sweeter than honey (Ps. 119:103) and his fruit delights the taste of the Bride (Song of Sol. 2:3).

4. *Smelling the glory of God*—The Lord's wedding garments smell of myrrh, aloes, and cassia (Ps. 45:8). The Shulamite sang of our Lord, whose name is like fragrant ointments (Song of Sol. 1:3). He is described as a "bundle of myrrh" and as the merchant who has fragrant powders (Song of Sol. 3:6). The cry "Abba Father" (Mk. 14:36; Rom. 8:15; Gal. 4:6) means "Daddy, I love your smell."[6]

5. *Touching the glory of God*—Many knew that if they could only touch Jesus—even the hem of His garment—they would be healed (Matt. 9:21; 14:36; Mk 3:10; 5:28; 6:56; 8:22; 10:13; Lu. 6:19).

I have experienced the touch and weight of the glory of God in prayer and worship on numerous occasions, where His hand has pressed me into a chair or onto the floor where I could not move for hours. At other times, His love causes delightful pangs within my heart, and He takes my breath away. In no way are these frightening experiences. He overtakes us with love. Every touch of His hand and every contact with His glory only means that another portion of my heart has been conquered and laid bare for the imprint of His nature.

There are not words enough for encounters with God's glory. He leaves us speechless. The goal is not just to have experiences, but to become more like Him—more loving, gracious, obedient, full of joy, holy, and peaceful.

Merrill Unger shows us the relationship between God's glory and holiness. He says that glory is:

> . . . the manifestation of his divine attributes and perfections, or such a visible effulgence as indicates the possession and presence of these. . . . God's glory is the

correlative of his holiness. . . . is that in which holiness comes to expression. Glory is the expression of holiness, as beauty is the expression of health.[7]

We know that the sight, sound, taste, smell and touch of the glory of God are freely available for all believers at all times. Though God reveals Himself layer by layer to us, we can never know the depth and wonder of the knowledge of the glory of God that He wants to reveal to us. We have no idea what awaits us in His presence.

LAYERS OF GLORY

. . . the glory of the Lord—There are more than four hundred and fifty references in Scripture concerning the glory of the Lord. I was surprised to find that around half of these are found in the New Testament. Just based on a few of these scriptures, we can learn the following facts about the glory of God:

Seeing the glory: The glory of God has been seen by Old and New Testament saints (Ex. 16:7; Lev. 9:6; Num. 14:10; 16:19; 20:6; Pss. 63:2; 97:6; Is. 40:5; Ez. 1:28; 3:23; 8:4; Lu. 2:9; Jn. 2:11; 11:40; 17:24; Acts 7:2; 7:55; 22:11) and can be seen by us now (2 Cor. 3:18).

When we see the glory of God, that same glory is seen in us (Ps. 34:5; 2 Cor. 3:7–18). We behold the glory of God whenever we are with Him (Jn. 17:24).

The glory of God has appeared in a cloud (Ex. 16:10; Ezek. 10:4). The glory of God sometimes looks like a fire (Ex. 24:17; 2 Chron. 7:3). The glory of God sometimes looks like a rainbow (Ez. 1:28). The glory of God is seen in His face (Ex. 33:18–23).

The location of the glory: The glory of God is able to come into the sanctuary and leave the sanctuary (Ez. 10:4, 18; 44:4). The glory of God sanctifies the tabernacle (Ex. 29:43). The glory of God sometimes fills the whole sanctuary (2 Chron. 5:14; 7:1–3; Ps. 63:2; Ez. 43:5; 44:4; Rev. 15:8). The glory of God is going to fill the whole earth (Num. 14:21; Hab. 2:14; Pss. 57:5, 11; 72:19; 108:5).

The glory of God is to be declared in all the nations (1 Chron. 16:24; Is. 42:12; 66:18). The glory of God is to be declared by all people everywhere (1 Chron. 16:28–29; Pss. 29:1–2; 96:3, 7–8). The heavens declare the glory of God (Pss. 19:1; 97:6). The glory of God is declared continuously before the throne of God (Is. 6:3; Rev. 4:8). The glory of God accompanies His presence (1 Chron. 16:27).

The effect of the glory: The glory of God has, at times, caused men to be unable to stand (1 Ki. 8:11; 2 Chron. 5:14; 7:2; Ez. 44:4; Acts 22:6). The glory of God is a fearful thing (Ps. 102:15; Is. 2:10, 19, 21; 59:19; Lu. 2:9).

The crown of glory: God is clothed and crowned with glory (Job 40:10; Heb. 2:9). God's people form a crown of glory for the Lord (Is. 62:3)—(Note: the Lord has been crowned three times—with glory, thorns, the Church)—God will become an eternal crown of Glory to His people (Is. 28:5; 1 Pet. 5:4). Our God is the King of glory (Ps. 24:10).

The glory in the last days and through eternity: The Lord is going to appear in glory (Ps. 102:16)—Everyone on earth will see the Lord coming in glory (Matt. 24:30). The glory of God will endure forever (Ps. 104:31; Matt. 6:13; 1 Pet. 5:11; Rev. 4:9, 11; 5:12–13; 7:12; 19:1). The glory of God will provide light for all eternity (Is. 60:19; 21:23). The glory of God on earth is going to be greater in the last days than at any other time in history (Hag. 2:9). All believers will be presented faultless before His glory (Jude 24).

The possession of the glory: The glory of God is the inheritance of the wise (Prov. 3:35). The glory of God cannot be shared with anyone—it is God's alone (Is. 42:8; 48:11). Sin has caused mankind to fall short of the glory (Rom. 3:23). Our greatest hope is the glory of God (Rom. 5:2; Col. 1:27). God gives us all a spirit of wisdom and revelation so that we might receive greater understanding of Him and the work of His glory in our lives (Eph. 1:17–19).

The revelation of the glory: The glory of God will be seen upon God's people (Is. 60:1–2; 62:2; Hag. 2:7). God is intent upon revealing His glory in and through His people (Is. 43:7; 60:7; Jn. 17:10, 22; Rom. 8:18, 30; 1 Cor. 2:7; 10:31; 2 Cor. 10:17; Gal. 6:14; Eph. 3:21; 5:27; 1 Pet. 5:1)—accompanied with great rejoicing (1 Pet. 4:13; 5:1). The glory of God surrounds those who serve Him (Is. 58:8). The glory of God is manifested in and through Jesus (Jn. 1:14; 2:11; 12:23; 13:31–32; 14:13; 17:1, 4–5). The glory of God is revealed through us whenever we bear fruit (Jn.

15:8). Joy in Christ is a joy that is filled with the glory of God (1 Pet. 1:8). Only God is worthy to receive all glory (Rev. 4:11; 5:12).

When we see the glory of God, that same glory is seen in us.

GLORY TRANSCENDENT AND NUMINOUS

. . . *the glory of the Lord* —True worship will invariably contain an element of transcendence. Transcendent worship is vertical worship, where we tend to sing and minister *to* God rather than singing *about* Him. Transcendent worship also draws us away from focusing on our needs. It is transcendent worship that lifts us into an encounter and understanding of the awesome and glorious God who is our King and Father. In this day, where we have lost so much respect for authority, it seems that it is easy to become too self-absorbed and familiar with God. We seem to have forgotten that our every breath is in His hand (Job 12:10; 34:14–15); that His face shines with the same brilliance as the sun (Rev. 1:16); that He is clothed in greatness, power and majesty (1 Chron. 29:11; Pss. 93:1; 104:1); that He alone is full of wisdom, perfect in beauty, beyond compare, and completely past finding out (Job 9:10; 11:7).

> Oh, the depth of the riches both of the wisdom and knowledge of God! How unsearchable are His judgments and His ways past finding out! (Rom. 11:33)

No one can say it quite like Charles Spurgeon:

> The Master has riches beyond the count of mathematics, the measurement of reason, the dream of imagination, or the eloquence of words. . . . the unsearchable riches of Christ is the tune for the minstrels of earth and the song for the harpists of heaven.[8]

LaMar Boschman often refers to transcendent worship in his writings and teachings. I agree wholeheartedly with Boschman when he insists that Christians need to focus more upon the majesty of the Lord in worship, rather than spending long periods of time singing to the Lord about our needs and His power to meet those needs:

> When we touch transcendent worship the temporal is transformed and abased. . . . When we experience this level of worship there is an awareness of the awesome presence of God.   . . . Our worship should transcend our feelings, needs and circumstances.[9]

Robert Webber and Richard Foster also call the believer to transcendent worship—worship wherein there is an encounter with God and a transcending of intellectual or selfish thought—where our whole being is consumed with the sight of Him:

> More than an intellectual assent to doctrine, creed, or prayer, worship is an experience of the presence of a holy God. Response to this encounter should touch the center of the worshiper's being, creating a sense of awe and mystery.[10]

> We desperately need to see who God is. . . . to meditate on his attributes, to gaze upon the revelation of his nature in Jesus Christ. When we see the Lord of hosts "high and lifted up," ponder his infinite wisdom and knowledge, wonder at his unfathomable mercy and love, we cannot help but move into doxology.[11]

> To worship is to experience reality, to touch life. It is to know, to feel, to experience the resurrected Christ in the midst of the gathered community. It is a breaking into the Shekinah of God, or better yet, being invaded by the Shekinah of God.[12]

Richard Leonard describes transcendent worship and the encounter with the glory of God that believers experience in worship as the *numinous* aspect of biblical worship.

> . . . in genuine biblical worship, the focus is always on the **One who is worshiped.** The biblical worshiper comes before the Creator with an overpowering sense of reverence, awe, even dread before the divine mystery. This aspect of worship is known as the **numinous.**[13]

An encounter with the numinous aspect of God's presence may range from the sweet impressions He makes upon our hearts of His nature and will, to a visible encounter, which is known as a *theophany*.

THEOPHANIES

Many theophanies have been recorded in the Bible. Several of those are outlined in Table 3, *Encounters With God*. The purpose in making such a thorough study of theophanies is—for those of us who would be students and seekers of His presence—that we would be able to recognize the kinds of preparation needed to encounter God, and the diverse manifestations and effects of His glory on humankind.

Our goal should not be just to experience supernatural manifestations, but to attain the deep knowledge of Him that weighs upon the soul. We would do well to pursue God with the same intensity and devotion of some of these Biblical characters.

In Table 3, *Encounters With God*, I have attempted to show the place of their encounter; how long they spent seeing God; what they did to prepare their lives for such a privileged sight; what they actually saw, or the supernatural manifestation that was revealed to them; the revelation they received; the resulting effect on their personal lives, and what lasting changes came as a result of the visitation of God.

The glory of the Lord is surely the most powerful force in the universe.

. . . *the glory of the Lord* —The glory of the Lord is surely the most powerful force in the universe. Whenever we worship, we create an atmosphere where God's power and potential are revealed.

Our whole lives are to be a statement of God's power and life. Our very lives are worship and bring glory to God. First Corinthians 10:31 says:

> Therefore, whether you eat or drink, or whatever you do, do all to the glory of God.

TABLE 3

ENCOUNTERS WITH GOD

NAME	PLACE	LENGTH/TIME	PREPARATION	MANIFESTATION	REVELATION RECEIVED	RESULT	AREA OF LIFE CHANGED
ADAM/EVE Gen. 2-3	Eden Gen. 2-3	?	God formed and initiated relationship with them	God walked openly before them Gen. 3:8	Whatever God showed them of Himself	1. Oneness with God 2. Sinlessness	We can only presume they grew from glory to glory
ENOCH Gen. 5:22-24	?	Three hundred years	He walked with God in habitual fellowship	?	?	God took him	He was given a glorified body
ABRAM Gen. 12:7	Shechem	?	Obedience to God's commands	The appearance of God	An unconditional promise to Abram and his descendants	He built an altar	He grew as a man of faith
ABRAM Gen. 17:1-22	?	?	Obedience to God's commands	The appearance of God	Abramic covenant and the promise of a son	He fell on His face, laughed	His name was changed
ABRAM/SARAH Gen. 18:1	By the oaks (terebinth trees) of Mamre	?	Obedience to God's commands	Three men (God) stood by him	Is any thing too hard for the Lord? Confirmation of previous promises destruction of Sodom & Gomorrah	He ran to greet and to minister to God bowed down	?
SARAH Gen. 21:1	Gerar	?	Faith in the promises of God Heb. 11:11	?		Her body was renewed she was able to conceive	Sarah had a child

NAME	A PLACE	LENGTH/TIME	PREPARATION	MANIFESTATION	REVELATION RECEIVED	RESULT	AREA OF LIFE CHANGED
JACOB Gen. 28:10-22	Probably Mt. Moriah	One night	Separation from family & inheritance	v12 Open heaven/ladder between heaven & earth/angels ascending and descending/the Lord stood beside him	Renewal of Abramic covenant /v16 "The Lord is in this place"	v17 Awe and fear of God	Beginning of a heart change/Jacob started to give to God v22
JACOB Gen. 32:22-32	Peniel (The face of God), over the brook—Jabbok	One night	v9 Prayer/v22-23 He passed over Jabbok (emptying) and left everything that he trusted in behind	Jacob fought all night with the Lord—he saw God face to face v30	Jacob had a revelation of himself as he faced God. The Lord changed his name	1. v2 repentence 2. v26 He fought God for His blessing	1. v28 His name and character were changed (he became a prince with God) 2. v25;31 His walk—he limped
MOSES Ex. 3—4:7	Mt. Horeb (desert) possibly a part of Sinai	3 days	40 years in Egypt, 40 years in the desert. Moses was prince of Egypt who had become humble	1. The bush burned but was not consumed 2. Appearance of an angel 3. God's voice 4. The rod changed from serpent to rod again 5. Hand became leprous then healed	v14 This is the first time that God gave Himself a name — I AM. "I have manifested, I do manifest, I will manifest"	1. Moses hid his face in fear 2. Removed his shoes	The call of God—from shepherd to deliverer.

NAME	PLACE	LENGTH/ TIME	PREPARATION	MANIFESTATION	REVELATION RECEIVED	RESULT	AREA OF LIFE CHANGED
MOSES Ex. 19-24.8	Mt. Sinai (thorns)	3 days	1. v10 The people were sanctified 2. v11 They waited for 3 days	1. 19:9 God's presence in a thick cloud 2. v16, 20:18 Earthquakes, thunders, lightnings 3. v18 Mt. Sinai smoking fire 4. 20:21 Thick darkness 5. 19:19 God's voice	20:1-17 The Ten Commandments	1. Fear and Trembling 2. Moses stood afar off 3. Death if any came too close	19:6 Moses was called to be priest as well as a deliverer 20:21 Moses responded with faith and obedience to God
MOSES Ex. 24:9-31:18	Mt. Sinai	40 days & nights	24:16 6 days waiting in God's presence	24:17 The sight of God's glory was like a devouring fire	The instructions concerning the Tabernacle (of Moses)	Moses drew near to God	32:7-28 The call of God—Moses became a judge
MOSES Ex. 33-34	Base of Sinai/ Horeb, then up the Mt.	40 days & nights	v7 Separation from the camp of sin	1. v10 Cloudy pillar 2. v11 God speaking face to face 3. v23 View of the back of God	1. 34:6-7 The goodness and severity of God—in His name 2. 34:28 The Ten Commandments	34:8 Moses immediately bowed down to worship	34:29-35 Moses countenance shone like God's face and had to be veiled
JOSHUA Josh. 5:13-6:5	Gilgal (rolling away) near Jericho	?	1. 5:2-9 Obedience 2. Keeping of Passover	A man with a sword drawn in his hand—The capitan of the Lord's host (Jesus)	6:2-5 The battle plan for victory at Jericho	1. He fell on his face and worshipped 2. He removed his shoes	The call of God— Joshua was now a warrior as well as a deliverer

NAME	PLACE	LENGTH/TIME	PREPARATION	MANIFESTATION	REVELATION RECEIVED	RESULT	AREA OF LIFE CHANGED
ELISHA 2 Ki. 2:1-14	Jordan	A moment	1. Elisha was a servant to Elijah 2. Persistance from Gilgal	1. Chariot of fire 2. Horses of fire 3. Elijah taken up	v9 double portion anointing	1. v12 He cried out 2. Rent his clothes 3. v14 Smote the water with Elijah's mantle	The call of God—Elisha was now a prophet as well as a servant
ISAIAH Is. 6:1-13	Probably in Jerusalem	?	Death of Uzziah—Isaiah's father figure	1. The Lord high and lifted up 2. v1-4 Seraphim 3. v8 He saw the Trinity in discussion 4. v4 He saw the doors of heaven shake	1. v5 Sin nature of man 2. v8-10 The heart of God for His people	1. v5 Repentance 2. v6-7 Cleansing 3. v8-9 Call	1. His cry—from "woe unto them", to "woe is me" 2. His cleansing v6-7 3. His call—"send me"
EZEKIEL Ez. 1:1-13	By the river Chebar	?	Captivity	This whole book is filled with visions. Cherubim; fire; whirlwind; cloud; throne of God: four creatures; the glory of the Lord; open heavens; The Spirit of God entered Ezekiel as He spoke to him; he was lifed by his hair between earth and heaven	1. God's glory and His prophetic plan for His people 2. He saw and heard God as He spoke	1. 1:28; 3:23 He fell upon his face 2. 3:15 Remained silent and astonished for 7 days	3,8 God gave Ezekiel a firm, inflexible will and character to endure great hardships in order to bring his prophetic message to God's people

NAME	PLACE	LENGTH/ TIME	PREPARATION	MANIFESTATION	REVELATION RECEIVED	RESULT	AREA OF LIFE CHANGED
SHADRACH MESHACH ABEDNGO Dan.3	Babylon	?	Godliness in captivity	1. v25 The Son of Man in the fire with them 2. The fire had no ability to burn	The power of God	3:29 A decree was issued—the nation would serve the Lord	v30 Promotion in the court of Nebuchadnezzar
DANIEL Dan. 7:9-28	Babylon— In the first year of Belshazzar	?	Godliness in captivity	1. v9 The Ancient of Days 2. v9 God's throne 3. v10 The angelic ministers of God	1. v9 God's name, "Ancient of Days"— the only name given to God the Father in scripture 2. v14 The kingdom of God 3. God's eternal plan	7:15; 28 Grieved, troubled, alarmed	v28 Daniel was troubled by his thoughts, his countenance changed, but he kept this visitation a secret
DANIEL Dan.10	Beside Hiddekel// Tigris river	?	1. 9:3 Prayer 2. 10:2-3 3 weeks mourning 3. 10:12 Daniel's heart of understanding; his humility and words before God caused the Lord to respond with His presence	v5-6 An extraordinary man (Christ)	1. Future events 2. Daniel caught a glimpse of the battle between good and evil supernatural powers	1. v7 Great trembling and fear, hiding 2. His strength was sapped 3. v8 His face went pale 4. v9 Deep sleep 5. v9 He fell on his face on the ground 6. Unable to speak	v 18-19 Renewed strength

NAME	PLACE	LENGTH/ TIME	PREPARATION	MANIFESTATION	REVELATION RECEIVED	RESULT	AREA OF LIFE CHANGED
MARY Lu. 1:26-38	Nazareth— a place of no reputa- tion—bor- dered by heathen	?	v28 Meekness. Mary's relationship with God caused her to be greatly blessed and graced	1. v26-38 The angel Gabriel spoke with her 2. v35 The overshadowing of the Holy Spirit	v32-33 That she would conceive and bring forth the Messiah whose kingdom had no end	1. v29 Troubled 2. v38 Humble submission	She became fruitful and bore our Messiah
PETER, JAMES, JOHN Matt. 17:1-13	A high mountain	?	Closeness with Jesus	1. v2 Transfiguration of Jesus 2. v3 Moses and Elijah 3. v5 A bright cloud 4. v5 The voice of God	v13 Some revelation of the teachings of Jesus	v6 They fell on their faces and were afraid	Nothing perceptible
(The disciples had other encounters with the glorified Christ during His life on earth, and as He ascended into heaven)							
STEPHEN Acts. 6:15;7: 55-60	Jerusalem	Possibly only hours	6:3,5, 8, 10; 7:55 He grew in the wisdom, honesty, faith, power and fullness of the Spirit	1. 6:15 His face had the appearance of an angel 2. He saw the glory of God, and Jesus standing at the right hand of God 3. v55-56 He saw the heavens opened	Stephen had a revelation of the glory of God. (His sermon starts and finishes with the glory of God)	v54-57 The hearers: 1. Were cut to the heart 2. Gnashed on him with their teeth 3. Cried with a loud voice 4. Stopped their ears 5. Ran upon him	6:15 His countenance shone

NAME	PLACE	LENGTH/TIME	PREPARATION	MANIFESTATION	REVELATION RECEIVED	RESULT	AREA OF LIFE CHANGED
PAUL Acts 9:3-8	On a road near Damascus (Some meet God on the road alone	?	Martyrdom of Stephen and the persecution of the church	1. v3 (Acts 26:13) A light shone round about him which was brighter than the sun 2. A voice from God	1. Jesus—the Light of the World 2. v6 Self—the sinner	1. v4 Fell to the earth 2. v6 Astonishment; trembling 3. v8 Blindness for 3 days	1. His name (from Saul to Paul) and nature were changed. He moved from anger towards the church to become a great apostle 2. v6 His heart was surrendered to the Lord
JOHN Book of Revelation	1:9 Island of Patmos	?	1. 1:9 Tribulation 2. 1:10 Walking in the Spirit	1:13-16 One like unto the Son of man, with the voice like a trumpet. v10	1. The Lamb of God 2. The Alpha and the Omega 3. The throne of God 4. The church 5. The end times 6. Heaven 7. Eternity	v17 He fell at His feet as if he were dead	Blessed

Those who dwell in the light, or glory, of God are able to see greater and greater degrees of His glory. To the believer the light of God is not a blinding force, but the illuminating knowledge of the true nature of God—it is divine revelation. We will never know God or understand this life by our own wisdom. Our understanding of God and our world-view must stem solely from the light of His presence and Word. Only then will we be able to understand ourselves and everything around us from God's perspective. All other light and wisdom on this earth are incapable of being fully perceived without our minds being filled with the light of the presence of God:

> . . . in Your light we see light. (Ps. 36:9)

> . . . the Holy Ghost lights up the dark recesses of our heart's ungodliness. . . one ray from the throne of God is better than the noonday splendour of created wisdom.[14] (Charles Spurgeon)

Again and again we experience His grace—grace that beams the light and the glory of God upon our hearts—until we see, at last, the revelation of our true nature and of His marvelous excellencies. Then we, the righteous, will shine with the brightness of the sun (Matt. 13:43; 2 Pet. 1:19). No earthly light is enough to shine the way to His presence, and no worldly wisdom will adequately guide us to eternity. Only the light of God's perfect and sanctifying presence will quell the deafening sigh in our hearts for more of God!

> O, send out Your light and Your truth! Let them lead me; let them bring me to Your holy hill and to Your tabernacle. (Ps. 43:3) ⤳

Chapter Nine

WORSHIP IS TRANSFORMING
"... are being transformed into the same image"

The gods we worship write their names on our faces, be sure of that.
That which dominates will determine man's life and character.
Therefore, it behooves us to be careful what we worship,
for what we worship we are becoming.
Ralph Waldo-Emerson

*A*re being transformed into the same image—We are created in the image and likeness of the Lord, but sin has separated us from Him. As we worship, we draw near to the Lord and become more and more like Him. John Dryden wrote of man's creation in the image of God:

> Man only of a softer mold was made
> Not for his fellows' ruin but their aid:
> Created kind, beneficent and free,
> The noble image of the Deity.[1]

There is almost a cyclic effect that occurs as we behold Him: the more we unveil our faces and see Him, the more we will be transformed. The work of our transformation will then create new desire to see Him again and be further changed into His image. This is one of the great Biblical principles of worship.

Most teachers of worship concur with this opinion. Sally Morgenthaler calls worship "an exchange," as self is abandoned in

His presence, and layer after layer of His heart and likeness are embraced by the worshiper.

> Essentially, Christian worship is the spirit and truth interaction between God and God's people. It is an exchange.[2]

. . . *are being transformed into the same image*—It is impossible to truly worship without being eternally transformed—such is the power of any encounter with God. If we say we have worshiped, yet we have no evidence of change in our lives, we are deceived. It simply means that we did not see Him and did not unveil our faces in worship.

God offers us change to the very core and fiber of our being—change in the way we think, feel, believe, act, speak and live. We are changed in order to bring our lives into accordance with His Divine will and purpose.

> All the doors that lead inward, to the sacred place of the Most High, are doors outward—out of self, out of smallness, out of wrong.[3] (George MacDonald)

John Stevenson adds that we will either be transformed or convicted in His presence:

> . . . you will either leave transformed by the power of God or you will leave convicted by the power of God.[4]

If we are not changed in worship, all we have done is sing a few songs, say a few prayers and perform our lifeless rituals—we have not worshiped. Worship offers an eternal exchange. At the altar of worship, we leave something of self behind and gain the likeness of Christ.

We are changed in order to bring our lives into accordance with His Divine will and purpose.

WORSHIP GIVES A DIFFERENT PERSPECTIVE

Praise and worship give us a different viewpoint and perspective on everything. Part of laying self aside means that we lay down our opinions and perspectives that may be born out of the seat of brokenness and sin in our hearts.

As I speak of this encounter with God and the change that is woven into our lives, some may be tempted to think only in terms of smoke, fire, wind, heavenly voices and so forth. While such events indeed transpired throughout the Bible and occur even today, we must not expect them to be the norm for *every* encounter with God. (We may very well encounter God in such ways at certain times, but, in general, I believe that many have inflated expectations.)

We often say we have "heard His voice"; "met God"; "sensed His presence"; "seen His glory"; or any other such phrase that indicates some form of encounter with Him. (Using such language is not being "superspiritual" as some would accuse, for we are not necessarily speaking of dramatic physical manifestations.) Such communion should be normal for believers, as we are His children—His greatest love in all the earth. He desires continual fellowship with us, and His arms are always inviting our response to His loving pursuit of our lives.

But when God confronts us, it may be in the form of a whisper, or an impression in our hearts or minds. He might put His finger on something and we notice it for the first time. His hand might make an almost unnoticeable adjustment in our thinking, or at the seat of our desires. He might speak to us through His Word; through music, friends, leaders or through His creation. We may know things that we did not learn; be sensitive when our hearts were hard; feel longings that have been breathed into us by God Himself; have grace for others when it has been sadly lacking on previous occasions; witness for Christ with words and passion that has been foreign to us; see new light at the end of our personal struggles; or experience victories in battles that appeared hopeless—the possibilities of our meeting with Him are as endless as God Himself.

No matter how He shows Himself to us, there will be transformation. Sometimes it seems as if He reveals Himself to us in layers—and layers of self are changed. The transformation of the early apostles was noticed even by unbelievers:

> Now when they saw the boldness and unfettered eloquence of Peter and John, and perceived that they were

> unlearned and untrained in the schools—common men
> with no advantages—they marveled; **and they recog-
> nized that they had been with Jesus.** (Acts 4:13, Amp.)

There must have been something about the way they spoke and
the look in their eyes that caused amazement. My prayer is for that
same reaction to take place when people observe the worshiping
Church. When we leave our churches and go to restaurants, gro-
cery stores, our homes and places of employment, people should
be able to take one look at us and know that we are different—
that we bear upon our lives the likeness of Christ.

These were "unlearned and untrained. . . common men with no
advantages"—all the more reason for amazement (!). The abilities
and character now displayed in the lives of Peter and John could
not have come from themselves. Within a few days, the sight and
communion of the glorious Christ had worked great changes within them.

God's Plan for the Earth Concerns His Glory

God's plan for the spread of His glory throughout the earth is
simple: Worship causes us to become partakers of the divine nature
(2 Pet. 1:4); we then go out into the world as ministers of that same
glory.

> . . . and through us spreads and makes evident the fra-
> grance of the knowledge of God everywhere, for we are
> the sweet fragrance of Christ. . . (2 Cor. 2:14b–15a
> Amp.)

When we see Him through worship, prayer, or communion, His
likeness penetrates through our countenance to the very core of
our being—we will never be the same again. They "looked to Him
and were radiant. . . " (Ps. 34:5).

. . . *are being transformed into the same image*—Our goal is not
to be transformed into the likeness of any man, or gifting. We are
not to imitate the most popular TV preacher or the last prophet to
visit our church. Our goal is the likeness and imitation of Christ:

> [For my determined purpose is] that I may know
> Him—that I may progressively become more deeply
> and intimately acquainted with Him, perceiving and

recognizing and understanding [the wonders of His Person] more strongly and more clearly. And that I may in that same way come to know the power outflowing from His resurrection [which it exerts over believers]; and that I may so share His sufferings as to be continually transformed [in spirit into His likeness even] to His death. . . (Phil 3:10, Amp.)

Clearly, Paul was not advocating a meager transformation of thought processes or an easy path to spiritual enlightenment. His example and challenge beg us all to come to complete death of self. As Richard Foster puts it:

Worship . . . is not for the timid or comfortable. It involves an opening of ourselves to the adventurous life of the Spirit.[5]

> When we see Him through worship
> . . . His likeness penetrates through our
> countenance to the very core of
> our being and we will never
> be the same again.

WE BECOME LIKE THE ONE WE WORSHIP

Every time we worship, we are being changed into the likeness of the one we worship. This principle applies whether we worship false gods, or the Lord, Himself. Consider these scriptures:

Their [the Gentile's] idols are silver and gold, the work of men's hands. They have mouths, but they do not speak; eyes they have, but they do not see; they have ears, but they do not hear; noses they have, but they do not smell; they have hands but they do not handle; feet they have, but they do not walk; nor do they mutter through their throat. **Those who make them are like them; so is everyone who trusts in them.** (Ps. 115:4–8) (See also Ps. 135:15–18)

The Psalmist is describing a spiritual reality—those who make or worship any god other than the Lord will come to look like, sound like, act like, think like, and live like that god. For example, some people worship the gods of power and self. These influences are easily recognized in the words and actions of their lives.

We also see this principle in at work in the peoples and nations who do not know the Lord as their God. I have visited countries where some worship snakes. As these snake worshipers leave their temples, it is common for them to fall to the ground and writhe like snakes. What barrenness and despair!

Compare this with David's prayer:

> As for me. I will see Your face in righteousness; I shall be satisfied when I awake in Your likeness. (Ps. 17:15)

> As for me, I will continue beholding Your face in right-eousness—rightness, justice and right standing with You; I shall be fully satisfied, when I awake [to find myself] beholding Your form [and having sweet communion with You]. (Ps. 17:15, Amp.)

I would like to suggest that we do not have to wait until the final, end-time manifestation of God's glory before we become like Him.

By clothing himself in the righteousness of God, David was able to look upon the face of God in the same manner as Paul does in our text, 2 Corinthians 3:18. His satisfaction is complete when he awakens in the morning with the likeness and communion of God marking his life.

The Apostle John wrote:

> . . . but we know that when He comes and is manifest-ed we shall [as God's children] resemble and be like Him, for we shall see Him just as He [really] is. (1 Jn. 3:2b, Amp.)

I would like to suggest that we do not have to wait until the final, end-time manifestation of God's glory before we become like

Him. Even now, God is manifesting His glory in the earth. Even now, when we see Him, we are changed into His likeness.

> The Mighty One, God, the LORD, speaks and summons the earth from the rising of the sun to the place where it sets. From Zion, perfect in beauty, God shines forth. (Ps. 50:1–2, NIV)

THE CALL TO WORSHIP IS FOR EVERY NATION

The Lord calls all people from all nations to come before Him and behold His glory. His worshiping people—the people who love His presence—are named Zion. These are perfect in beauty, and the Lord shines out of them, for they have seen Him(!).

. . . *are being transformed into the same image*—This transforming process is a mystery. Its workings are past finding out. So much of the transforming process is a work of grace. Certainly, there are decisions to be wrestled with in order to fully perfect the transforming process as it works daily in our lives. We must realize, however, that the majority of the work has been done for us on Calvary. Our part is to agree with and yield to the miracle of the Lord's transforming work in our lives. The work of God within us is nothing short of miraculous. He takes the likes of you and me—with all of our imperfections and wretchedness—and has chosen to use us as His primary vessels that will minister His glory throughout the earth.

Paul wrote to the Church in Rome of the magnitude of the change that is wrought within us by Christ:

> Do not be conformed to this world—this age, fashioned after and adapted to its external, superficial customs. But be transformed (changed) by the [entire] renewal of your mind—by its new ideals and its new attitude . . . (Rom. 12:2a, Amp.)

The Greek word for *transformed* has been studied and documented by much greater writers than I. Yet, the radical meaning of *transformation* is scarcely perceived by most Christians. Consider the full meaning of this word:

Transformed is translated from *metamorphoo* (met-am-or-fo'-o)—(Strong's #3339, from #3326 and #3445). The same Greek word is often translated as *transfigure,* meaning to *change into another form.* Vine's dictionary says:

> . . . the obligation being to undergo a complete change which, under the power of God, will find expression in character and conduct. . . 2 Cor. 3:18 describes believers as being "transformed into the same image" (i.e., of Christ in all His moral excellencies), the change being effected by the Holy Spirit.[6]

It is obvious, but still worth stating, that our English word *metamorphosis* is closest in meaning to the Greek word, *metamorphoo. Metamorphosis* means:

> [1.] A change in form from one stage to the next in the life of an organism, as from pupa to butterfly. 2. A change of form, structure, or substance as by magic. 3. A remarkable change, as in appearance.[7]

> [2.] Change in the way a person or thing looks or acts. . .[8]

The changes that need to take place in us are as extreme as the metamorphosis from caterpillar to pupa or pupa to butterfly. The following are only a few examples of the extraordinary changes the Lord works into our lives:

- *He is able to take any darkness within us and infuse it with His light*—"For You *are* my lamp, O LORD; The LORD shall enlighten my darkness" (2 Sam. 22:29). Also: "For God Who said, Let light shine out of darkness, has shone in our hearts so as [to beam forth] the light for the illumination of the knowledge of the majesty and glory of God [as it manifests in the Person and is revealed] in the face of Jesus Christ, the Messiah" (2 Cor. 4:6, Amp.). (See also: Job 12:22; Ps. 112:4; Is. 9:2; Dan. 2:22; Micah 7:8; John 12:46; Rom. 2:19; 1 Pet. 2:9.)

- *He brings life out of death and calls into existence things that do not yet exist*—". . . God, who gives life to the dead and calls those things which do not exist as though they did" (Rom. 4:17).

- *He turns our troubles into doorways of hope* (Hos. 2:15).

- *He turns dry and thirsty places within our hearts into streams and pools of water* and teaches us how to rejoice and blossom there (Is. 35:1, 7; 43:19; 44:3, etc.).

- *He deliberately chose the foolish, insignificant, weak and despised things within us to rise up and triumph* over man's wisdom, self-promotion, strength and arrogance (1 Cor. 1:27).

- *He who knew no sin, not only took our sin from us, but He became that sin* so that He could pay the full penalty for us. We, who are born in sin and are rotten to the core, were received and have become the righteousness of God (2 Cor. 5:21).

There is no book large enough to describe the transformation that the Lord skillfully weaves into every willing life. His whole purpose is to form us into His likeness.

That which is our beginning, regeneration, and happiest end—likeness to God.[9] (John Milton)

To stand before the Holy One of eternity is to change. . . In worship an increased power steals its way into the heart sanctuary, an increased compassion grows in the soul. To worship is to change.[10] (Richard Foster)

> There is no book large enough to describe the transformation that the Lord skillfully weaves into every willing life.

WORSHIP FORMS US IN THE IMAGE OF CHRIST

We are being formed into the image of Christ—not the other way around. We often try to form God into our image, as the prospect of change and transformation is a daunting one (to say the least).

> The pursuit of God will embrace the labor of bringing our total personality into conformity to His. And this is not judicially, but actually   . . . I speak of a voluntary exalting of God to His proper station over us and a willing surrender of our whole being to the place of worshipful submission which the Creator-creature circumstance makes proper.[11] (Tozer)

 . . . *are being transformed into the same image*—The transformation that Christ works in us is a process; we are *being* transformed. Neither our worship nor our transformation was ever intended to be a one time event. Neither is our transformation an option. If we worship we will be transformed.

> By becoming Christians we are made into the image of Christ by his Spirit that is Jesus himself; we are united to him, gazing here by faith upon him and his meaning, able to advance to greater perfection.[12] (Jerome Biblical Commentary)

Paul's words to the Philippians reveal his understanding of the process or progression that the Christian must go through to become like Christ and to be known as being *in Him* (I really like the Amplified translation here):

> Yes, furthermore I count everything as loss compared to the possession of the priceless privilege—the overwhelming preciousness, the surpassing worth and supreme advantage—of knowing Christ Jesus my Lord, and of progressively becoming more deeply and intimately acquainted with Him, of perceiving and recognizing and understanding Him more fully and clearly. For His sake I have lost everything and consider it all to be mere rubbish (refuse, dregs), in order that I may win (gain) Christ, the Anointed One, And that I may [actually] be found and known as in Him, not having any (self-achieved) righteousness that can be called my own. . . (Phil. 3:8–9b, Amp.)

Paul also understood that the more we worship God and are changed, the more clearly we see how far we still need to go to be conformed to His likeness. Paul desired the likeness of Christ, even to the point of death. We have no cause to "glory," or boast, in our transformation, as we are not becoming God, we are becoming like Him. Our eyes need to remain upon Him.

> But God forbid that I should boast except in the cross of our Lord Jesus Christ, by whom the world has been crucified to me, and I to the world. (Gal. 6:14)

ALL CREATION IS SUBJECT TO HIS TRANSFORMING GLORY

. . . are being transformed into the same image—Anything that has ever been created is likely to be transformed at the sight of God. For example:

- Fire sometimes does not burn when the All Consuming Fire reveals Himself through it: Ex. 3:2–4; Dan. 3:21–26
- In the presence of the Jesus, the Water of Life, water may:
  –become a highway—Ex. 14:21–22
  –burst out of rocks—Ex. 17:6
  –become a roadway for men to walk upon—Matt. 14:25–29
  –be turned into wine—Jn. 2:6–10
- He is the Rock, and in His presence, rocks or mountains will sometimes:
  –tremble or quake—Ex. 19:18; Pss. 68:8; 114:7; Is. 64:1; Matt. 27:51; Acts 16:26
  –smoke—Ex. 19:18; 20:18; Ps. 104:32
  –bow down before the Lord like the stone god, Dagon—1 Sam. 5:3–4
  –skip or leap—Ps. 114:4, 6
  –melt like wax—Pss. 46:6; 97:5
  –be threshed like wheat and made into chaff— Is. 41:15–16

-sing—Is. 44:23; 49:13; 55:12

-be turned to bread—Lu. 4:3

-grow lips and sing praises—Lu. 19:40

-grow legs and run into the sea—Matt. 17:20; 21:21-23; Mk. 11:23

- The Lord is the Alpha and Omega, The Beginning and the End. In His presence the sun, which is the keeper of time, might:

  -stand still in the sky—Josh. 10:12-13

  -go backwards—Is. 38:8

It is almost as if these elements are crying out to praise Him who is Fire, Water, The Rock, The Alpha and Omega. There is no way they can measure up to Him, and, in shock at His awesome presence, they are changed.

If these elements are capable of such dramatic and supernatural changes, how much more should we change in the presence of the Lord who became flesh for us that we might become more and more like Him?

The Amplified translation of our text reads:

> . . . are constantly being transfigured into His very own image in ever increasing splendor. . . (2 Cor. 3:18, Amp.)

The progress of our change into His likeness and splendor must be constant; the magnitude of our change is defined by our degree of transfiguration.

. . . are being transformed into the same image—In light of these glorious truths, we might well ask why Christians seem so often weak and powerless in their daily walk. I believe that the sad state of the Church today can largely be traced to a lack of worship and of the *manifested* presence of God in our lives. If we regularly met face to face with the Lord—Who is "All Powerful," "Full of Wisdom," a "Wonderful Counselor," our "Healer" (the One who makes us whole), our "Redeemer" and "King"—then we would reflect these same characteristics in our lives, as the representatives of His virtue here on earth.

If it is true that worship brings transformation into the likeness of God, then we must examine ourselves: Are we becoming more

holy; more loving; more whole in body, soul and spirit; more zealous for the lost to be saved? If not, are we truly worshiping?

Prophetic worship demands immense adjustments within us.
But the rewards are all ours, as we enter into a new wholeness and
authority with God and man that we may never have experienced
before.

Richard Foster challenges the Church to engage in true worship
and to live obediently:

> If worship does not propel us into greater obedience, it
> has not been worship. . . Holy obedience saves worship
> from becoming an opiate, an escape from the pressing
> needs of modern life.[13]

Tozer writes of this aspect of our spiritual growth through worship and the presence of God:

> The instant cure of most of our religious ills would be
> to enter the Presence in spiritual experience, to become
> suddenly aware that we are in God and God is in us.
> This would lift us out of our pitiful narrowness and
> cause our hearts to be enlarged. This would burn away
> the impurities from our lives as the bugs and fungi were
> burned away from the fire that dwelt in the bush.[14]

WORSHIP SHAPES OUR INNER BELIEF AND OUTWARD RESPONSE

. . . *are being transformed into the same image*—Worship not
only changes our inner lives, it also affects the expression of our
faith and service to God in the world around us. Satan tried to
tempt Jesus in the wilderness by offering all the kingdoms of the
world if Jesus would bow down and worship him. Jesus' response
was powerful: "Away with you, Satan! For it is written, 'You shall
worship the LORD your God, and Him only you shall serve.'"
(Matt. 4:10).

> This illustrates a great principle of worship. Whatever
> we worship we ultimately will end up serving. The
> more we worship something or someone, the more our
> commitment increases, and the more we become like
> the thing we worship.[15] (Terry Law)

Our love and worship of God will cause us to serve Him with greater and greater devotion and desire. If we aspire to a more excellent heart for service and Christian witness, then we must surrender to His presence and His ongoing claims upon our lives.

Chapter Ten

WORSHIP IS ETERNAL
"... from glory to glory"

God is a sea of infinite substance.[1]
St. John of Damascus

≈

*F*rom glory to glory *(from one degree of glory to another,
Amp.)*—God's glory is able to be measured in endless
degrees of incomparable beauty and perfection. The depths
of the unfolding of His glory can never be exhausted. Therefore,
our progress in His glory must never cease; it should expand
throughout eternity, one degree at a time, beginning at our salvation. The change that is worked within our lives through worship
and beholding His glory will remain and mature forever. This
thought could not be expressed more excellently than through
these words of Bernard of Clairvaux:

> God in Himself is incomprehensible, the beginning and
> the end. He is the beginning without conclusion, and
> the end without any more excellent end. [2]

When we are born again, we receive Christ and His glory into
our hearts. Paul is telling us in 2 Corinthians 3:18 that our salvation is not the end of the story. We need to continually behold Him
and be transformed. There is no such thing as "arriving" as a
Christian. We must continue to allow the Lord to work His likeness into our hearts as we grow daily through beholding Him. The
God we behold is lavish and extreme in His gifts to us. The favor
we are granted in worship is the ultimate—His glory and likeness!
The glory that we receive from Him is eternal. It will never fade
and cannot be sold. Our lives will be changed forever whenever we

are confronted with His glory. True worship, or the sight of God, will bankrupt every mediocre place in our hearts.

> . . . the knowledge of God is God himself dwelling in the soul. The most we can do is to prepare for his entry, to get out of his way, to remove the barriers, for until God acts in us there is nothing positive that we can do in this direction. [3] (Watts)

The favor we are granted in worship is the ultimate—His glory and likeness!

WORSHIP AND ETERNITY

. . . *from glory to glory*—There is something timeless or eternal in this statement "from glory to glory." The Bible declares that He is the same yesterday, today and forever (Heb. 13:8). With regard to worship we need to understand what this means: He was worshiped, He is to be worshiped, He will be worshiped for all eternity. When we worship the Lord, we participate in the eternal. We proclaim and enact His Kingdom; we declare His sovereignty in the earth, and we pronounce His attributes for all to hear. When we worship, we join the heavenly beings and shout through the hallways of all time, echoing the song of worship that is never interrupted day and night and never ceases: "Holy, holy, holy, Lord God Almighty, who was and is and is to come! " (Rev. 4:8).

. . . *from glory to glory*—The same glory that shone out of darkness to create the earth is the glory that shines in our hearts to reveal Christ to us:

> For God Who said, Let light shine out of darkness, has shone in our hearts so as [to beam forth] the Light for the illumination of the knowledge of the majesty and glory of God [as it is manifest in the Person and is revealed] in the face of Jesus Christ, the Messiah. (2 Cor. 4:6, Amp.)

If complete and utter darkness can be penetrated with God's light, and life is able to be born from there, then that same light of glory is able to give birth to the knowledge and character of God within us.

Again, it is a mystery that the glory of God should find its home in our hearts. God's secrets and mysteries are there for everyone to discover. They are not an exclusive or hidden plan for just a few to experience. When God indicates in the Word that something is a mystery, it means that it is not able to be understood by man unless God reveals it to us. The Father of all glory desires to give to every believer the spirit of wisdom and revelation so that we might know Him more completely and partake of the riches of His glory (Eph. 1:17–19).

It is a mystery that the glory of God should find its home in our hearts.

OUR SANCTIFICATION AND HIS GLORY

The mystery of our sanctification and completion in Him is wrapped up in these scriptures on the glory of God. Sin caused mankind to lose his ability to embody the life, image and glory of God. Yet, He has made a way, through our salvation and subsequent relationship with Him, for us to be restored to full fellowship and sonship. Whenever we worship and behold God's glory, we will be changed, cleansed, renewed, and sanctified by the experience and encounter with God. The wholeness of every Christian depends upon the principle of beholding the glory and yielding to His work in our hearts.

Paul desired that the mystery of God's glory should be enacted in the heart of every person and openly proclaimed throughout the earth:

> To them [the saints—Christians] God willed to make known what are the riches of the glory of this mystery among the Gentiles: which is Christ in you, the hope of glory. Him we preach, warning every man and teaching every man in all wisdom, that we may present every man perfect in Christ Jesus. (Col. 1:27–28)

The new contemporary translation of the New Testament, *The Message*, offers a clear translation of this verse:

This mystery has been kept in the dark for a long time, but now it's out in the open. God wanted everyone, not just Jews, to know this rich and glorious secret inside and out, regardless of their background, regardless of their religious standing. The mystery in a nutshell is just this: Christ is in you, therefore you can look forward to sharing in God's glory. [4]

The Father, Son and Holy Spirit are involved in our lives to bring about His likeness and glory. Ralph Martin has laid out the *trinitarian structure* of this mystery, as shown in Table 4. [5]

TABLE 4
GOD IN YOU

You in God (Col.3:3; Jn. 17:21)	God in you (Phil. 2:13; 1Cor. 6:20; Jn. 14:23)
You in Christ (2Cor. 5:17; Rom. 8:1; Jn. 15:4f.)	Christ in you (Col. 1:27; Gal.2:20; Jn. 14:18-20)
You in Spirit (Rom. 8:9; Gal.5:16,25; Jn. 4:23f.)	Spirit in you (1Cor. 3:16; Rom. 8:9; Jn. 14:16f)

Because of this mystery of God's glory, we are made into His image layer by layer. Because our hope of glory comes from a Savior who resides within us, and because we are hidden in Him, we are able to be perfected and finally presented before Him without fault:

> You are all fair, my love, and there is no spot in you. (Song of Sol. 4:7)

> . . . that He might present her to Himself a glorious church, not having spot or wrinkle or any such thing, but that she should be holy and without blemish. (Eph. 5:27; See also: 2 Pet. 3:14)

> Now to Him who is able to keep you from stumbling,
> and to present you faultless before the presence of His
> glory with exceeding joy   . . . (Jude 24)

This must be the greatest hope of the Christian: that the Lord will be filled with joy on that day when we are presented before His glory. What work must be done in our hearts and lives in order for us to achieve perfection! It is not as if we had never sinned, but so complete is the redemption and forgiveness of God that not one stain will be found in us.

> You and I are in little (our sins excepted) what God is
> in large. [6] (Tozer)

OUR REWARD—A CROWN OF GLORY

. . . *from glory to glory*—Our eternal reward as faithful sons of God is the incorruptible crown of glory (1 Pet. 5:4). God is holy. Nothing is able to stand before Him that does not reflect His holiness and perfection. Everything that surrounds Him partakes of His glory: Angels (Lk. 2:9; 9:26; Rev. 18:1); the cherubim (Heb. 9:5); the heavenly city (Rev. 21:11); and mankind, who are the only ones who are permitted to grow in the light of His glory for eternity. There is no essential glory in man—only those who are transformed from glory to glory will spend eternity gazing upon Him. He must make us fit for His presence.

Jesus' great prayer in the Gospel of John, Chapter Seventeen, is a plea for the Believers to become one in Him and with each other by dwelling with Him and beholding His glory:

> And the glory which You gave Me I have given them,
> that they may be one just as We are one . . . [that they]
> may be with Me where I am, that they may behold My
> glory which You have given Me . . . (Jn. 17:22, 24)

Obviously, the Lord longs for us to participate with Him in ministering His glory in the earth. Beholding His glory and being changed into the likeness of His glory is a key for every Christian. He became flesh so that we could commune with Him and become like Him—holy and blameless, able to stand in His presence forever:

And the Word became flesh and dwelt among us, and we beheld His glory, the glory as of the only begotten of the Father, full of grace and truth. (Jn. 1:14)

Beholding His glory and being changed
into the likeness of His glory is a
key for every Christian.

THE BEAUTY OF HOLINESS

. . . *from glory to glory*—As the glory of the Lord is layered upon our lives, we become more and more beautiful in body, soul and spirit.

In the Old Testament the glory of God is spoken of as a visible thing—many of the saints saw His glory from time to time. But it was only on rare occasions that anyone could be described as having His glory manifested upon their lives. Moses was one man who beheld the glory of God and received the same light of glory in his own face (Ex. 34:29–35).

In the New Testament we live with the glory of God dwelling in us. We do not just see the glory, we live with the glory upon our lives. It is shared with us on the basis of our relationship with Him.

In *The Message*, Eugene Peterson focuses on this aspect of the glory when writing of 2 Corinthians 3:18:

> And so we are transfigured much like the Messiah, our lives gradually becoming brighter and more beautiful as God enters our lives and we become like Him. [7]

The Psalmists often sang of the beauty that adorns the worshiper:

> Give to the Lord the glory due to His name; worship the Lord in the beauty of holiness or in holy array. (Ps. 29:2 Amp.) (See also Ps. 96:9)

> . . . praise from the upright is beautiful. (Ps. 33:1; 147:1)

The King is enthralled by your beauty [greatly desires
your beauty, KJV]; honor Him, for He is your lord. (Ps.
45:11 NIV)

Out of Zion, the perfection of beauty, God will shine
forth. (Ps. 50:2)

And let the beauty of the LORD our God be upon us. . .
(Ps. 90:17)

For the LORD takes pleasure in His people; He will
beautify the humble with salvation (Ps. 149:4)

(See also: Song of Sol. 1:5, 10; 2:14; 4:3; 6:4; 7:1; Is.
28:5; 52:1, 7; 61:3; Jer. 6:2; Eze. 16:13)

We can see from these scriptures that one of the greatest beau-
ties that accompanies our lives is the beauty that comes from holiness. God is a holy God and can only be truly worshiped by a holy
people. Holiness is the inner architectural structure of the believer.
Without it our faith will weaken and fall. On the other hand, a
holy life is a life of great beauty and attractiveness.

The seraphim declare this one attribute of His character continuously before His throne (Is. 6:1–3; Rev. 4:8–9); the priests of the
Old Covenant cleansed themselves, their utensils and their garments before they approached the Lord (Ex. 19:22; Ex. 28:36–43;
29:1–9, 21, 29, 35–37, 44; 40:12–13, etc.), and David cried out:

Who may ascend into the hill of the LORD? Or who
may stand in His holy place? He who has clean hands
and a pure heart. . . (Ps. 24:3–4)

Romans 3:23 declares that every man has sinned and fallen
short of the glory of God. Just as sin has taken us from God's glory,
holiness will lead us to His glory. Paul's heartache in this matter is
that we have fallen short, not of becoming evangelists, ministers,
singers or prayer warriors, but of the likeness of God. Worship and
holiness lead us to God's glory so that we can come out of His
presence as ministers of His glory.

The writer of Hebrews encourages the worshiper to seek after
holiness. Without holy lives we will not be able to see the Lord,
and seeing Him is an essential component of prophetic worship.

Worship and the Word of God both confront us with God's holiness. As Judson Cornwall states, the Lord expects us to pursue holiness.

> While God condescends in grace to redeem us, He expects us to ascend in holiness to worship Him. I do not mean to imply that one must become absolutely holy in order to have a worship experience with God. . . . I am saying that holiness is an absolute prerequisite in order to become a consistent worshipper.[8]

Changing from glory to glory means that we adorn ourselves with His holiness and beautify ourselves with His grace. In other words, the character, power and graces of the Lord are our glory and beauty. God intends that these grow in our lives daily. The more we worship and become like Him, the more beautiful we become, inside and out.

DISPLAYING HIS GLORY—THE ULTIMATE EVANGELISM TOOL

. . . *from glory to glory*—We are not changed from glory to glory just to fulfill our own eternal purposes. We are molded into the likeness of His glory in order that the whole earth might see Him and likewise be changed.

Recall how God displayed His glory in the midst of a powerful worship service in a prison, where Paul and Silas prayed and sang praises (Acts 16:25–34). At least one purpose for that display of God's presence and glory was for the salvation of others, seeing the prison guard and all of his household were saved. (I would not be surprised if a few of the prisoners were saved also, though they are not mentioned. We do know that they were listening and not mocking when Paul and Silas were praying and singing.)

Worship, evangelism, and missions are related at every turn. The eternal destiny of everyone on earth depends upon the obedience of believers to this call to worship God and be changed into His likeness. Through our compliance, we gain the heart and will of God for all mankind, and the wisdom, grace, and strength to execute His purposes in the earth. When we are changed into the likeness of His glory, we become more able ministers of His glory to those around us.

The glory of the LORD shall be revealed, and all flesh shall see it together; for the mouth of the LORD has spoken. (Is. 40:5)

. . . to Him be glory in the church by Christ Jesus to all generation, forever and ever. Amen. (Eph. 3:21)

Chapter Eleven

WORSHIP IS INITIATED BY THE HOLY SPIRIT
"... even as by the Spirit of the Lord"

> Worship... is God's Spirit in man responding
> to God's Spirit in God. It is the Holy Spirit
> worshipping through us.
> *Judson Cornwall*

≈

*E*ven as by the Spirit of the Lord—*"God is Spirit, and those who worship Him must worship in spirit and in truth"* (Jn. 4:24).

The Holy Spirit is a person and He dwells in the heart of every believer. It is the Holy Spirit that leads us to the Father and teaches us how to worship in spirit and in truth. Whenever spirit and truth are joined in worship there is blessing. He is the One who is active in our lives in bringing us into the likeness of Christ—layer by layer, from glory to glory.

When we worship, we are responding and interacting with the Holy Spirit to bring our love, adoration, and service directly to the Father, through the mediation of Jesus, the Son. The Holy Spirit is the source and inspiration for our communion with God and is the primary initiator of the intimacy between God and man. He has gone first and given us life. He laid down His life for us so that we might enjoy Him forever.

In every religion other than Christianity, man attempts to reach up to God. Our God, however, has initiated our relationship; He

has reached down to us. By the work of the Holy Spirit, every
Christian is led to worship and the likeness of Christ. Judson
Cornwall agrees with Scripture when he writes that it is impossi-
ble to worship without the help of the Holy Spirit:

> . . . while praise can be the product of the human spir-
> it, worship is impossible without the aid of the Holy
> Spirit of God.[1]

> . . . no one can say that Jesus is Lord except by the Holy
> Spirit. (1 Cor. 12:3)

It is the Holy Spirit that leads us to the Father and teaches us how to worship in spirit and in truth.

It is the Lord who begins our worship journey, and the Lord
who completes us through the work of the Holy Spirit. He does
not override our will, however. The Holy Spirit responds to our
desires for His work in our hearts: as Tozer puts it, "He waits to
be wanted."[2]

Richard Foster comments on the wooing of the Holy Spirit in
worship. He calls worship:

> . . . our response to the overtures of love from the heart
> of the Father.[3]

His love is made known to us through the work of the Holy
Spirit. Adam Clarke teaches of the influence of the Holy Spirit as
He brings about God's nature in every part of our lives:

> By the energy of that Spirit of Christ which gives life
> and being to all the promises of the Gospel; and thus
> we are made partakers of the Divine nature and escape
> all the corruptions that are in the world.[4]

The Apostle John tells us that it is impossible to come to Christ
unless we are drawn by the Father (Jn. 6:44). The means by which
the Father allures us is the Holy Spirit. The Father, Son, and Holy
Spirit work together to win our hearts in uncompromising devotion:

For through him we both have access by one Spirit to
the Father. (Eph. 2:18)

We must be wholly and humbly dependent upon the Holy Spirit
to draw us in worship. He must be the source of every aspect of
relationship with God. We were born again by the Spirit; we must
continue in the Spirit.

THE HOLY SPIRIT—OUR COMPANION IN WORSHIP

. . . even as by the Spirit of the Lord—The Holy Spirit is our
Guide and our Friend as He leads us into the knowledge and love
of the Father and the Son. There are times in worship that are
absolutely delightful, as the Holy Spirit brings us to meet with the
Lord in different ways. As described below, there are many places
where the Holy Spirit desires to lead us so that we may encounter
the Father. He brings us to:

- *The face of God,* where He speaks to us of Himself (Ex.
  32:30; 33:11; Pss. 17:15; 27:8; 41:12); where He turns
  our hearts in repentance (2 Chron. 7:14); and where He
  kisses us in love (Song of Sol. 1:1).

- *The hand of God,* where we take our place alongside
  Him as His royal bride (Ps. 45:9; Is. 62:3); where we
  find His blessings and protection (Pss. 16:1; 18:35;
  63:8; 138:7; 145:16; Is. 41:10); where He molds us into
  vessels of honor (Is. 64:8); and where He hides us (Is.
  49:2).

- *The feet of God,* where we fall down in worship (Matt.
  15:30; 28:9; Lk. 7:37–38; Jn. 12:3; Rev. 5:14; 7:11).

- *His banqueting hall,* where we sit down and feed from
  Him (Song of Sol. 2:4); and where He prepares a table
  for us in the presence of our enemies (Ps. 23:5).

- *His throne room,* where we come boldly and bow
  humbly before our King (Es. 5:1; Heb. 4:16; Rev.
  19:4–5).

- *His inner chamber,* where we engage in intimate and
  secret communion with Him (Song of Sol. 1:4); and

where He spreads His wings over us (Ru. 3:9; Pss. 17:8; 36:7; 57:1; 61:4; 63:7; 91:4; Eze. 16:8).

- *His seat of justice and judgment,* where we obtain for-giveness and justice (Pss. 35:22–24; 68:5; 82:1; 89:14).

- *His secret places,* where we grow nearer to Him and receive His treasures (Pss. 27:5–6; 31:20; 81:7; 91:1; Prov. 3:32; Song of Sol. 2:14; Is. 45:3).

- *The outer court of His presence,* where we celebrate and rejoice because of His greatness (Ps. 100:4).

- *The gates of His Holy place,* where we become atten-dants of His majesty and servants of His court (Ps. 24:3; Prov. 8:34).

- *The place of prayer and intercession*—the private closet and the right hand of God (Matt. 6:6; Rom. 8:26–27, 34; 1 Tim. 2:1).

The Holy Spirit draws, directs and leads us into every encounter with the Father. All we have to do is respond with all our hearts and run after Him. Prophetic worship opens the way for us to enter His presence again and again.

Draw me away! We will run after you. (Song of Sol. 1:4)

His attracting force is extremely powerful, and yet the soul follows freely and without force. Why? Because the attracting of your Lord is just as delightful as it is powerful! Although His attracting of you is powerful, it carries you away by its sweetness.[5] (Madame Guyon)

AN EXTRAORDINARY COMMUNION WITH GOD

. . . even as by the Spirit of the Lord—Anything the Holy Spirit initiates is pure (Ps. 24:3–4) and perfect (Deut. 32:4; Pss. 18:30; 19:7). Some may be afraid of possible excesses when considering prophetic worship. All I would say to this is that if we compare the Lord to our personal, cultural or denominational preferences in worship, then we would have to agree that He is rather extraordi-

nary in all that He does. His love, judgment, mercy, presence, and joy—as described in the Bible—might all be characterized as being consummately extreme when compared to our standards of expression.

Even though we might find the Lord to be extreme in all of His ways, yet He requires that we commune with Him in a way that is pleasing to *Him*—not to us. We need to learn *His* definition of "normal" when it comes to worship.

It is imperative that we understand that the Holy Spirit is the one who is leading us to the glory and face of God. We have nothing to fear, and nothing to lose except ourselves. We must trust the Holy Spirit to bring both liberty and order to our worship. E. F. Harrison writes of this liberty:

> The Spirit is the key to this process, [the process of 2 Cor. 3:18], affording liberty to the saints to keep Christ before them and grow up into Him in all things.[6]

. . . even as by the Spirit of the Lord—Worship flows from our lives when we are filled with the Holy Spirit: ". . . be filled with the Spirit, speaking to one another in psalms and hymns and spiritual songs, singing and making melody in your heart to the Lord . . . " (Eph. 5:18b-19). Our worship is based upon our relationship with God, and our relationship is dependent upon the indwelling of the Holy Spirit in our lives.

. . . even as by the Spirit of the Lord—The Holy Spirit reveals a definite purpose and intent in this verse. We are confronted with His desire in the matter of our relationship with the Lord. In the previous six points of 2 Corinthians 3:18, our focus has been on the things we need to be doing: unveiling our faces, looking into His glory, yielding to His transforming work in our lives, and so forth. Now we see the emphasis has shifted to the desire and determination of the Holy Spirit in this matter.

SEVEN DESIRES OF THE LORD

I only know of the Lord expressing seven desires in the entire Bible. Each of His desires concerns the Church and her relationship with Him. Our worship must be profoundly affected by these seven things that God has specifically mentioned. The seven desires of God are summed up in God's longing to have fellowship with us, His children.

He desires:

• **The beauty of His Bride, the Church**

> "So the King will greatly desire your beauty. . . " (Ps. 45:11)

This is the only time in the Word that there is mention of the Lord greatly desiring anything. The Lord greatly desires to see and partake of the beauty that is woven into our lives as we are transformed into His likeness in the light of His glory.

• **Zion to be His dwelling place forever**

> For the LORD has chosen Zion; He has desired it for His dwelling place: "This is my resting place forever; here will I dwell, for I have desired it." (Ps.132:13–14) (See also Ps. 68:15–16)

Zion is a poetic and prophetic name for the worshiping Church. The Lord desires to dwell in the midst of His people forever.

• **Truth in our inner being**

> "Behold, You desire truth in the inward parts. . . " (Ps. 51:6)

The beauty of God's people begins on the inside. In this Psalm, David is asking the Lord to cleanse him completely after he had been caught in a sin. It is David's astounding repentance—from the core of his being—that restored his relationship with the Lord and caused him to be known forever as: a man of integrity and uprightness (1 Ki. 9:4); with a perfect heart (1 Ki. 11:4; 15:3), and a man after God's heart (Acts 13:22). Our on-going relationship with the Lord is only possible if we walk in transparency and holiness to the core of our being.

"The power of godliness is the main thing God looks at and requires, and without it the form of godliness is of no avail."[7] (Matthew Henry)

• **Mercy above sacrifice**

"For I desire mercy and not sacrifice. . . " (Hos. 6:6)

God desires our righteousness and inner virtue over the external sacrifices that He instituted. The Hebrew word for *mercy* in this passage is *checed* (Strong's #2617)—meaning *kindness, piety, beauty, favor, lovingkindness, mercy*. These qualities are more desirable in us than any form of outward religion.

• **For us to know and worship Him**

"For I desire. . . the knowledge of God more than burnt offerings." (Hos. 6:6)

God desires the reality of our faith and relationship with Him over the forms and rituals of religion. He wants our sincere and genuine participation in worship rather than a theoretical understanding of the Bible and His presence. Not only does God want to know us, but He desires that we know Him as well. What a glorious thought! Even if we were to study Him and know Him for millions of years, we would never be able to exhaust the vast depths and riches of His character. We may think that we know Him now, but great wonders and delights await the true seeker of God.

"The great need in every generation is for a true knowledge of God. Without this knowledge the world loses its sense of meaning and the church falls into a state of apathy."[8] (Sammy Tippit)

If we are to know God, then we must become students and stewards of His divine mysteries (1 Cor. 4:1). Paul's constant prayer was that believers would grow in the knowledge of God:

[For I always pray] the God of our Lord Jesus Christ, the Father of Glory, that He may grant you a spirit of wisdom and revelation—of insight into mysteries and secrets—in the [deep and intimate] knowledge of Him. . . (Eph. 1:17, Amp.)

If we are to know God, then we must become students and stewards of His divine mysteries.

• **He wants all of our heart**

"I am my beloved's, and his desire is toward me." (Song of Sol. 7:10)

The Shulamite recognized that her lover was totally devoted to her. She was the center of all His desires. This is the same way that the Lord feels about us—the Church. His greatest love and most profound desire is for intimacy and relationship with us—His bride. We need to respond to Him by yielding every area of our lives fully to Him. He desires all of us, not just a part of us.

• **For us to see His glory**

"Father, I desire that they also whom You gave Me may be with Me where I am, that they may behold My glory which You have given Me   . . . " (Jn. 17:24)

The final desire the Lord expresses in the Word is that we would see Him as He truly is. Not only does He require that we be unveiled, but He desires to unveil Himself before us in worship and show us His glory.

God is deeply involved in 2 Corinthians 3:18 by the work of the Holy Spirit. He has expressed His desire throughout the Word that we grow in intimacy and relationship with Him. It is His desire that we turn our hearts and lives completely over to Him and partake of His glory forever. The Holy Spirit is earnestly and passionately working to bring about God's will in our lives. 2 Corinthians 3:18 is not an option for the Christian. God will have His way. We will be changed into the likeness of His glory.

> But He is unique, and who can make Him change? And
> whatever His soul desires, that He does. (Job 23:13)

OUR HEART'S CRY

Perhaps this song, written by Paul Baloche, sums up the desire
that arises in our hearts in the midst of worship to behold His
glory and participate in the eternal song of heaven—"Holy, holy,
holy":

> Open the eyes of my heart, Lord.
> Open the eyes of my heart;
> I want to see You, I want to see You.
> Open the eyes of my heart, Lord.
> Open the eyes of my heart;
> I want to see You, I want to see You.
>
> To see You high and lifted up,
> shining in the light of Your glory.
> Pour out Your power and love;
> as we sing holy, holy, holy.
>
> Holy, holy, holy;
> holy, holy, holy,
> I want to see You.[9]

We all must realize that every church and individual worshiper
must undergo some changes in order for prophetic worship to
become the norm. I would like to suggest that those who refuse
change and personal growth in worship will not go far with God.
He has been developing, renewing and changing the worship formats of His people since the beginning of time.

The sacrificial system of worship that Cain and Abel were used
to was later changed to an elaborate tabernacle worship spectacle.
The Lord told David that He desired him to offer "spiritual sacrifices" rather than animal sacrifices. Later, David's son, Solomon,
built the Temple, which combined worship forms taken from the
tabernacles of both Moses and David.

In the New Testament, Jesus told an inquiring woman that the
hour was coming when worship would no longer take place in a

particular geographic location, but in the hearts of men (Jn. 4:19–24). The pace of change has accelerated into the Church Age. As we are all aware, the architecture of churches, styles of music and types of instruments used in worship have changed vastly.over the centuries. All we can be sure of with the Lord is that changes are bound to take place.

> True worship renewal does not come about through superficial measures, but through recognizing that worship studies are an essential discipline of Christian theology. Renewal grows out of attention to the biblical and historical sources of Christian worship and the provision of the Holy Spirit.[10] (Robert Webber)

Let us yield to the work of the Holy Spirit as He forms Christ in us.

Part Three

Prophetic Worship:
A New Exemplar

Chapter Twelve

AN INTRODUCTION—
BREAKING WORSHIP
TRADITIONS

Worship is a journey into God

I was raised in a conservative Presbyterian Church and am forever indebted for the training I received there over the years. I deeply respect the history and rich heritage of shared, Biblically-based truth that is found in all the mainstream churches. It is time, however, to challenge the rigidly held traditions and beliefs on worship that are found in all of Christendom, from the oldest denominations to the newer independent and charismatic churches. Pastor Jack Hayford says this of tradition:

> We would die for it, but we can't live with it. Its role in worship is pervasive; no part of human experience is more shaped by tradition than the way we worship. Even in the Body of Christ, frequently the force of tradition over-rides the truth of God's Word.[1]

It is the truth about worship in the Word of God that I am interested in. I maintain that prophetic worship is the model which best describes Biblical worship in both the Old and New Testaments.

Prophetic worship is the model which best describes Biblical worship in both the Old and New Testaments.

THE USE OF THE WORD *EXEMPLAR*

I have used the word *exemplar* in the title for the third section of this book because its meaning best captures the nuances of the message I am trying to convey. Many use the term *paradigm* or *paradigm shift* as they search for new models for worship. The term *exemplar* goes a step further and calls for *a patterning after, a way to be followed or imitated.* Thus, I use the term because I truly believe that the model for prophetic worship presented here should become the norm for *all* worship in *each* congregation in *every* nation.

Prophetic worship is not the exclusive worship model for some new type of charismatic church. It is not restricted to those congregations who have a charismatic or other particular theology of worship. Rather, it can be understood and attained by any church, irrespective of their culture, background, denomination, or size; no matter what the proficiency of their musicians and singers.

Please understand, I am not on a quest for all churches to worship in the same manner, to the detriment of the distinctive character of individual congregations. I believe in a unity that includes diversity. Yet, our distinctiveness should not merely be a reflection of our denomination or our culture, but a consequence of the individual journey of every congregation, the character of the people and the unique work of God within them.

In the past, many have clamored for more consideration to be given to the individual rights and personalities of the people in worship. I am more concerned that we give full consideration to the will and character of God. The chapters that follow outline a prototype for achieving this goal in worship.

CONTRASTING TRADITIONAL WITH PROPHETIC WORSHIP

When we contrast traditional worship with prophetic worship, it is important to note that traditional worship—as it applies to any particular form or denomination—is not really the issue that is at fault. The traditional practices, themselves, may be valuable and even advantageous in the pursuit of true worship. We must bear in mind, true worship is a matter of the heart and of genuine devotion to God.

These thoughts offer some helpful insights into the role tradition often plays in our worship theology:

It is even possible to be traditional about our non-traditionalism. Tradition has to do with the repetition of a pattern, not with the essential character of the pattern. . . The worship of Jesus Christ must never become so familiar that we simply go through the motions.[2] (Sammy Tippit)

Tradition is the living faith of the dead; traditionalism is the dead faith of the living.[3] (Jaroslav Pelikan)

Do not seek to follow in the footsteps of the men of old; seek what they sought.[4] (Matsuo Basho)

I think we sometimes deceive ourselves concerning our rituals and traditions. We assume that because they are important to us, that they must be important to God as well. So often, true prophetic worship has been stifled by our insistence upon ancient rituals that may have no heart and no devotion in them. Consider Ambrose Bierce's definition of *ritualism:*

Ritualism: A Dutch garden of God where He may walk in rectilinear freedom, keeping off the grass.[5]

Andrew Hill has also given an excellent definition of *ritualism:*

. . . ritualism occurs when the worshiper is no longer able to participate knowingly, actively, and fruitfully. In other words, the worshiper no longer recognizes and appropriates the form or liturgy of worship as his or her personal expression of faith. Thus, participation in the outward form of worship is devoid of inward reality.[6]

As you read the following chapters, keep these questions in mind with regard to the issue of ritualism within your own worship traditions:

Are we fashioning our worship to fit our own preferences to such a degree that we actually mar the reflection of the nature of God?

Are we pursuing our traditions in worship over and against Biblical injunctions and examples for true praise and worship?

Are we truly seeking to minister to God in our worship, or are there other, more selfish motives that drive our weekly attendance at church (such as what *we* expect to get out of it)?

Do we find such security in our age-old liturgies and forms of worship that we do not even look for God to manifest His glory before us? In other words, do our trust and comfort come from our traditions rather than from God Himself?

Do the rituals of our weekly worship meetings even allow *a time* for God to manifest himself? Or is the Order of Service completely filled with our own expressions and activities?

Is there any portion of our worship meetings that *requires* the manifest presence of God? In other words, if He failed to show up one Sunday, would we even realize that He was missing?

I seek to be challenging rather than critical as we compare the traditional ways of worship with the prophetic way of worship outlined in Scripture. I have endeavored to treat every Christian denomination and worship tradition with respect. For it is my desire to open up to all, the tremendous possibilities of prophetic worship and the impact that it can have on any church.

It is not my intention that we use these points of contrast as items of negative criticism towards one another, but rather, that we all make an honest evaluation of our own hearts and expressions of worship. As Tippet has said, the actual style of our traditionalism is not the shortcoming; it is the lack of integrity and devotion at the core of our corporate experience. This will make any worship lukewarm, at best, and totally dead, at its most tragic.

Neither is it my intention that we study worship dynamics in order to compare ourselves with others. Please do not use these chapters as a means to evaluate your worship in the light of other churches; let them challenge your own heart to a deeper and more honest relationship with the Lord. Allow the Holy Spirit to inspire change where it is necessary and to have His way in every aspect of your devotional life.

Also, I am not interested in churches obsessing on worship in ways that will only cause them to make insincere and superficial

TABLE 5

TRADITIONAL WORSHIP VERSUS PROPHETIC WORSHIP

TRADITIONAL WORSHIP	PROPHETIC WORSHIP	CHAPTER
1. Worship is defined by what **we** are doing: our various expressions and forms of worship. Many feel that praise is defined by fast songs and worship by slow songs	Worship is defined by what the **Lord** is doing. Praise includes all our expressions of what He has done, is doing and is going to do. Worship is our response to His manifest presence	13
2. The worship leader is in control	The worship leader leads, but is also a door keeper and facilitator. The Holy Spirit is primarily the worship leader—the one directing and in control of the service	14
3. A small number function as ministers in the service: Those on the platform (pastors, singers, musicians, etc.)	The whole congregation is a holy, royal priesthood. Each one is responsible for participating in the service and ministering to the Lord	15
4. There are definite time limits on the worship service	There are no time limits. Worship continues as long as the Holy Spirit directs	16
5. The songs/hymns are regarded as being less important in the overall service than the preaching	The songs/hymns, the worship time and the preaching are all regarded as having equal importance	17
6. Our denomination determines the way we worship and has definite ideas about worship forms	The Word of God is our foundation and guide for worship structure and forms	18
7. Our worship may be determined and greatly influenced by our culture	Our national origin or native culture is not our focus. We belong to a new nation—the Kingdom of God, where the standard for appropriate worship is determined by the King, Himself. Though flavored by our culture, our worship must be made suitable for the King	19

8. There is an emphasis on the music. Music and other art forms are used for performance, entertainment and accompaniment. There is art for art's sake—art forms used in worship are often an end unto themselves. Success is measured by excellence in the art form	There is an emphasis on the manifest presence of God. Music and all other art forms are used for ministry to God and His people. All art forms must be ministered in a prophetic sense—they are a means to an end. The goal is the glory of God. Success is measured by the presence of God and His fruit in our lives	20
9. There is little or no change of musical styles and repertory over the years	The music and songs we sing are seen as an ongoing reinforcement of the things that the Lord is revealing, therefore they are continually changing	21
10. In order for the congregation to participate in worship they do not need to mature spiritually—they are merely an audience. Nothing more is required of the worship leader and team than to be artists	Prophetic worship is only possible with a congregation that continues to mature in the likeness of Christ. The worship leader and team are required to be students of the presence of God and carry a prophetic anointing.	22
11. Worship is an individual experience	Worship does not stop at being an individual experience, it must include the corporate journey	23
12. There is little or no expectation of hearing God's voice speak today in the worship service. The majority of our spiritual communication is one-way: "man to God"	Hearing God's voice speak today is one of the primary objectives of prophetic worship. There is openness for two-way or reciprocal communication with God: "man to God" and "God to man"	24

changes to their worship services. This does nothing but foster "liturgical hedonism," as Paul Waitman Hoon puts it.[7]

Table 5, *Traditional Worship Versus Prophetic Worship*, contains a synopsis of the major issues that distinguish prophetic worship from traditional worship. It could almost be considered a summary of this whole book. Keep in mind that these are generalizations. Again, it is not my intention to be critical, but rather, to offer suggestions for a new exemplar.

It is the weakness of our human nature that begs us to cling to the traditions and practices of the past and flee from every notion of change. While I am encouraging every church to make courageous changes and break with dead traditions, I am not trying to eliminate the distinctive and meaningful contributions that each denomination has made within the Body of Christ. If we can learn how to hold on to the traditions that are meritorious while embracing the truth of prophetic worship, I think change will become more palatable.

It is my sincerest belief that *prophetic worship is the wave of the future for all churches that wish to move on with God.*

Prophetic worship is the wave of the future for all churches that wish to move on with God.

An in-depth explanation of each point from this chart is contained in the chapters of Part III. ✍

Chapter Thirteen

REDEFINING PRAISE AND WORSHIP

Worship, in essence, is simply communing with God.
Bob Sorge

〜

T he foremost subject of the Bible and central goal of lives must surely be the glory of God. Every definition of worship and understanding of its workings, power and purpose must stem from this comprehension. Sammy Tippit agrees with this thought:

True worship will always be wholehearted worship built upon the single foundation of the glory of Christ.[1]

The foremost subject of the Bible and central goal of lives must surely be the glory of God.

Worship is rooted in God's worthiness, therefore our primary reason for coming into the presence of the Lord is to bless Him and to minister to Him. When Jesus defined worship in John 4:20–23, He emphasized the *object* of our worship over the *place* of worship. The key issue for all true worship is that it must be founded in spirit and in truth:

"But the hour is coming, and now is, when the true worshipers will worship the Father in spirit and truth; for the Father is seeking such to worship Him. God is

Spirit, and those who worship Him must worship in spirit and truth." (John 4:23–24)

Numerous writers have given explanations of these words, "spirit and truth." Most seem to conclude that Jesus was referring to the mind and manner,[2] or the motive and form of worship. (It is interesting to note that Jesus referred to *Himself* as a worshiper in verse 22: "'You worship what you do not know; we know what we worship, for salvation is of the Jews.'")

Matthew Henry and Adam Clarke offer these wise commentaries on John 4:23:

> If we do not worship God, who is **a spirit, in the spirit,** we miss **the end** of worship. . . .[3] **In spirit.** . . . We must worship him with fixedness of thought and a flame of affection, with all that is within us. **In truth,** that is in sincerity. We must mind the power more than the form. . . The gate of spiritual worship is straight. Such worship is necessary, and what the God of heaven insists upon.[4] (Matthew Henry)

> **God is a spirit.** This is one of the first, the greatest, the most sublime, and necessary truths in the compass of nature! There is a God, the cause of all things—the Fountain of all perfection—without parts or dimensions, for He is eternal—filling the heavens and the earth—pervading, governing, and upholding all things, for He is an infinite Spirit! A man worships God **in spirit** when, under the influence of the Holy Ghost, he brings all his affections, appetites, and desires to the throne of God; and he worships Him **in truth** when every purpose and passion of his heart, and when every act of his religious worship, is guided and regulated by the word of God.[5] (Adam Clarke)

Because of these truths, how we define *praise* and *worship* is supremely important; our theology and understanding of Biblical worship are based on this.

Various methods of categorizing praise and worship music have been used over the centuries. In Charismatic and Pentecostal circles, we have long defined praise and worship by the style of our songs. One rather simplistic (and grossly inaccurate) form of this is to say that "praise is the fast songs and worship is the slow songs."

This simple example illustrates how rarely we consider the Lord's role and place in worship. It is as if we have thought of Him as a heavenly spectator for our music and songs. We have not welcomed Him as the leader and full participant in this great communion.

THE MANIFESTATION OF THE PRESENCE OF GOD

While we are ministering to Him, He inhabits our praises and communes with us. As a result of His presence we are changed forever. Worshipers are changed as they minister to God, almost as a beneficial "side effect." This is one of the greatest principles in the Bible—we become like the one we worship.

God is omnipresent—in all places at all times—yet He *manifests*—reveals, uncovers or shows—Himself in the midst of our praises and speaks of Himself there.

A. W. Tozer speaks of the omnipresence and manifest Presence of God:

> The omnipresence of the Lord is one thing, and is a solemn fact necessary to His perfection. The manifest Presence is another thing altogether, and from that Presence we have fled, like Adam, to hide among the trees of the garden, or like Peter, to shrink away crying, "Depart from me, for I am a sinful man, O Lord." (Luke 5:8)[6]

Whenever He manifests Himself to us we will worship and be changed forever. It is really quite impossible not to worship Him once we have encountered Him. He is irresistible.

Yet the question remains for many of us: How do we recognize His manifestation and what form does it take? We have studied in previous chapters the great variety of ways that God can speak to us in worship (such as through Scripture, prophetic words, or feelings, thoughts, impressions, etc.). It is almost as if He is speaking to all of us at once on many different wavelengths. As each person expresses what God has placed within his or her heart, a coherent picture begins to take shape. Then we realize that He is revealing an aspect of Himself in our midst.

It is really quite impossible not to worship Him once we have encountered Him.

For example, the Lord might choose to manifest Himself in our worship as a God who is rejoicing or dancing over us with singing (as in Zeph. 3:17). At such a time the sound of our music will most probably include the sound of rejoicing. During this part of the service, the worship music may very well become fast and loud as the instrumentalists become inspired by and respond to this revelation.

Likewise, if He comes amongst us as a gentle Shepherd, then we will play and sing with gentleness.

Our gauge for determining worship is rooted in the fact of God's presence, not the issue of our music. We know that worship is taking place because God is present and the people are responding to Him. The character of His presence, then, will determine the exact nature and sound of our worship; whether fast or slow, majestic or somber, joyous or gentle.

We know that worship is taking place because God is present and the people are responding to Him.

I will never forget the day when He came amongst us as a Deliverer during a service at Shady Grove Church. The pastor had invited all those who felt they needed deliverance from some form of spiritual oppression to come forward for prayer. The front of the church was filled with those who felt this need. But before anyone could begin to pray for them, some dancers came onto the platform and began to dance in a warlike manner, beating out a rhythm on the wooden platform with their hands and feet. After a time, the musicians joined in with a victorious sound and the whole congregation entered into intercession on behalf of those at the altar. The Lord healed and delivered many that day.

How awesome He was in the midst of the praises of His people! It is not that the dance and music were so powerful in themselves, but they became *a prophetic expression* of the Lord's strong right arm and His delivering strength.

We worshiped that day, because we allowed the Lord to show Himself in the midst of His people. Our worship was not based on the kinds of songs we had chosen to sing that day, but on the manifestation of His presence among us and His work in our lives.

The character of the Lord determines the nature of our worship

---

Richard Foster calls upon the worshiping church to regularly expect miracles in the midst of worship:

> If Jesus is our leader, miracles should be expected to occur in worship. Healings, both inward and outward, will be the rule, not the exception. The book of Acts will not just be something we read about, but something we are experiencing.[7]

Quite simply, praise is not "the fast songs." Rather, praise is our faith-filled expression of thanks and honor because of what the Lord has done, is doing and will do. It is the pouring out of our hearts in sacrifice before Him as priests.

We so need the Holy Spirit to draw us into praise and teach us the language of praise. If He is allowed to lead us, there will be times when our praises become prophetic. This means we will be declaring the greatness of the Lord *before* we even see what He is going to do; or, we will delight in His works *before* we fully understand the magnitude of His acts.

OUR RESPONSE TO THE PRESENCE OF GOD

Worship is our response to the manifest presence of God. The manifest presence of God is His revealed presence. Whenever we come to our place of worship we must have an expectation for His voice and His manifest presence.

Worship is only possible once the Lord has "shown" Himself. I believe that it is impossible to really worship God unless we have had a revelation of God. Once we have had a revelation of Him, it is impossible not to worship, as this encounter with Him requires a response from us.

LaMar Boschman and Richard Foster comment on this issue:

> We come into His presence singing praises, and, when we find Him, we worship.[8] (Boschman)

> We can use all the right techniques and methods, we can have the best possible liturgy, but we have not worshiped the Lord until Spirit touches spirit. . . When Spirit touches spirit the issue of forms is wholly secondary.[9] (Foster)

Some of us have "super-spiritualized" the word *revelation*. Having a revelation of God is not just for the high and the mighty, once or twice a year, but should be the norm for all of God's children on a regular basis. Revelation from the Lord is an integral part of our personal and corporate relationship with Him. It is what keeps our relationship alive.

It is impossible to really worship God unless we have had a revelation of God. Once we have had a revelation of Him, it is impossible not to worship Him.

Several others have commented on the revelation of God in the midst of worship:

> Worship is revelation and response. . . If we fail to respond, worship has probably not occurred.[10] (Allen and Borror)

> Fundamentally, worship is a person responding to a person, so we cannot worship until we get a glimpse of God. We can praise out of our memory circuits, but we must worship out of a present relationship; that is, we must be in God's presence to worship. True worship will not begin to flow until we get a good glimpse of Christ Jesus.[11] (Judson Cornwall)

> Christ came to **declare** God to us.[12] (Matthew Henry)

I can remember countless occasions when the Lord revealed Himself to an entire congregation.

One time during a worship conference in Puerto Rico the Lord came among us as a Shepherd. This was evidenced by a prophetic word, followed by a lilting melody played on a recorder (wooden flute), and various scriptures that were read. Many were healed as the Lord walked among His people and anointed their heads with the oil of His Spirit. Some dancers depicted this action of the Lord through dance and mime.

I do not think anyone present that evening missed out on this incredible revelation of the Lord as the Good Shepherd. Of course, I had read Psalm Twenty-three numerous times and was intellectually aware of the Lord's role as the Shepherd of His people. Yet, that evening, something of His Shepherd's heart touched my heart, and I will never be the same.

REVELATION AS IT RELATES TO WORSHIP

There are so many examples in Scripture where worship is preceded by a revelation of God and His manifest presence. These are just a few:

- *Genesis 18–22*—This is the first time worship is mentioned in Scripture. Abraham had a visitation from the Lord concerning God's promise of a son. This visitation from the Lord caused Abraham to be able to worship God by offering his son, Isaac, in chapter 22. The Lord revealed Himself again on Mt. Moriah as He provided a ram for the sacrifice. Abraham worshiped God after this great provision and revelation, offering the ram as a sacrifice to God.
- *Exodus 15*—Following the Lord's revelation of Himself as a deliverer through the Red Sea, Moses worshiped and sang the first prophetic song that is recorded in the Word. The first verses contain a description of the revelation that Moses and the Children of Israel received from God. In verse three Moses sang one of the names of God that had been revealed: *"The LORD is a man of war; the LORD is His name."*
- *Exodus 34:1–9*—The Lord descended in a cloud and passed before Moses, proclaiming His name. Following the revelation of the character and nature of God that

was found in His name, Moses bowed down and worshiped.

- *2 Chronicles 7:1–6*—After the Lord revealed Himself in
the glory that filled the temple, Solomon and all the
people worshiped Him with generous offerings.
- *Isaiah 6:1–8*—Isaiah saw the Lord in His throne room.
After this astounding sight, he had a revelation of him-
self and his unworthiness. Then he responded to the
Lord and gave his life to speaking on behalf of the
Lord. Throughout Isaiah's writings we find a prophet
who is obviously a worshiper.
- *Luke 1:39–80*—Mary worshiped the Lord after the
Holy Spirit was revealed to her and Elizabeth. John the
Baptist's father, Zacharias, also saw a miracle of God in
his life, was filled with the Holy Spirit and began to
worship God.
- *Luke 4:40–41; 5:25; 7:16; 13:13, 17; 17:15–16; 18:43;
19:37–38*—(These examples are just from the book of
Luke.) Jesus healed the sick, raised the dead and commanded the elements from Judea to Galilee. Whenever
He performed miracles such as this, He uncovered His
grace and His great glory. At the sight of such a One,
the people worshiped.

TWO CRUCIAL ISSUES CONCERNING WORSHIP

I believe the two following issues are crucial and must be
emphasized:

1. By definition, all worship is prophetic because it includes the
concept of God's self-revelation. Every ministry in the presence of
God—whether music, dance or any other artistic expression—is an
extension of the true act of worship, which is the communion
between God and his people. Worship will take place whenever
God fills our praises with His presence (Ps. 22:3).

2. Many seem to feel that God's manifest presence—or revelation
of Himself in the corporate worship service—is somewhat a "hit
or miss" experience. The opposite should be true. Profound, creative, revelatory, and intimate worship should be the norm for
every congregation of all denominations. Our relationship with

God bids us to expect face to face encounters with God on a regular basis. It is our responsibility as worship leaders to make a way for God to "uncover" Himself, or manifest Himself before His people. He is a gentleman and will not "invade" our services. He is patiently waiting to respond to our longings.

Once we have worshiped in spirit and in truth, we will be ruined for anything else, forever.

Once we have worshiped in spirit and in truth, we will be ruined for anything else, forever. We will have no patience for dead traditions of any sort. It will be easy to recognize any man's hand upon the worship service, as some would try to manipulate and control spiritual things. Graham Kendrick says this:

> If the presence of God is made known in our worship, if his Living Presence truly saturates the proceedings, then not only will there be the reverence and order that characterize the holy God of an ordered creation, but a sense of the unexpected that reflects his endless creativity as he molds and fashions our lives together.[13] ✎

Chapter Fourteen

MAKING THE HOLY SPIRIT YOUR "WORSHIP LEADER"

What I believe about God is the most important thing about me.
A. W. Tozer

≋

Who controls the worship service in your church? Is it the pastor? Is it the worship leader? Who decides when it is time to sing, when it is time to stop singing?

This is truly one of the more difficult issues to be resolved for churches (and church leaders) that desire to pursue prophetic worship, because it requires a new understanding of leadership and of spiritual authority. In prophetic worship, everyone must submit to the leading of the Holy Spirit.

THE HOLY SPIRIT AS WORSHIP LEADER

In prophetic worship, the worship "leader" functions more as a worship "door keeper" or worship "facilitator." The Holy Spirit is the true leader, and His role is to craft the sight and sound of God in our midst with the excellence of a master conductor before a symphony orchestra.

If, for example, He wants the sound of His voice to be expressed through the sweetness of a flute or an innocent prayer of a child, then the worship leader must be sensitive enough to respond immediately and make space for these to come forth.

As this illustrates, we need to completely "rethink" the traditional role of a choir director or worship leader so that there can come an understanding of spiritual release and delegation of responsibility to the whole congregation in worship.

The Lord has a lot to say about the direction of our worship services, if we will only take the time to listen. We must learn that He has a masterful plan and purpose for *every* service. His direction is already set. It is up to the worship leader to "tap into" the Lord's leading and release a wide participation in the service by all members of the congregation.

In prophetic worship, everyone must submit to the leading of the Holy Spirit.

We might describe this kind of leadership as a rather fluid form of leadership, as many different people may participate in, and even "lead" at various moments in the service. By "lead," I mean that they might be inspired by the Holy Spirit to step out and call upon the congregation for a particular response.

I have seen a man come forward and challenge the men of the congregation to pray; a woman gather children to dance; and a trumpet player stand and play, then direct other musicians to follow his example. During these moments, those who have stepped forward may, in effect, be leading the service as the Lord is using them as vessels to uncover His will and purpose for the service.

On one occasion I heard a drummer prophesy on his drums. It was during a service where we had all been singing songs concerning the King and were expecting Him to reveal Himself to our hearts in an extraordinary way. As the congregation exalted and praised the King, it was almost as if He heard our cry and processed in the midst of our praises. At that moment the trumpets played in spontaneous fanfare and announced His presence. A holy hush descended upon the people and they appropriately fell upon their face before Him.

After a time of silence, the Lord began to speak. That night, His voice was like a thunder. The most suitable instrument to speak at that moment was the drums. For several minutes the drummer played on the toms—not with a set rhythm, but with the cadence of one who is speaking. The walls shook with the sound and our hearts were melted in the presence of the Lord. Some time after the drums finished, the pastor came to the microphone, explained what the Lord was saying and asked the people to remain in silence until He had finished His work in our hearts.

No one had told the drummer to play at that moment, and no worship leader had directed during the thirty minutes or so that this went on. The Holy Spirit was clearly in charge and the Lord received all the glory. I am sure that every believer in that service remembers God's thunderous voice to this day. It was an awesome sound, rather than a frightening sound, that shook our hearts to the core. We walked away softly after that night, with a greater hunger for God and a much fuller understanding of His impressive majesty.

There is no need for any pastor or elder to feel their authority is being compromised in this type of service. Neither is there any room for personal "kingdom building," or the usurping of authority of any sort by anyone present, when a congregation of mature and spiritual people gather to worship the Lord.

We must assume that the Lord has a
masterful plan and purpose for
every service.

Ultimately, the Lord is the primary Worship Leader of the church. Richard Foster concurs:

> Christ is the Leader of worship in the sense that he alone decides what human means will be used, if any. Individuals preach or prophesy or sing or pray as they are called forth by their Leader. In this way there is no room for the elevation of private reputations. Jesus alone is honored.[1]

THE FEAR OF GOD

This may lead to a greater release on the part of the worship leader and team, but also to a greater increase of the fear or awe of God. I say *release*, because it is not up to anyone (worship leader, musicians, or pastor) to make anything happen. It is not necessary to fabricate the sense of God's presence. His presence is indisputable. His desire to reveal Himself to His people is certain.

As worship leaders, we do not need to carry the burden of manufacturing His presence for the people. God is completely responsible for every supernatural meeting with the congregation, and for touching our lives with His grace. The worship service—for which we plan and prepare—is merely the tool, or stepping stone for God to use as He "breathes" upon the songs, words, instruments, and so forth.

I also use the word *fear* as we approach this place of meeting with the Lord. It is a fear that must be born out of a profound reverence and respect for the Lord. Every meeting with God is both glorious and formidable (Deut. 7:21; Job 37:22; Pss. 47:2; 68:35). While He will always be our most gracious Friend and Father, He remains overwhelming and we will never come to the end of our discovery of Him. There is so much of the fear of God that has been lost in this world. How can we expect unbelievers to walk in the fear of God, when we see so little awe and reverence for Him in the church?

True, God is our friend and is closer than a brother, but He is also our King who is full of splendor and majesty. The sight of Him has caused mere men to tremble, be blinded and fall down as if they were dead. After God spoke the Ten Commandments to the whole assembly from the midst of the fire (Deut. 5:22–27), the Israelites begged not to hear the sound of His voice, as they believed they would die if they heard any more from Him (Ex. 20:20). Worship is rooted in the honor and fear of God.

Worship is rooted in the honor and fear of God.

> . . . genuine corporate worship, will only happen when a people gather together in a community response of awe to His name.[2] (Allen and Borror)

We will never fully know what God is going to do in our midst. Even so, let God have full control of the whole service—especially the worship. Prophetic worship does not need to be a "hit or miss" experience for the church. Surely, it should be the norm for us to regularly encounter God in a most profound and prophetic manner in our church services.

Sally Morgenthaler has succinctly addressed one of the major problems that churches encounter when trying to release control of the service to the Holy Spirit—pride and self-promotion. Each member of the congregation and leadership needs to examine his or her heart so that sinful reactions to this great liberty do not ruin God's best for His prophetic people.

> If we are really going to give people opportunities to encounter and interact with God in our sanctuaries . . . we have to set aside some of our control issues and get out of the way.[3]

As leaders, we may carefully plan the songs and the order of participants in the service, but more is required of us than to have a tidy song list and instruments that are in tune. Our hearts must be consecrated and our ears made sensitive through prayer as we draw near to Him in expectation and reverent fear.

Set your eyes and ears upon the true Worship Leader. Watch Him, wait upon Him and work with Him as the Holy Spirit ushers us into the courts of His awesome majesty, and He deftly weaves His life and likeness into every heart. ✍

Chapter Fifteen

RELEASING THE PRIESTHOOD OF ALL BELIEVERS

True worship has no room for a spectating heart.
Sammy Tippit

≈

Most believers shy away from thinking of themselves as priests. We have a traditional view of the priesthood where we see it as a vocational calling alone, but God's idea on this subject differs drastically from our typical understanding. A priest is really a bridge-builder—one who stands between God and unredeemed man. Every believer is to be actively involved in worshiping God, and actively involved in ministering to those around us. That is the priestly call upon the Church.

When it comes to the believer's role in worship, we find that little has been expected from the congregation at all. Individuals can faithfully attend a church for decades and never once participate in the worship service, apart from congregational singing. Is it possible that many people treat worship as a spectator sport where they would rather have professionals sing to them than to participate in worship themselves? Tom Schwanda has this to say about the role of the Christian in worship:

> . . .a foundational biblical principle of worship is that it
> is participatory.[1]

The true meaning of 1 Peter 2:1–10—where the Church is challenged to participate in Christian life and worship as a holy, royal priesthood—has yet to be fully explored and experienced by the modern Church.

Each believer is meant to be a priest of the "spiritual house" mentioned in 1 Peter 2:5. This is more a corporate expression of priesthood than an individual one. Peter's intent was not to dismiss spiritual authority in the believer's life and send each person off to lead their own "church." As he goes on to explain, the primary reason for the corporate priesthood is:

> . . . to offer up spiritual sacrifices. . .(1 Pet. 2:5) (See also Heb. 13:15–16)

> . . . that you may proclaim the praises of Him who has called you . . . (1 Pet. 2:9)

We will not go wrong if we see our priestly role as those who are ministers before the Lord in praise and worship, and servants of all people on earth—both the saved and unsaved. As priests and servants to the lost, we have a great responsibility to proclaim His saving grace to all (2 Cor. 5:16–19).

Jesus and Paul clearly taught that we are the dwelling place, or temple, of God, and that we are the priests who are responsible for ministering before the Lord (Jn. 14:23; 1 Cor. 6:19–20; 2 Cor. 6:16; Eph. 4:6). Our personal ministry before the Lord is necessary preparation for our priestly ministry within the church body. The Lord has sought for this priesthood since the beginning of time.

Our personal ministry before the Lord is preparation for our priestly ministry within the church body.

ACTIVE PRIESTLY PARTICIPATION

God never intended for the Church to have an élite caste of ministers. The vast and persistent gap that separates church leaders and platform ministers from the congregation ("the clergy" from "the laity") clearly militates against truly prophetic worship.

Several well-known authors have addressed this issue with respect to worship:

> Worship is a verb. It is not something done to us or for us, but by us.[2] (Webber)

. . . if worship is a meeting between God and his people, then return worship to the people.[3] (Webber)

Liturgy is supposed to be the work of the people . . .[4] (Tom Schwanda)

. . . the people of God are deserving of a richer share in the service than simply being hymn-singers and offering-givers, while for the rest of the service they remain a body of inert auditors and passive spectators . . . give them an understanding that each facet of the public worship of God has meaning in which they are invited to contribute a significant activity—in praising, praying, giving, as in remembering, listening, confessing, believing, and acting out. These are all verbs of involvement and choice.[5] (Martin)

Active participation in worship is the Biblical norm for the whole congregation.

There is no escape for the believer. Active participation in worship is the Biblical norm for the whole congregation. Whenever we gather, we have to understand that we have not come for a performance put on by the pastor, music minister or worship team, but we have come to participate in the greatest "work" of our week. It is our highest calling to participate in ministering to God by offering "spiritual sacrifices" to Him (see Chapter Two for further discussion of these sacrifices).

We are not only priests, we are *royal* priests (1 Pet. 2:9). We must learn to assume our position as ministers within a royal court before a great King. Every worshiper can learn to be a gatekeeper of His court (Ps. 84:10; Prov. 8:34); a minister of incense before His Throne (1 Pet. 2:5); a royal Bride who knows intimate communion with Him (Ps. 45:9–15; Song of Solomon); royal sons of God who rule and reign with Him on earth and in His Kingdom forever (1 Jn. 3:1–2).

Pastor Jack Hayford makes some very wise comments on the role of the believer as a royal priest:

What the priest-king role of worship does do is to build a bridge between heaven's Throne and earth's need. Worship becomes God's rule into man's circumstances. Because we the redeemed are privileged to be the ones exercising the action which issues that welcome, a regal role is ascribed to us by God Himself. . . man's assignment to rule may be regained because his responsibility to worship has been reclaimed.[6]

When the pastor, priest, or music team are expected to lead every aspect of the whole service, the congregation functions as nothing more than spectators or an audience for a well-scripted, religious show.

For good or for ill, we live in a society capable of producing spectacular shows and productions on a regular basis. Multi-billion-dollar sports, media, advertising and entertainment industries rule our finances and constantly saturate our senses.

What a pity that our children and congregations have not been shown that the experience of the presence of God in worship is much more profound, moving, and magnificent than anything Hollywood could ever imagine or produce(!). Awaiting the true worshiper is the presence of One who provides joys so delightful and filled with His glory that they are unable to be fully told or spoken of (1 Pet. 1:8).

Awaiting the true worshiper, is the presence of One who provides joys so delightful and filled with His glory that they are unable to be fully told or spoken of.

The presence of God is also the place where we experience the "fullness of joy" and "pleasures for evermore" (Ps. 16:11). We must assume that there is no pleasure, happiness, delight, indulgence, ecstasy, excitement or enjoyment that can come even close to comparing with the thrill of God's presence. Think of all the wonders on this earth and all the sensational creations and abilities of man—not one can compare with Him!

For worship to be this exciting, *it must involve the whole congregation.* Participation is a key to prophetic worship. Sammy

Tippit and Judson Cornwall add these thoughts on congregational participation:

> Music that produces worship will be participatory in nature. True worship has no room for a spectating heart; the home of worship is in the participating heart. Worship cannot sit in the grandstands of the church watching the performance of the more talented. True worship does not perform for others. It only participates in the grace and love of God.[7] (Tippit)

> Worship is one thing that cannot be done for the people; it must be done by them, for worship by identification is impossible. The Old Testament priesthood assisted the worshipper in his approach to God, but they did not perform the ritual as a surrogate for the worshipper. . . The choir's anthem cannot substitute for congregational singing, nor can the preacher's sermon replace congregational praise and worship. Worship demands involvement on the part of the worshipper.[8] (Cornwall)

WHOLEHEARTED WORSHIP

Not only must every member of the congregation participate in worship as priests, but individuals are challenged to yield every area of their bodies, souls and spirits to worship ministry. This is God's first and greatest commandment:

> And you shall love the Lord your God out of and with your whole heart, and out of and with all your soul (your life) and out of and with all your mind—[that is] with your faculty of thought and your moral understanding—and out of and with all your strength. This is the first and principle commandment. (Mk. 12:30, Amp.) (See also: Deut. 6:4–5; Matt. 22:37; Lu. 10:27)

Wheaton professor, Andrew Hill, calls the whole congregation to fully participate in worship based on his understanding of ancient Hebraic culture and their belief that humans are an indivisible totality:

> . . .the nature and constitution of the human being
> demanded that the whole person respond to Yahweh in
> worship, not just the spirit and the soul. . . . Active,
> whole person worship of the Lord God is not only
> implicit given the Hebrew worldview but also is implic-
> it in the divine commandments regulating Israel's
> covenant relationship with Yahweh.[9]

Wholehearted worship is not necessarily loud and exuberant
worship. The Lord looks at the intent and purpose of our hearts.

I know stroke patients who are barely able to speak or move,
yet seem able to fulfill this obligation of enthusiastic and sincere
worship. They strain with every fiber of their being to participate
in the songs and lift or clap their hands in response to the Lord.
Barely a sound can be heard from their lips, and their clapping
may be awkward and off the beat, but no one can dispute the
earnest nature of their offering to the Lord.

New Testament expectations of unbelievers and believers in worship

First Corinthians 14 is one of the primary passages where Paul
gives instruction to the Church on how to conduct public worship
services. Paul is particularly concerned that the gifts of the Spirit
be ministered in an orderly manner, and that the congregation
understand their role in the service. There are some very significant
statements in this passage concerning congregational participation
in prophetic worship. Paul also indicates the most likely response
of any unbeliever if they encounter the presence of God in the
midst of the Church:

> But if all prophesy, and an unbeliever or an uninformed
> person comes in, he is convinced by all, he is convicted
> by all. And thus the secrets of his heart are revealed;
> and so, falling down on his face, he will worship God
> and report that God is truly among you. How is it then,
> Brethren? Whenever you come together, each of you
> has a psalm, has a teaching, has a tongue, has a revela-
> tion, has an interpretation. Let all things be done for
> edification. (1 Cor. 14:24–26)

In the midst of this prophetic meeting—where the whole church was flowing in the gifts of the Spirit—an unbeliever had the secrets of his heart uncovered and he fell down and worshiped the Lord. Even this unbeliever was able to recognize the presence of the Lord and be changed in the midst of true worship. How much more should we, who know the Lord, be able to hear His voice as He flows through the ministry of the whole congregation?

At Shady Grove Church in Grand Prairie, Texas, it is not uncommon for unbelievers to receive Christ during the worship service. Altar calls are customary and may be given at any time throughout the worship, as the Holy Spirit directs. Several people may come forward to receive Christ during this time, even though these services are not targeted specifically towards the lost, as would be the case in a "seeker service."

Other kinds of body ministry also take place during these worship services, such as prayers for healing, or comfort for those who are suffering in some way.

As this illustrates, our prayer for one another is an extension of our worship ministry to the Lord. Sometimes the Father turns the worship service towards body ministry because He is our Pastor and Chief Shepherd and is acutely aware of every need and every troubled heart.

The other main point in this passage is that Paul seems to expect this prophetic flow through every member of the church, each time we gather together:

> Whenever you come together, each of you. . . (1 Cor. 14:26)

Young people and those without Bible school degrees are not excluded. The whole Body is expected to function in a manner that will bring edification to all—even the unsaved. This kind of ministry within the church service can only be accomplished when the congregation is taught that they are a part of a holy, royal priesthood whose greatest work on earth is to be ministers unto the Lord in worship.

The true function of a vocational minister is to equip the Body to function in maturity in all areas of their Christian lives—including worship ministry:

> And He Himself gave some *to be* apostles, some prophets, some evangelists, and some pastors and

teachers, for the equipping (perfecting—KJV) of the
saints for the work of ministry, for the edifying of the
body of Christ, till we all come to the unity of the faith
and of the knowledge of the Son of God, to a perfect
man, to the measure of the stature of the fullness of
Christ. (Eph. 4:11–13)

Our greatest work on earth is to minister to the Lord in worship.

Prophetic worship summons the congregation to significant
maturity and participation in every service. The whole church—
the youngest to the oldest, the strong and the weak, the educated
and the uneducated—needs to be taught how to function as one in
mature and prophetic ministry to each other. Each one is a part of
this holy, royal priesthood. This is the model for true prophetic
worship.

I often encounter brothers and sisters after a service who believe
that the Holy Spirit was prompting them to share a particular
scripture, prophecy, or song during worship, but they were too shy
to come forward and share what was on their hearts. While the
place of hearing and obeying the urging of the Holy Spirit is a
learning process for every Christian, I cannot help feeling grieved.
Their opportunities to minister have been missed, and the chance
for others to respond to the voice of God has been lost because of
disobedience, pride, or shyness.

Every believer must become responsible and remain alert to the
voice of God in worship. As a primary means of speaking to all
people, the Lord has chosen us—His priests—to proclaim His
voice. We do not earn the right to "speak" for Him. Corporate
prophecy is not the sole prerogative of older or more mature
Christians, but the responsibility of the entire church body.

At the *Light the Nation* conference in Dallas (May 5–8, 1998),
Tommy Tenney made this statement on the true purpose of church:

> The original purpose of church was a meeting place
> between God and man. Church was not created for you
> to get anything, church was created for you to give
> something of yourself to Him. . .if we want a restora-

tion of the original power of the church, we have to return to the original recipe.[10]

The original recipe that Tenney is referring to is found in 2 Chronicles 7:14:

> If my people who are called by My name will humble themselves, and pray and seek My face, and turn from their wicked ways; then I will hear from heaven, and forgive their sin and heal their land.

Desperate, wholehearted seeking of God by the entire priesthood needs to be heard in the Church today if we desire the glory of God to invade our land.

Chapter Sixteen

STEPPING INTO ETERNITY

Time is an available instrument for reaching the eternal.
John W. Lynch

≫

E very moment of every day really belongs to God, for the earth and everything in it is His (Ps. 24:1; 1 Cor. 10:26, 28). He is the Author and Finisher of our faith all the days we live on this earth (Heb. 12:2). Our best moments and greatest regard should always be given to the Lord as an act of worship. My pastor, Charlotte Baker, speaks of "wasting ourselves, our time and all we have upon Him" in the same way that Mary "wasted" the contents of the alabaster box upon the head and feet of Jesus.

Unfortunately, we live in a world that is confined by multitudes of time restraints. It is reasonable to surmise that living daily under such restraints has had some influence upon our attitudes toward corporate worship.

Perhaps this is why some tend to treat worship as just one "segment" of a highly produced and well-packaged "Sunday Celebration Service." Such services are designed to subject church members to as short a time as possible in fulfilling their church commitment, since leaders are afraid to take too much time from the busy schedules of the "average Christian."

Many are the occasions when I have seen anxious pastors looking at their watches and glaring at the worship leader when the "worship segment" of the service seems to be running late. That would, of course, throw off the entire schedule for that morning's production (!).

Often, out of fear for his job, or just because he feels it is time to move on, the worship leader will interrupt the moving of the

Holy Spirit to yank everyone to their feet for a rousing finale. This can be quite frustrating for those in the congregation who are truly communing, for it interrupts the intimacy they are experiencing with Christ.

AN AUDIENCE WITH THE KING

The truth of the matter is that the Lord is enthroned in the midst of us as we worship Him (Ps. 22:3). At that moment we have the opportunity to sit, stand or kneel in the presence of the King and commune with Him—face to face. Worship summons us into the presence of His Majesty, the King of Kings. Who on earth would want to pass up that opportunity just to fulfill a man-made schedule?

Worship summons us into the presence
of His Majesty, the King of Kings.

If we were in the presence of an earthly King, Queen, President or Prime Minister, I doubt that we would be constantly looking at our watches and anxiously gazing towards the exit in anticipation of the close of the meeting. It is more likely that we would measure our words and count every second as an honor, that we have an audience with one of such eminence and dignity.

If the Queen asked us to spend one day with her, how quickly we would cancel all other engagements, how insignificant all other pursuits would seem at that moment. We would count the days till our appointment, tell all our friends, lay out our finest clothes, prepare ourselves for any possible questions from Her Majesty, pray for favor, practice our protocol and enter with wonder, awe and anticipation.

May I suggest that every moment of boredom for every man, woman or child in the presence of Jesus is a moment when that individual has lost sight of the One we worship? As spectacular as it would be to have an audience with Her Majesty, the Queen, nothing will ever come close to the encounter we are invited to every Sabbath.

This reminds me of a nursery rhyme I learned as a child:

Pussy cat, pussy cat, where have you been?
I've been to London to see the King.
Pussy cat, pussy cat what did you there?
I spied a little mouse under the chair!

The cat came all the way to see the King, but diminished his gaze and his whole purpose for the visit by focusing on the lowly mouse.

What would be the reply if we were to ask the members of our congregations the same questions?

Christian, Christian where have you been?
I've been to church to see the King.
Christian, Christian what did you there?
I spied the pastor's wife with funny hair!

It may not be the pastor's wife that we are looking at, but one thing is certain: anything or anyone who might distract our focus away from the awesome majesty of the King of Kings can never stand worthy of such misdirected attention. It is a stolen moment to be sure. How often we waste time in the presence of Jesus by emphasizing the trivial and concentrating on earthly matters.

Some people go to church to see who didn't.[1]

> Every moment of boredom for every man, woman or child in the presence of Jesus is a moment when that individual has lost sight of the One we worship.

HONOR THE SABBATH

The time we spend with God should not be an accident, nor should it be determined by some theoretical theological calculation. The Lord is aware of how much time we need to commune with Him. Everything He has done has been in its right time—He is never early or late.

The Lord has even commanded us to set aside a whole day as a holy day unto the Him (Ex. 20:8). W. Vine tells us that the root meaning for the Hebrew word *Sabbath* (Heb: *Shâbath*) means: *to cease, desist*. Vine goes on to explain that the singular word has a doubled "*b*," which indicates "an intensive force, implying complete cessation or a making to cease, probably the former. The idea is not that of relaxation or refreshment, but cessation from activity."[2]

Various rabbinical writings over the years have served to turn the blessing of this commandment into a legalistic burden by making the rules of the Sabbath more important than the rest and worship that this day offers. We must ensure that the Sabbath serves God's people rather than God's people serving the Sabbath. This day should release us to prophetic worship without undue concern for other business that might rob us of our full communion with the Lord.

The fast pace of modern society may be responsible for our erroneous attitudes towards this day of rest and worship. Worship services are peppered with the sound of beepers and cellular phones. Numerous activities have been crammed into our Sabbaths, leaving little room for waiting upon God.

SILENCE IN WORSHIP

Prophetic worship requires that we have time to wait and listen for God's voice and respond to Him appropriately. Spontaneous and unprepared moments are quite common in services where the Holy Spirit is the leader.

The art of waiting on God seems to be lost in the majority of churches these days. We are far more accustomed to filling every moment with our prepared programs and seem to be afraid of any silence. Leaders dare not venture one minute beyond the predetermined schedule or order of service.

The Psalmist wrote, "Be still and know that I am God" (Ps. 46:10). Something of the knowledge of God is found in the stillness. Holy silence and stillness are often life-changing moments in our worship. Wheaton professor, Andrew Hill, has made some excellent observations regarding silence in worship:

> The silence of worship is equally as important as the noise of worship. Silence takes the worshiper out of

time and into God's eternity. . . . Silence is valuable in Christian worship because it is disturbing, arresting. We feel uncomfortable, helpless; we are no longer in control.[3]

When God draws us into His silence, our schedules and time constraints become irrelevant; we are consumed with the delights of His presence alone. A. W. Tozer goes further, as he speaks of an inward adoration that is experienced in silence:

> With our loss of the sense of majesty has come the further loss of religious awe and consciousness of the divine Presence. We have lost our spirit of worship and our ability to withdraw inwardly to meet God in adoring silence. . . it is impossible to keep our moral practices sound and our inward attitudes right while our idea of God is erroneous or inadequate. If we would bring back spiritual power to our lives, we might begin to think of God more nearly as He is.[4]

The work done by a worshiper will have eternity in it.[5]

Silence, alone, is not the key to the spiritual depth that is being described here. We must combine silence with reverence and worship. Silence is more a result of the awe and wonder we experience in God's presence rather than being an expression of worship by itself.

The art of waiting on God seems to be lost in the majority of churches these days.

There are times in worship when all words are inadequate and a serenity or holy hush falls upon everyone present. Pastors and worship leaders must surrender to the time frame of the Holy Spirit during these moments as He works secretly and lovingly within our hearts.

But not all His silences are quite so secretive. In 1997 Pastor David Fischer, of Living Waters Fellowship in Pasadena, called worshipers from all over the Southern California area to a day of worship that he called a "Sabbath of Worship." There were no plans for sermons or announcements—the day was entirely devoted to worship.

Throughout the day the Lord moved among the people and uncovered Himself in various ways. At one point He drew us into about forty-five minutes of silence. During that time, mimes Todd and Marilyn Farley ministered silently and prophetically from the Song of Solomon. No words were spoken, and no sound was made as the Farleys called the congregation to a greater understanding of our "bridal" relationship with the Lord. The story was told through mime. It was silent and very effective. The silence was broken only by various instruments as they began to play the song of the Bride and the song of the Bridegroom.

As this illustrates, there can be many different kinds of silent response to the Lord in worship, ranging from awe to silent prophetic mime.

Here are two other statements on the value of silence that are well worth considering

> Everything true and great grows in silence. Without silence we fall short of reality and cannot plumb the depths of being.[6] (Ladislaus Boros)

> Four things go together: silence, listening, prayer, truth.[7] (Hubert Van Zeller)

True worship touches eternity and transcends time.

Not all waiting has to be in silence. There is a silence that is without sound, but sometimes we can wait on God while the instruments play quietly. During this time we are engaged in hushed prayers, or perhaps we might softly sing a particular song until the Lord has finished speaking to us.

Solomon wrote of the gift of time that the Lord has extended to us:

> To everything there is a season, a time for every purpose under heaven. (Eccl. 3:1)

We would be wise to reconsider our use of time in worship—the most important purpose under heaven. Surely, there are few who would dare say their church spends *too much time* worshiping. For most congregations, quite the opposite is true.

THE ALPHA AND OMEGA

Because worship is an encounter with the Alpha and Omega— God, Who is the Beginning and Ending of all time—we should become accustomed to Him invading and overruling our human concepts of time and order whenever He pleases. When we enter eternity, time, as we understand it, ceases.

The worship service should take as long as the Lord needs to accomplish His work in us.

True worship touches eternity and transcends time. It will know no time restraints or limitations, nor will it be bound by man's expectations.

> . . . future time should reshape present behavior (1 Thess. 5:6–11; 2 Pet. 3:11–12; Rev. 22:10–11).[8] (Andrew Hill)

> God invades our time with eternity. We are not born for time but for eternity. We are victims and prisoners of time but creatures of eternity.[9] (Charlotte Baker)

In traditional worship structures, there is rarely a place for worship to be extended or altered beyond a set time frame. With prophetic worship, the Lord frequently has us operate according to *His* time frame: eternity. Every moment of His presence is a moment that knows no earthly time frame.

This does not mean that every worship service must go on for hours and hours in order for it to be seen as "successful." However, each service should provide as much time as the Lord needs to accomplish His work in us.

If He completes all that He has for us in fifteen minutes, then we should stop and go on to the next phase of the service. But if He would have us sing one song for half an hour, remain in silence for twenty minutes, or bow before Him for a full hour, then what on earth should keep us from these things?

What I am suggesting here is that we make an effort to give greater priority to the time frame of God's communion with us than we do to the everyday schedules of our lives. It has been my observation that the process of God's communion with the congregation is frequently interrupted by those who insert *their own* schedules and agendas. Invariably, some are just wanting to beat the Baptists to the restaurant. Andrew Hill has made some relevant statements concerning time:

> Worship is the key to a Christian understanding of life and time. Only worship can place all of human experience in the larger context of life's ultimate purpose and meaning.[10]

> Accordingly, those who truly observe the biblical Sabbath build "a sanctuary in time."[11]

Chapter Seventeen

ESTABLISHING BIBLICAL PRIORITIES IN WORSHIP

Worship renews the spirit as sleep renews the body.
Richard Clark Cabot

〰️

Since the Reformation, when pulpits were placed in the highest and most central part of the church, preachers have regarded the sermon as the main part of the service. Statements like that of E. W. Howe, below, show the prevailing attitude of the day:

> If you go to church, and like the singing better than the preaching, that's not orthodox.[1]

Such statements have been believed for centuries. These words foster an inaccurate concept of worship and promote unnecessary competition and separation between the preaching of the Word and worship ministry.

Robert Webber highlights this thinking with this statement concerning his seminary education:

> I graduated from three theological seminaries without taking a course in worship. . . . My seminary education left me with the impression that the only important matter in morning worship was the sermon. All else was preliminary. . . . I say, Shame![2]

Surely the subject of worship should become a major subject of study in all seminaries. I believe the best preachers are those who are worshipers and who have an intimate relationship with God as their teacher and example.

In some churches, the Sunday service is called the "Worship Service." Sadly, many Christians believe they have worshiped simply because they have attended the "Worship Service," sung a few songs and listened to a sermon.

Anointed preaching will inspire great worship in a congregation, and anointed worship will inspire great preaching.

Without trying to detract in any way from the importance of the Word of God in all of our lives, I would like to suggest that worship—in spirit and in truth—can have as powerful an effect upon our lives as any preaching.

There may be times in the life of the church when the pastor feels that more time or emphasis is needed for his message. During other seasons, worship may be given greater emphasis. But on the whole, *worship and preaching should be given equal prominence in church life.* In churches where prophetic worship is practiced, there will be a healthy balance between worship and the preaching of the Word.

Teacher and author Dr. Sam Sasser expresses this thought clearly:

> We must re-focus to see that while the ministry of the Word of God is imperative, the ministry we give to a holy God, from the deep inner recesses of our hearts in sustained worship, is even more imperative. This is not to say that I seek to elevate "worship" without "word," but rather to return the reader to the distinction of worship with the word, to clarify that our focus must be on the throne before the pulpit.[3]

Once again, the power of our traditions seems hard to break. Most pastors and congregants today seem to regard the sermon as the most important part of the whole service. Some people even come to church late without remorse, as they believe that they are not missing anything important since the preaching has not yet begun.

Here are some other worship leaders' thoughts on this subject:

> It is no longer adequate to defend our worship services by saying, "Well, we've always done it this way." It is equally insufficient to conceive of our worship services as "the preliminaries," something to "condition" the congregation in preparation for the truly important part of the service: the sermon. It is time to seriously consider from a broader perspective the vital role that worship plays in the life of the congregation.[4] (Bob Sorge)

> There are Godly men and women in the church who have an inadequate and sub-biblical view of music. They think of music as a filler, as a warm-up, as passing time. They think of music as the preliminary and the sermon as the main event. By this attitude the people become listeners and note takers—well informed, highly motivated, godly people, to be sure—but with no common outlet for corporate praise of the God they love. This short-circuits the cycle of praise in their life.[5] (Ronald B. Allen)

When prophetic worship is restored to its rightful priority in a church, there is never a conflict between worship and preaching, because the Holy Spirit has no inner conflicts with Himself.

I have witnessed many worship services where the theme of the worship has tied in directly with the preaching, even though the worship leader had no idea what the pastor was planning to preach that particular day. In a worshiping church, on occasion the pastor may feel free to preach for a shorter period of time—or not at all, if he senses that the Holy Spirit has accomplished all that was needed during the worship time.

We should not see worship as being a hindrance to the preaching, or in competition with it in any way. Rather, worship should prepare the hearts of the people for the word and make them better able to receive all that God has to say to them through the pastor.

Anointed preaching will inspire great worship in a congregation, and anointed worship will inspire great preaching. ✎

Chapter Eighteen

TRANSCENDING DENOMINATIONAL BARRIERS IN WORSHIP

It is always dangerous to go to church, for there is always
a chance that God's presence will break through the
protective shell of our denomination.
Eugene Carson Blake

≈

For any of us, it is possible to believe all the right things about
God and embrace a correct theology of worship, yet still
have little passion for His presence or true devotion for God.
Worship is very much a matter of the heart that must transcend all
things—including denominationalism. Dynamic and heart-felt
worship that is filled with expectations of God's presence must
surely become the primary goal of all churches.

A. W. Tozer provokes Christians from all denominations to a
greater understanding and experience of the presence of God:

> That type of Christianity which happens to be the
> vogue knows this Presence only in theory. It fails to
> stress the Christian's privilege of present realization.
> According to its teachings we are in the presence of
> God positionally, and nothing is said about the need to
> experience that Presence actually. . . Ignoble content-
> ment takes the place of burning zeal.[1]

While it would be inappropriate for us to judge various denominations on their outward forms of worship alone, each of us must

learn to recognize the impact that our own denomination has had on our worship experiences.

Dynamic and heart-felt worship that is filled with expectations of God's presence must surely become the primary goal of all churches.

Some might seek to defend the status quo by saying that we must accept the fact that Christians prefer to gather in groups of like theology, personality, and background. Therefore, those who like highly emotional forms of worship should form their own denomination, and let those who prefer a more subdued atmosphere continue to have their traditional meetings (most likely, as far away as possible, on the other side of town!).

This is the way things are today. But my contention here is that all of us—whether quiet worshipers or emotional worshipers—need to make some necessary changes that will bring each of us closer to the Biblical *truth* of worship, without losing the *Spirit* of worship, Who calls us far beyond all matters of personal preference.

Generally speaking, it is possible to describe the music and worship of any church based on the name of the denomination that is found above the door. Traditionally, our denominations have had a lot to say concerning the style of music, length of singing, use of instruments, volume of the overall sound, congregational involvement, use of hymn books or overhead projector for the words of songs, and other such important issues in worship.

(Please bear in mind, the things we *do* in worship are not nearly as meaningful as the fact that we *are* worshipers. Sadly, many believers have fought each other long and hard over issues that have little to do with eternity.)

Sally Morgenthaler points out that our Christian identities have largely been shaped by what occurs in the worship services of our particular denomination:

> Historically, whole movements and denominations have been birthed over what did or did not happen on Sunday mornings. The way we worship is often as

much a part of our Christian identity as whom we worship—sometimes even more so.[2]

Too often we worship our methodologies while feign-
ing devotion to God. And when we do this, our pride
and self-reliance belie a humanism more secular and
infinitely more grotesque than anything we abhor in the
world.[3]

Henry Jauhianinen also expresses his concern that the Christian
Church has focused too much attention on traditions and forms of
worship, rather than the truths of Biblical worship:

We need to affirm and cherish those basic features
which lie at the heart of Christian worship, regardless
of special tradition. Our first question, then, should not
be: "What makes worship Pentecostal or charismatic?"
We need to ask: "What makes worship Christian?" We
should reaffirm and celebrate those elements that are
absolutely essential to Christian worship, practicing
them in our own context. This is not a call to bland
eclecticism, nor a denial of so-called Pentecostal or
charismatic distinctives. It is a call to join other evangelicals in recovering from historical amnesia and
regaining a sense of continuity with the worshiping
church through the ages, thus enriching our present
experience.[4]

Judson Cornwall expresses this thought excellently:

. . . true worshippers . . . will not allow themselves to
be limited by the traditions of men, or bound by the
worship ritual of their religious heritage. . . they will
choose to be Bible-directed in all of their responses.[5]

. . . too often religion stifles, rather than kindles, worship responses.[6]

PROPHETIC WORSHIP AND DENOMINATIONAL STYLES

When it comes to worship and music, I think that each of us
would have to confess to some degree of denominational tunnel

vision, born out of a lifetime of experiences within our own
Christian traditions.

For each of us, the history of our worship experiences and the
satisfying times we have had with God tend to become embodied
in our favorite music and rituals. It is difficult, therefore, for us to
consider our need for growth or change in any area of our worship
expressions. But we definitely *do* need to grow—and the manner
in which we propose change in our services is just as important as
the changes themselves:

> There are times when we are guilty of trading ritualism
> for rutualism. Some who consider themselves "non-
> liturgical" and would defend their freedom at any price
> have bound themselves to a liturgy even more restric-
> tive than the avowed liturgist.[7] (Ronald Allen and
> Gordon Borror)

Biblical worship must transcend denomination, generation and culture.

Presbyterians, Baptists, Pentecostals, Charismatics . . . all have
their prescribed ways of doing things. Some sing only hymns, while
others use predominately contemporary choruses from publishers
such as Hosanna! Music, Maranatha! or Vineyard Music Group.
Some churches use only a piano or organ, while others use many
instruments, even large bands or orchestras. Some churches allow
the free use of the gifts of the Holy Spirit in worship while others
completely forbid the ministry of these gifts.

It is one thing to have a preference in these issues, but it is
another matter entirely to legislate or restrict worship based on
any denominational decree:

> Ordinances and sacraments are certainly scriptural, but
> many times God cannot be accommodated by our pro-
> gram or liturgy! In a lot of churches there is no room
> for the Lord.[8] (Ernest Gentile)

One of the funniest things about this whole scenario is that each
church continues to believe that they are the ones who worship
"decently and in order," according to 1 Corinthians 14:40. They

tend to consider every other denomination who is different from them to be at fault in some way.

I suggest that we need to read the whole of chapter 14 to understand what Paul means by "all things." Our concept of what constitutes "decently and in order" should reflect what the Lord considers decent and in order, *not* just that with which our denomination is most comfortable.

Robert Webber writes concerning the effect culture has had on our worship services:

> Protestant-evangelical worship has followed the curvature of culture, rather than being faithful to the biblical, historical tradition of the church. The true character of worship is not determined by people, but by God.[9]

> Our task is not to be judgmental in a manner of spiritual superiority, but to dig beneath the traditions to recover the spiritual impulse that originally brought them forth.[10]

WORSHIP INVOLVES OUR WHOLE HEART

The essential point is that we need to worship God with all our heart, soul, mind, and strength (Deut. 6:5; Mark 12:30, 33; Lu. 10:27). Our entire body enters into the act of worship as we become a living sacrifice (Rom. 12:1). Whatever it takes for such praise and worship to be sincerely expressed must be allowed.

> God calls for worship that involves our whole being. The body, mind, spirit and emotions should all be laid on the altar of worship. . . . We are to present our bodies to God in a posture consistent with the inner spirit in worship.[11] (Richard Foster)

Or as Paul Sarchet-Waller puts it, worship is the expression of:

- The adoration of the heart,
- The attitude of the soul,
- The understanding of the mind,
- The strength of the body.[12]

I learned one of the greatest lessons on whole-hearted worship several years ago when I participated in an international worship symposium in Bogotá, Colombia. I was given responsibility for the large orchestra, gleaned from among several thousand delegates.

The orchestra consisted of about sixty guitars, seventy tambourines, one clarinet, a piano, bass, drums, and one little lady—stuck behind the piano, scarcely able to see or be seen—who played a pair of finger cymbals.

I will never forget the face of this lady as she stood at her post and waited with patience for me to ask her to play. Despite the fact that she was never heard by anyone except God, she stayed poised for action—eyes ablaze with expectancy—from the first note of the first song, right though to the last note of the conference. She gave her all and played her part with great diligence and devotion.

Many musicians would have clamored for the best seat and the loudest microphone before they would have consented to play during worship. This woman, however, was only interested in pleasing the Lord through her worship as she counted it an honor to play with the other musicians. She was clearly ministering to God with all her heart, mind, and strength. My life was changed as I worshiped with her.

> Biblical worshipers are generous worshipers because they are wholehearted worshipers[13] (LaMar Boschman)

FORMS OF WORSHIP

I would like to suggest that in order for us to move from the confines of our traditions closer to the purity of true worship, there are many changes that need to take place. The changes I submit here are based on a call to true Biblical expressions of worship. Yet, Ralph Martin, Associate Professor of Biblical Studies at the University of Sheffield, England, makes a good argument for conserving tradition:

> . . . in worship we dramatize and enact God's saving mercies to His people long ago. The past events are reenacted so that their present influence may be felt and their appeal registered to each succeeding generation of believing people.[14]

If we can learn to maintain our valuable, *Biblical* traditions without compromising the life and liberty that is offered to us by the Holy Spirit, worship will be fulfilling for all.

Did you know that kneeling in prayer or worship is not uniquely Catholic or Episcopalian? It is a Biblical expression as old as our faith, and all Christians should feel free to kneel in prayer or worship (Ps. 95:6). Likewise, did you know that the clapping and lifting of hands is not essentially a Charismatic or Pentecostal form of worship? It also is a Biblical expression (Ps. 47:1; Ps. 134:2; 1 Tim. 2:8).

These outward expressions of worship follow the inward attitudes that they symbolize. When our heart bows in reverence before the Lord, it is appropriate for us to kneel or prostrate ourselves before Him. When we are lifting up praises to Him, or reaching for His love, it is befitting to lift our hands in worship.

> We should worship in a particular manner because the Bible teaches us that it is acceptable, not because our denomination has traditionally allowed it in our worship service.

All denominations should appropriate and encourage *all* these forms of expression. Because they are clearly mandated in the Bible, consideration of personal preferences and temperament becomes irrelevant. Rather than being threatened by our differences, we need to learn from one another.

This same reasoning could be applied to so many forms of worship. We should worship in a particular manner because the Bible teaches us that it is acceptable, not because our denomination has traditionally allowed it in our worship service.

One day every knee will bow before the Lord (Phil. 2:10–11). There will be no question as to the individual's culture, denomination, or preference in the matter. Surely, if it is appropriate to kneel when we see Him in heaven, it is appropriate now when we worship on earth.

If we really want to study Biblical models for worship, we will find that many exuberant and artistic expressions of worship are clearly accepted by the Lord throughout Scripture.

Here are just a few examples:

- The angels and heavenly beings—over one hundred million of them—*cry with loud voices* (Rev. 5:11–12)

- David and all of Israel *danced and played instruments* with all of their might during a joyous procession into Jerusalem (2 Sam. 6:14–15)

- *Colorful banners, declaring the names of God, were displayed* in David's worship (Ps. 20:5—A Psalm of David)

- Solomon *offered a lavish number of sacrifices* on the occasion of the dedication of the temple. At times his offerings were so extravagant that they could not be counted (2 Chron. 5:6; 7:4–5)

- Jehoshaphat *put anointed singers in front of his army* and saw victory in a consequential and celebrated battle. The victors returned to Jerusalem *with exuberant praises* (2 Chron. 20:28)

- The praises that were offered at the rebuilding of the temple in Ezra's time were accompanied by *shouting and weeping mingled together*

Not one of these examples was followed by a heavenly expression of shock or displeasure. Not once did God declare that He was offended with these acts of worship, due to the fact that He was Presbyterian, Baptist, Pentecostal, or a member of any other denomination. Since there was no cry of dismay over such passionate displays of emotion and no indication that any such fervor was inappropriate before Him, the opposite reaction must be assumed.

It appears that the Lord has ordained for His people to worship Him with enthusiastic abandon. Nowhere are there scriptures that seek to curtail genuine devotion to God.

In fact, when King David's wife, Michal, saw him dancing publicly in worship before the Lord and despised him in her heart, God's punishment of her was quite severe: Michal was made barren for the rest of her life (2 Sam. 6:14–23). This contains a lesson for all of us.

Would God "Fit in" to Your Worship Service?

My suspicion is that God, Himself, just might not "fit in" to most of our worship services because of His rather unorthodox voice and presence.

God's voice sounds, at times, like a gentle whisper (1 Ki. 19:12 NIV), many waters (Rev. 1:15), or gigantic thunder (Job 37:4–5; 40:9; Ps. 29:4–9). He shouts like a warrior in battle (Is. 42:13, Amp.), cries out like a woman in labor (Is. 42:14, Amp.), hisses or whistles to the nations (Is. 5:26), and goes forth with the sound of the trumpet (Ps. 47:5).

It is this same God who opened the sea for His people to walk through (Ex. 14); wrote on a wall with just a hand (Dan. 5:5); healed the sick (Matt. 14:14); walked on top of the sea (Matt. 14:25); forgave sins (Lu. 5:24), and raised the dead (Jn. 11:43).

> The principle here is that our praise and worship should attempt to match its object. I say "attempt" because even an eternity of praise will never do justice to the attributes and character of God. . . . Is there not, then, something desperately wrong if we get regularly bored in church?. . . What kind of God do we think we have? Is He not endlessly creative, irrepressibly vital and alive, always doing "new things". Indeed God is "the same yesterday, today and forever", but one of his unchanging characteristics is that he is always full of surprises![15] (Graham Kendrick)

I understand it is simplistic to assume that we could all come to some kind of consensus with regard to our forms and styles of worship. There are, however, clear descriptions of worship in the Bible that truly transcend denomination or culture. There are examples of cities and nations where the Christians of all denominations practice a unity that recognizes one Church, though consisting of many congregations. May this become the true Church of the future.

Denominational differences and diverse forms of worship should not divide Christians; rather, the reality of His presence in the Church should unite us and make us appreciate one another. We have so much to learn from other Christians. As we encounter differences in worship, let it inspire us to greater devotion and deeper love for God.

> Denominational differences and diverse
> forms of worship should not divide
> Christians; rather, the reality of His
> presence in the Church should unite us
> and make us appreciate one another.

I would like to assume that all the denominational fathers have given careful consideration to the great body of writings on praise and worship, both Biblical and scholarly. Some might then regard it as presumptuous of me to call for further Biblical study in consideration of changes to our worship services.

But let us not hold on to our styles of worship for tradition's sake alone; let us hold on to them only after careful and honest study of the Word of God proves them valid.

Terry H. Wardle calls the entire Church to openness in their forms of worship:

> I am not advocating change for the sake of change. What I am encouraging is flexibility and mobility in form and order. Our worship services should certainly be sensitive to tradition but not completely determined by tradition. Forms of worship should not be institutionalized. Instead, they should be carefully designed, consistent with the moving of the Holy Spirit in this day—at this time and place in history.[16]

My desire in writing this book is not only to promote acceptance of denominational and cultural diversity in worship, but to prophetically call all people to transcend their denominational and cultural limitations so they can embrace the Biblical model for prophetic worship.

> Only when its unity is rooted in its sense of devotion to the one true Sovereign can a community of faith transcend the webs of pettiness, parochialism, and self-interest that so rapidly belittle and destroy human fellowship. . . . United in worship and reconciled with its God, the community of faith is restored to the health and wholeness that enables it to be a nucleus of health for the broader human community around it. Its own

blessing and health are not gifts intended for it alone, but willed by God for all.[17] (Paul Hanson)

Until we as pastors and worship leaders make it a point to "fill in our gaps" with the intentional, dedicated study of worship, church after church will be held hostage by our ignorance. Until we put worship back in its rightful place as the number-one activity of the church, our churches will be malnourished and lacking in the spiritual power necessary to do God's work.[18] (Sally Morgenthaler)

What business do we have in confining God to our narrow and biased denominational boundaries or restricting the worship of His people to the meager expressions that we have claimed as our own?

Let Him be praised in the dance! Let new and prophetic songs abound in the Church! Let every instrument prophesy and resound with impassioned praise! Let every man, woman, and child rejoice before Him with every ounce of their strength and every decibel with which they are capable!

Oh clap your hands, **all you peoples!** Shout to God with the voice of triumph. (Ps. 47:1)

Praise the LORD, **all you Gentiles (nations KJV)!** Laud Him, **all you peoples!** (Ps. 117:1)

Let the peoples praise You, O God; let **all the peoples** praise You. (Ps. 67:3) ✍

Chapter Nineteen

TRANSCENDING CULTURAL RESTRAINTS IN WORSHIP

*Culture. . . The harmonious development of all
the (natural) powers and capabilities of man.*
Felix Perles

≫

No matter where we are from, we must recognize that our culture greatly affects our attitudes toward worship. We need to be careful, however, that we do not allow our culture to dictate our style and expressions of worship.

It is also becoming quite popular today for churches to attempt to be sensitive to the unchurched in their worship services. Some churches exclude or minimize expressions of worship that might "offend" visitors without much thought as to the will of the Father or the Biblical injunction for such expressions. This is also an area in which to tread carefully. After all, our primary objective as Christians is not to conduct worship services that will be pleasing to unbelievers, but to God.

I agree with Tom Schwanda as he makes the following points:

> . . . an inherent danger in striving to be culturally relevant is that the church will instead become culturally driven. Indeed, in observing the push toward becoming all things to all men one might wonder whether some promoters of cultural sensitivity have not become imprisoned by the need to reach their market, regardless of how much their efforts might compromise the message of Jesus Christ.[1]

In my travels I have observed that churches of the same denomination often differ greatly from one country to another. Each may be experiencing worship in spirit and truth, yet cultural traditions may lead some to more expressive forms of worship than others.

Even though the truth of worship *transcends* culture, it is expressed *through* culture. We must be careful to emphasize the aspects of our culture that release and enhance true worship, while seeking to release ourselves from any traditions—religious, cultural or otherwise—that inhibit prophetic worship.

The truth of worship transcends culture.

Gerrit Gustafson sums this thought up as follows:

> For some reason, our own particular religious traditions and experiences tend to color our ideas of what God's preferences are and aren't. . . . How quickly our preferences become biases. And how easily our biases become walls that keep us from the larger Body of Christ and from fuller expressions of worship. . . . The sum total of these distinctives and preferences is termed **culture**. . . . It is interesting that the root word for culture is **cult** which is, in its simplest definition, a system of worship or devotion. You could say our culture reflects our worship. We should neither despise nor deny our culture. . . . When God says that His ways are higher than our ways (Isa. 55:9) He is saying that His divine culture is higher than our human culture.[2]

> The stagnating pools of our cultural prejudices must be flooded by the river of God's divine purposes.[3]

Worship leader and teacher Kent Henry also feels that our culture has been responsible for leading us away from the Biblical foundation for praise and worship:

> In the past, churches have usually been opposed to this kind of activity (clapping, bowing and kneeling, dancing to the Lord and the lifting up of hands). For the most part, this opposition has been based on cultural experience or style. Now, praise and worship services

have returned to a more biblical precedent rather than following cultural orientation.[4]

When we come to an agreement on the simple, yet absolute, foundations of worship—that Jesus is King of all the earth and worthy above all to be worshiped—we find that true worship is a great key to bringing reconciliation to all nations.

My point here is that, although it is understandable for our culture to be influential on our theology and expressions of worship, ultimately, it should not have as great an impact as we often see. The reason for this is that the center and object of our worship is the same, no matter what our nationality or traditions. The Lord's description of worship is outlined in the Word, which does not change from one nation to another.

Judson Cornwall believes that worship will ultimately cause a blending of different cultures:

> Worship is the one religious activity that lends itself to such a delicate blending of different heritages, for worship is so Christ-centered and requires such a God-consciousness that participants must look away from themselves in order to worship.[5]

We must also note that the first allegiance of Christians, from all peoples and nations, is to the same King. This alone is a great foundation for unity within the global Body of Christ, and should be the chief influence on our worship traditions. Our goal is for our worship to please the King of Kings; for it to be a vehicle for the expression of devotion for all the citizens of the Kingdom of God. When we worship we are united in focus, centered around our King, and joined as citizens of a new Kingdom.

Just as Gustafson has stated above, I believe that the Lord is forming His Church into a new nation called the Kingdom of God. The laws, customs and worship in this nation must ultimately transcend our nation of birth. The Kingdom of God is really our first nation. As Christians, we should not define ourselves primarily by geography and culture, but by our calling as sons of God. As worshipers, the Lord is calling us beyond our nation of birth to our nation of re-birth.

God desires that all people and all nations worship Him. He is calling people from every tribe, tongue, and nation to worship before His throne (Rev. 7:9). There is not a separate set of instructions on how to worship God that has been written for each nation. God's call to enter into His presence with prophetic, abundant and exuberant worship stands for all time and for all people.

Although the Lord's sound in worship may, at times, include the sounds of many nations, peoples, and generations, ultimately, a new sound will emerge from the Church—a Church which lives as a culture within a culture.

Ultimately, even our culture must submit
to the sounds and styles of worship
dictated by the King.

We in the Western Church have assumed that the Lord is a twentieth-century Westerner. The truth is that His life and nature are represented in all nations and all peoples from all time, throughout all the history of the earth.

> Let's stop routing Christ through western Europe and
> the United States. Let's abandon the folly of dressing
> Him in Western clothes, imputing to Him a Western
> life-style, implying to the world His message was born
> in the West.[6] (John Haggai)

Worship will be somewhat influenced and enriched by our culture, but ultimately, even our culture must submit to the sounds and styles of worship dictated by the King. Our worship must reflect a style that is suitable for the King. We must come to some understanding of how He desires to be worshiped and what is considered to be appropriate worship before Him. Therefore, we should not be quite as intent on fitting our worship sound and format to the culture we live in, but rather, to the dictates of the King of Heaven and Earth.

I have seen this truth exhibited in practical ways many times and in many nations. For example, one of the words in Hebrew for *exalt* is *ruwm* (room, Strong's #7311), meaning *to raise up* or *to heave up*.[7] We tend to use the word "exalt" synonymously with "praise," but I believe that Strong's definition has opened up further meaning to us.

After seriously studying the use of this word in Scripture, I have come to realize and teach that *the throwing of objects before the Lord in abandoned exaltation is quite appropriate and proper as a form of worship.* It is a valid way to honor the presence of our King.

(To some of you, this type of worship may seem somewhat shocking at first glance, but it is really a natural human expression. We have all seen how adoring fans honor singers and actors by throwing flowers at their feet after a great performance or how sports fans toss their coats and hats when their team wins a victory.)

In my travels, I have seen this type of worship occur spontaneously, time and again. Even people who are quite unaccustomed to such exuberant displays in their culture have eagerly heaved flowers, coats, paper, or other soft objects in the midst of unrestrained and passionate worship.

At a women's conference in Colombia, the ladies threw carnations and roses before the King and filled the room with a sweet perfume. I have witnessed usually undemonstrative Norwegians exalting the Lord by heaving things before Him. In Venezuela, thousands threw their coats into the air as they worshiped in an outdoor stadium.

The members of Shady Grove Church regularly greet the King with similar abandon. On each of those occasions, it seems that they surpass the jubilation of any wild football crowd or the festivity of a victorious political rally.

In no way am I advocating inordinate excess just for the sake of change. But I do believe that our worship must become all that God intended it to be, rather than remaining an expression inhibited by our denomination or culture.

The truth of our unity as worshipers does not exclude our distinctiveness or differences as separate cultures and congregations. The eternal heavenly sound of worship may very well include melodies, chords and rhythms that are indigenous to people from all over the earth. As we get closer and closer to eternity, the sounds of many nations will very likely be heard in our worship.

It is as if the Lord has hidden treasures of His glory in all the nations and peoples of the earth.[8] His voice can be heard and His hand can be seen in the sound and art of all peoples. When we become Christians, we bring these treasures and expressions of God's voice into our new nation—the Kingdom of God. The prophet Micah speaks of such treasures as he encourages Zion (the people who dwell in the presence of God—worshipers):

> Arise and thresh, O daughter of Zion! For I will make
> your horn iron, and I will make your hoofs bronze; you
> shall beat in pieces many peoples, and **I will devote
> their gain to the Lord, and their treasure to the Lord of
> all the earth.** (Micah 4:13, Amp.)

New and distinctive sounds and styles of worship are among the treasures that have been gathered from all the nations. There are rhythmic styles of the African and Caribbean nations that are full of life and great joy. The harmony of the Polynesian peoples and the melodies of the Celtic nations are exquisite. There are instruments and songs from every country that are now available to us. Such sounds could enhance the worship style of any church.

I also am very aware of the fact that many cultural traditions and musical sounds may not be at all appropriate for inclusion in worship. The biggest challenge for the Body of Christ is to remain open and sensitive to the Lord in this matter.

In the past, we have "demonized" musical sounds merely because they were different from our own musical heritage, or beyond our understanding and preference. We have made Christianity into a Western religion by forcing all facets of Western thought and culture upon our converts. All local arts were affected wherever Christianity was preached.

An example can be seen in the way missionaries and Bible teachers promoted the singing of traditional Western hymns over the inclusion of indigenous music in worship. In fact, any art form or style other than Western art has been dismissed over the centuries by all streams of the Church.

While this is a larger debate that lies beyond the scope of this book, I would like to suggest that the musical forms and artistic styles themselves may not be inherently evil. Rather, the heart of the worshiper and object of worship is what is good or evil.

When Moses and Joshua were coming down from the mountain where Moses had met with the Lord, they heard the sound of singing as the Israelites worshiped a golden calf (Ex. 32:17–18). It was not singing that offended the Lord, but the worship of a false god.

Likewise, Daniel and the other captive young people were told that whenever they heard the sound of the Babylonian music, they were to bow before the golden image of Nebuchadnezzar's god (Dan. 3:5, 7, 10, 15). Once again, it does not state that the music

was evil. It was the false god that Daniel objected to, and he did
not bow.

New and distinctive sounds and styles of worship are among the treasures that have been gathered from all the nations.

We often associate music with secular nations and the endeav-
ors they represent. This is understandable, but while we must certainly be discerning, we must also be sure that we do not lump all
unfamiliar cultural expressions into the category of the unregener-
ate and unusable.

Our worship can only be enriched by a genuine effort on all of
our parts to redeem the arts from all nations. When we do reclaim
the treasures from the nations, a new sound and culture will
emerge in the Church that will entice and summon the unredeemed
to the Kingdom of God.

The first step in developing the worship music of the Kingdom
of God is to foster respect for the distinct and ancient traditions
that have been handed down from generation to generation in all
the nations of the earth. Ethnomusicologists Roberta King and
Appianda Arthur have reported on some of the great strides that
have been taken in restoring artistic and cultural integrity to the
worship of many nations.[9]

We must also try to identify those things within our culture that
hinder true worship. It is possible for us to use our culture and
background as an excuse for rejecting intimate and ardent worship.

For example, some people refuse to dance or shout in the presence of the Lord, claiming "cultural immunity" from such "impru-
dence" (!). British and European people sometimes pride themselves on their "reserve," yet these same people might also be seen
decked out in the colors of their home team, giving full-throated
cheers at a ball game or political convention.

Sosene Le'au writes this testimony concerning the things the
Lord showed him concerning his culture:
God has:

- Called me to give up my culture so that I might be, before
  anything else, a citizen of His kingdom.

- Given my culture back to me with a fresh understanding of who I am in Christ, and who my people ought to be in Him.
- Showed me clearly that cultural diversity is one of God's great gifts to humankind.
- Showed me how He speaks through various cultures and peoples. . .[10]

Le'au also speaks about the necessity of giving up one's culture and surrendering this identity to the Lord before He can give it back to us.

The Lausanne Covenant of 1974 sums up this thought and appeals to the Church at large:

> Culture must always be tested and judged by Scripture. . . . The gospel does not presuppose the superiority of any culture to another, but evaluates all cultures according to its own criteria of truth and righteousness. . . . Churches have sometimes been in bondage to culture rather than to Scripture.

In order for us to find the artistic treasures in any culture, and break away from the confines of our cultural traditions, the vision for God's ultimate plan for His glory to cover the earth must be birthed in our hearts.

CULTURE AND ITS EFFECT ON ART IN WORSHIP

Contemporary worship musicians and songwriters have begun to incorporate the sound, styles, and rhythms of various nations into church worship music. I feel that this is a powerful example of both prophetic intercession and the proclamation of our God who is King over all peoples and nations.

It is interesting to note that in the secular world there has also been a growing recognition of the dignity and worth of all peoples and cultures. The popularity of the indigenous music and art of the nations has increased markedly in recent years.

It is possible to view secular folk music and other artistic expressions as the world's attempt at intercession, for they communicate the heart of a nation and its people.[11] The performers and artists may not actually be aware of the full import of what they are declaring, but most folk music and art is basically a cry for:

- *Recognition*—as the story of the people is told
- *Redemption*—as the heart's cry for all people is to be redeemed
- *Restoration*—as all nations have suffered greatly and are looking for the restoration of their history, culture, language and dignity

When I was young, I noticed that most movies or TV shows depicted non-European cultures in a disparaging light. For example, in "westerns," the Cowboys were regularly the "goodies" and the Indians were the "baddies."

Over the past fifteen or twenty years, however, Western film makers have abandoned these simplistic portrayals of other nations and cultures. In modern films, not only have the history and culture of many nations been exonerated, but their stories of heroism have been displayed, giving them international attention and focus.

At one time, all films depicted foreign cultures through Western eyes, but more recent films attempt to view the world through the eyes of a particular nation or people group. Here are but a few examples:

The Mission—South American Andeans and their suffering under Spanish imperialism

Gandhi—Mahatma Gandhi and India during the final years of British imperialistic rule

Dances With Wolves—Native Americans

The Last of the Mohicans—a story of Native Americans

Braveheart—describes a Scottish revolt against the English in the 14th century

Rob Roy—a folk tale of a Scottish hero who stood up to English cruelty

Seven Years in Tibet, Kundun—both describe the suffering of the Tibetan people and their leader under Chinese imperialism

Amistad—shows the suffering of African slaves in early

> U.S. history
> *The Mask of Zorro*—the story of Mexican folk hero,
>   Zorro

Other artists have also contributed to the promotion and appreciation of nations, cultures and their history.

Alex Haley's best selling book, *Roots*, based on the history and suffering of slaves in North America, could be credited with starting the current trend of recognizing and validating oppressed and overlooked peoples. *Roots* was eventually made into a TV miniseries and had a great impact throughout North America.

More recently, the Celtic dance productions *Riverdance* and *Lord of the Dance* have gained rave reviews and international fame. The French Canadian theatrical circus, *Cirque du Soleil*—acclaimed by audiences of over fifteen million worldwide—performs with a sensational and enchanting blend of artistic and acrobatic excellence.

Each of these productions, along with numerous others throughout the artistic world (such as the African-themed *The Lion King*) parade the richness of native cultures before our eyes.

I also find it interesting that so many "Save The Earth" stores have sprung up in shopping malls all over the U.S.A. This is a reflection of the growing ecology movement that reveres the plants and creatures and practically worships "Mother Earth." The people caught up in this movement are earnest souls, but I doubt that any of them really grasp the depth of the great forces that have been set in motion and are moving upon their hearts—for the whole of creation is groaning and in labor for the glory which is about to be revealed in the earth (Rom. 8:18–27).

All the earth is in expectation of the glory that is to come and is crying out to be "saved"—as in the days of Noah when wickedness abounded (Matt. 24:37) and the animals came to be hidden or saved in the ark of the people of God. Nature is telling us today that the time is at hand for the redemption and salvation of the whole earth.

All of nature and all cultures are crying out for recognition, understanding, restoration and redemption. I am convinced we are witnessing the beginning of a great global revival, where all nations and all people seek the one and only God who can bring full and complete redemption.

> However, the spiritual is not first, but the natural, and
> afterward the spiritual. (1 Cor. 15:46)

As this verse illustrates, the Lord will often demonstrate something in a natural way that He later manifests as a spiritual reality. Water covered the earth once in the days of Noah, but the great
flood of His glory is yet to be witnessed by all nations, for He has
promised to cover the earth with His glory in the same way that
water covers the sea (Hab. 2:14).

Prophetic artists throughout the church today have been hearing the rumblings of a great cry, as all nations and creatures cry out
for God's glory. The voices of nations and their thirst for the Living
Water are beginning to be heard in the worship of many churches,
through an abundance of prophetic songs about the rain, the river,
the falling dew, and flowing streams.

Worship of this kind may be best described as "prophetic intercession." As the congregation honors God, He may reveal His
heart for the nations through dance and mime, or in spontaneous
rhythms, harmonies, and melodies brought forth through the
singers and instrumentalists.

I have been in services where the sounds and dances of a particular nation were brought forth by the Holy Spirit, and the whole
congregation responded by lifting up their voices in intercession
for that nation.

WORSHIP AND GOD'S ETERNAL PLAN FOR THE NATIONS

As the Church enters the last days here on the earth, we are
looking for the Lord to use us in the fulfillment of His great promise in Habakkuk:

> For the earth will be filled with the knowledge of the
> glory of the Lord, as the waters cover the sea. (Hab.
> 2:14)

As I see it, the glory that is to cover the earth is not some silver
rain that will suddenly appear in the heavens. It will be the fullness
of the character of God working in and through every believer, and
the supernatural weight of His manifest presence among us.

Primarily, it will be His likeness in our faces, His power in our
prayers, His grace in our message, His holiness in our walk, and
His numinousness[12] in our midst that will bring about the display

of His glory in the earth. When His character and nature flood our lives, then His glory will permeate the earth like an ocean.

> When God's character and nature flood
> our lives, then His glory will permeate
> the earth like an ocean.

Kent Henry has indicated how important praise and worship are in the ultimate destiny of entire nations:

> Praise and worship have the power to transform the hearts of men and women on such a large scale that an entire nation may be impacted.[13]

Now is the time for the worshiping Church to comprehend God's plan for the nations and become God's arm and voice of reconciliation and redemption to all peoples. Surely it is impossible to say that we are worshipers, but not be able to hear God's intercession for the lost and His desire for all people to turn to Him.

Dutch Sheets, author and pastor of Springs Harvest Fellowship in Colorado Springs, Colorado, speaks of the Church as being the womb of God upon the earth where we release life through our prayers of intercession.[14]

Others have expressed how worship brings the believer into a correct world-view and gives Him or her a heart for the nations:

> This call to the nations is both missionary zeal and prophetic insight. When one worships the true God fervently, the Holy Spirit reveals the heart of Father God to bring all peoples before Him in worship.[15] (Ernest Gentile)

> When the Spirit of God comes into a man, He gives him a world–wide view.[16] (Oswald Chambers)

> The Spirit of Christ is the spirit of missions, and the nearer we get to Him the more intensely missionary we must become.[17] (Henry Martyn)

Our challenge, as the Church, is to become those who would birth and subsequently prepare for the multicultural song spoken of in Revelation 7:9:

> . . . I looked, and beheld, a great multitude which no
> one could number, of all nations, tribes, peoples, and
> tongues, standing before the throne and before the
> Lamb, clothed with white robes, with palm branches in
> their hands, and crying out with a loud voice, saying,
> "Salvation belongs to our God who sits on the throne,
> and unto the Lamb!"

It is interesting that this vast multitude of worshipers retain
their sense of ethnicity and language as they worship the Lord.
Their nationality is clearly evident and their different languages are
noted. But an even more remarkable detail confronts us—the evidence of eight crucial areas of unity in this worship expression:

- Provision.........They are all wearing white robes of
  righteousness
- Praise...............They are all singing the same words
- Purpose............They are all worshiping the Lamb
- Pageantry.........They are all waving palm branches
- Proclamation....They are all crying with loud voices
- Perspective.......They are all beholding the Lamb
- Place...............They are all before the throne
- Posture............They are all standing

Through the provision of our salvation in Christ Jesus, the
redeemed in this heavenly picture are all dressed the same and participate in the same worship service. All class, age and cultural dis-
tinctions have been left behind.

Worship must surely be the greatest unifying force in heaven
and on earth. We must ensure that worship never separates us as
believers. Not one of this great multitude—representing every
nation, tribe, language and dialect on earth—is prepared to cite
nationality, denomination, or age as a reason for doing something
different in worship.

By the description of this worship, we must assume that it is
thunderous, demonstrative, and quite spectacular, to say the least.
It is not divisive in any way, however, as the sight and presence of
the Lamb of God make all of this exuberance most appropriate.

There is no greater tool for healing nations and repairing the
breaches between us than worship. With our eyes fixed on Him we
will find no place for the pettiness that has separated us since the

first generation of mankind. Now is the time for the worshiping Church to comprehend God's plan for the nations and become His arm and voice of reconciliation to all peoples.

Multicultural neighborhoods are the norm in most cities today. We should commit to doing whatever is needed toward making our worship relevant for each generation and culture represented in our church family or local community.

> . . . churches deceive themselves when they believe they are multicultural simply by the mere presence of one or more ethnic groups.   . . . Only when these folks are made equal partners in the faith mission of that congregation may we begin to call that congregation multicultural. . . . I strongly hold that the music ministry of the church may be a powerful means of establishing a strong foundation for building a multicultural congregation.[18] (Anton Armstrong)

There is no greater tool for healing nations and repairing the breaches between us than worship.

The Lord is causing a new song to be birthed in the nations of the earth (Is. 42:10, 12). It is a song that will transcend generations, nations, and denominations. It will be understood by the young and the old, the strong and the weak, the rich and the poor. Those who have never responded to the Gospel of Christ will run to Him when they hear the song that is coming from the people who dwell in God's presence—Zion.

The sound and style of the new song will be different from anything that has been heard before. It is a sound that comes from the heart and presence of God. It is imperative that we understand our role as an integral part of the plan of God for the nations in these last days. The prophetic realm and the sound of God's voice in our worship are crucial keys as we become ministers of His glory in all the earth.

> The prophetic realm and the sound of
> God's voice in our worship are crucial
> keys as we become ministers of His
> glory in all the earth.

It will take a bending of our ears and hearts to hear and learn the song of God that He is singing over us all in these days. We must make a commitment to His perspective concerning the nations. The goal is to see His glory cover the earth as the waters cover the sea, participating in the sound and spreading His glory until He comes again.

At the 1997 Denver Summit on Worship, which was sponsored by Promise keepers, moderator Rick Kingham and I came up with a diagram (shown in Table 6). The diagram is based on the model of a baseball diamond, incorporating three bases and home plate. It is really a prophetic picture of the steps needed to implement God's objective of global glory through worship music.

BASE ONE—ACCEPTANCE

> . . . for thou shalt inherit all nations (KJV); For to You belong all the nations (Amp.); for it is Thou who dost possess all the nations (NASB). All the nations are the Lord's! (Ps. 82:8)

In order for the Church to get to first base in the Lord's plan, we need to make a great *commitment* to breaking down the insidious walls of racial prejudice that afflict not only our own hearts, but those of the entire Church community.

There is probably not one human being who has not been influenced by such prejudice in one form or another. I say that we need to make *a great* commitment, because the tentacles of racial prejudice are so far-reaching and so deceptive that I doubt they can be overcome in any of us without great contention.

I believe that the Lord will regularly bring us back to Base One in order to confront this issue with its various layers and deceptive facets. Base One involves:

- The acceptance of all nations and all people groups as equal and precious before God.

TABLE 6

OUR PROGRESSION THROUGH WORSHIP

TO THE GLORY OF THE LORD

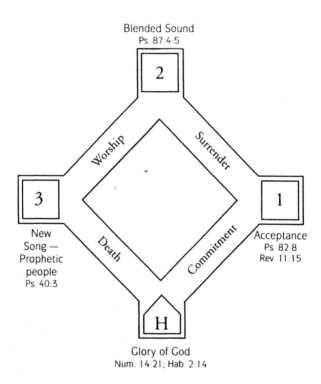

Blended Sound
Ps. 87:4-5

2

Worship   Surrender

3   1

New
Song —
Prophetic
people
Ps. 40:3

Death   Commitment

Acceptance
Ps. 82:8
Rev. 11:15

H

Glory of God
Num. 14:21; Hab. 2:14

- The acceptance of any artistic expression from any culture in the context of worship that accurately and
appropriately states God's voice for a particular service

BASE TWO—BLENDED SOUND

After we have come to the place of accepting one another, we
may begin to sing one another's songs. As we do, the sounds and
flavors of the nations will be heard in our worship. This is what I
am referring to as a *blended sound*.

There are several new praise and worship choruses becoming widely accepted today in many churches that demonstrate a blended sound. Whenever we use songs that clearly include melodies, harmonies, rhythms, or instrumentation of nations *or cultures* other than our own, we are employing a blended sound.

It is possible to include the typical sounds of more than one nation in a song—such as in *Kingdom Celebration,* by Andrew Smith, which blends the sounds of Ja, Cajun, Caribbean, and African.

Following are a few examples of the blended sound found in contemporary praise and worship music (the list is, by no means, exhaustive):

Song/Album	Artist/Publisher
The River is Here	Andy Park; © 1994 Mercy/Vineyard Publishing.
Kingdom Celebration	Andrew Smith; © 1994 Mercy/Vineyard Publishing.
Let the River Flow	David Ruis; © 1995 Mercy/Vineyard Publishing.
Holy and Kind	Robin Lyle, Jill Lyle, and Andy Nowlen; © 1996 Mercy/Vineyard Publishing.
The Happy Song	Martin Smith; © 1994 Curious Music/Thank You music.
Kiss The Son	Kevin Prosch; Various songs © 1996, 7th Time Music.
Journeys of Life	Kevin Prosch; Various songs © 1997, 7th Time Music.

In the beginning	JoAnn McFatter, Various songs © 1997 Ancient Age.
Celtic Worship	A recording of Celtic worship music by a group called Eden's Bridge; © 1997 Straight Way Music.
Shalom Jerusalem	© 1995; Hosanna! Music.
The Holy Fire	© 1997, Hosanna! Music. Various recordings of praise/worship music with a Hebrew "flavor".
Rejoice Africa	© 1993 Integrity Music Inc.
Hymns International	© 1993 Benson Instrumental Series. This is a series of instrumental recordings based on the musical style of various nations, such as Spain, Italy, the Caribbean, Celtic Nations, etc.
Essence Series	Brentwood Music publishes this instrumental series that features styles from various nations.

We might think that this is the first time the Lord has summoned the nations to participate in prophetic worship together. Such is not the case.

Approximately three thousand years ago, King David established his tabernacle of worship on Mount Zion. He called for all nations to come and be born in Zion and worship with him there (Ps. 87). I am sure that the Egyptians, Babylonians, Philistines, Ethiopians and other nations did not demand that their national musical sounds be played exclusively in the worship services. No, there was an understanding that the Lord had birthed a new and prophetic song that was relevant and acceptable for all nations.

These were the songs of Zion spoken of in Ps. 137:3, also:

> And the ransomed of the Lord shall return, and come to Zion with singing. . . (Is. 35:10)

We are in a day of renewal in worship. Every nation has been called to Zion—to be birthed in worship, dwell in His courts and run after His presence forever. We must not stay on first base and cling to "our rights" for our own nation to be heard and our own preferences of style to be placed in the forefront.

After accepting the sounds from all the Lord's nations and, possibly, reclaiming music from our own heritage, we may be tempted to find our identity among the nations and the new sounds we have embraced. But to reach the place of "blendedness," we need to embrace a deeper level of *surrender*, allowing the Lord to bring forth the sound that *He* desires in our worship.

This sound is to be a prophetic sound that blends the musical styles of many nations, yet carries melodies from the very heart of God.

BASE THREE—A NEW SONG AND A PROPHETIC PEOPLE

> He has put a new song in my mouth—Praise to our God; many will see it and fear, and will trust in the Lord. (Ps. 40:3)

We cannot underestimate the power of the prophetic song. This verse suggests that the song is such that it will be *seen*, and those who see it will be in awe of the Lord and will put their trust in Him.

It is most unusual to be able to see a song. I want to suggest that in these last days, prophetic worshipers will arise with the glory of the Lord on their faces and in their mouths. The prophetic songs that come forth will defeat the enemy and draw sinners to Christ.

There are seven Hebrew words for *praise* in the Old Testament (see Chapter 4). The particular word that is used in Psalm 40:3 is the word *tehillah*, which is a derivative of *halal*. Both of these words connote great boasting in the Lord and loud, exuberant praise.

Whenever the word *tehillah* is used in Scripture there seems to be something supernatural happening in the praise.[19] It is as if God's manifest presence has descended in the midst of the praises, and He shows something of Himself there.

I believe this is the case in Psalm 40:3. The Lord is present in these praises. It is His glory that is seen as the worshipers sing, and His kingdom that sinners run to at the first glimpse of His beauty.

> God is Spirit, and those who worship Him must worship in spirit and truth. (John 4:24)

We come to the place of the prophetic song through worship. It is worship in spirit that releases the prophetic song, and worship grounded in truth that forms a prophetic people. The Lord does not intend for just a few to participate in His prophetic presence. He has called us all to be a holy priesthood—a prophetic people. Such prophetic songs are the inheritance of the whole congregation.

Ultimately, God will birth a new nation in these days by assembling His people from all nations—from the north, south, east and west. There is a travail or intercession in Zion that a great nation will be born. This nation will affect all people on earth in these last days.

> Who has heard such a thing? Who has seen such things? Shall the earth be made to give birth in one day? Or shall a nation be born at once? For as soon as Zion was in labor [travailed KJV], she gave birth to her children. (Is. 66:8)

> (See also: Pss. 2:6; 110:2; Is. 2:2–3; 24:23; Micah 4)

Zion is the prophetic and poetic name of the worshiping people, or "nation," that will arise from the north in the last days. This nation will consist of a great company of worshipers who display God's splendor and defeat His enemies (Ps. 48:2; Jer. 6:22–23; 50; Joel 3:16; Zech. 2:10–12).

As I mentioned above, I believe that new or prophetic songs, sounds and culture will be found in the midst of Zion. As the Lord gathers us from all the nations, we carry with us the treasures that He has hidden within each culture. The Church today should look and sound like a melting pot of all nations. Out of that melting pot will arise a new and prophetic sound that comes from God Himself.

> Sing to the Lord a new song, [sing a song that has never
> been heard in the heathen world—Amp] and His praise
> from the ends of the earth. . . (Is. 42:10)

May the Lord tune our ears, eyes and hands to heaven's sights
and sounds. As we worship, may eternity overtake us, and may
God's supernatural culture be born in our hearts.

HOME BASE—THE GLORY OF THE LORD

Again, I want to quote this important scripture:

> For the earth will be filled with the knowledge of the
> glory of the Lord, as the waters cover the sea. (Hab.
> 2:14)

I have been fascinated with this verse throughout my whole
Christian life. I believe that the glory of God is the main subject of
the Bible and the full purpose for our existence. The glory of the
Lord is the goal of the Church as much as home base is the goal of
the base runner. We might be tempted to make unity or the
prophetic anointing our goal in worship. But let us not stop press-
ing into the Lord until we see the fulfillment of Habakkuk's
prophecy.

The glory of God will only be experienced through *death*. I am
not talking about a physical dying, but the death of the self life that
Paul spoke of in the Epistles.

Sin caused mankind to be separated from the glory of God
(Rom. 3:23). Worship will cause man to be exposed to the glory of
God (2 Cor. 3:18). At some point, worship will bring us all to the
place of dying to self. It is here that we are readied for the sight of
God's glory.

At some point, worship will bring us all
to the place of dying to self. It is here
that we are readied for the sight
of God's glory.

In Exodus 33 when Moses asked to see God's glory (Ex. 33:18),
the Lord replied that no man could see His face and live (v 20).
Jacob wrestled with the Lord face to face and was amazed that his

life was preserved (Gen. 32:30). Likewise, for us, the sight of the glory of God is an awesome thing. We must hide in the rock (Christ) as Moses did in order for our lives to be spared as we behold Him, and the glory of the Lord will shine from our faces and be heard in our songs.

The ultimate attainment in worship is not that we achieve excellence in our musical performances, or that we learn to arrange perfect medleys of songs, but that the whole congregation encounters the manifest presence of God and is changed into His likeness, from glory to glory. Even then, the Lord will not be satisfied until His glory shines through the Church to all the nations of the earth.

WORSHIP AND EVANGELISM

If you think about it, conversion is a wonderful worship experience. It is also a prophetic encounter with God. Conversion can only take place in our lives when the Holy Spirit reveals Christ to us, and our response to the revelation of Jesus is to abandon all of self to Him. There is no greater example of worship than this. Genuine salvation is worship. My own personal salvation experience was accompanied by tremendous gratitude, love, and worship.

Worshipers should make the best evangelists. As we commune with the Lord, He imparts His heart for the lost and for all nations to us.

> The church has not yet fully realized the power of praise and worship to reach the lost. It can restore those Christians who have been hurt, and recover those that have fallen away from the Lord.[20] (Kent Henry)

Some may argue that we need to make our church services more comfortable for unbelievers. They think that by patterning our worship after the worship of heaven, lost people will come to our services and be offended by our extravagance.

Let me just say that the God who dwells amongst us is both awesome and irresistible. If He is truly in our midst, even the hardest of hearts will be overwhelmed by His love and cry out for His saving grace.

There is no way that our worship services *can* be made "fit" for any and everyone—Christian or non-Christian alike. Robert Webber puts it this way:

> When worship planning is . . . "consumer-driven," serious abuses of true worship may result.[21]

If we make evangelism the primary goal of our Sunday services, both worship and evangelism will be in danger of declining very quickly. True worship will vanish because our focus will center upon the lost and we will become reluctant to participate in the expressions of abandon which worship requires. Keeping unbelievers "comfortable" will consume our thinking. Evangelism will remain the task of those on the platform. This was never God's plan and is doomed for failure. Evangelism must become the daily occupation of extravagant worshipers.

Evangelism must become the daily occupation of extravagant worshipers.

If unbelievers find their way into a worship service, it should not be uncommon for them to find Christ in the midst of the most lavish and extreme displays of worship. In 1 Corinthians 14, Paul gives some instruction on the guidelines for prophetic worship. He encourages the use of the gifts of the Spirit when in the company of unbelievers, for he expects them to be transformed by the presence of the Lord:

> . . . he (the unbeliever) is convinced by all, he is convicted by all. And thus the secrets of his heart are revealed; and so, **falling down on his face, he will worship God and report that God is truly among you.** (1 Cor. 14:24–25)

This example of conversion in the midst of prophetic worship should be the norm for all churches. Worship in spirit and in truth is the greatest ally of evangelism.

Sally Morgenthaler states it this way:

> The true goal of evangelism is to produce more and better worshipers.[22]

The conversion of three thousand souls began as the most stirring worship event in history: Pentecost (Acts 2:11).[23]

During the past decade there have been hugely successful *March for Jesus* parades all over the world. Hundreds of thousands of believers have marched in countless major cities and towns across the globe. While the central theme of these marches has been to praise and glorify the Lord, there are multitudes of testimonies from people who have been saved and added to local churches as the result of these marches.

The worship service should not be the primary time or place for evangelism. The mandate to show and tell others the wonderful gospel message is the obligation of every believer during every day of their lives. When any Christian loves the presence of God and is gripped with a passion for Christ, it will be difficult for him not to be a living witness of His saving grace.

It is not the form of our service that is the key factor in bringing souls to Christ; it is an encounter with His presence. Where traditional worship might seek to make the unchurched person "comfortable," prophetic worship exposes them to the supernatural, and to the questions everyone must answer:

. . . who is this who even forgives sins? (Luke 7:49)

. . . what shall I do to inherit eternal life? (Luke 18:18)

. . . what must I do to be saved? (Acts 16:30)

The worship service is principally the time and place for believers to function in their priestly ministry before the Lord and to one another, and to be equipped through the preaching to go out and live as ministers of God's glory and presence.

Worship will equip each of us to be better evangelists, pastors, doctors, teachers, housewives, office workers or whatever. We are called upon to affect our surroundings and the people with whom we work through the fragrance of the knowledge of God.

How can we become the fragrance of Christ without worship? Every activity of the Christian must be centered around and flow out of our worship experience. Every work of the church is an extension of the same presence and voice of God that is heard in worship. Worship, then, empowers and fuels evangelism.

Rather than concentrating on being culturally sensitive, the church should become sensitive to the formative power worship exercises over people. It should re-evaluate its idea of who constitutes the object of worship—the worshiper or God. . . Let the church dedicate itself to discover anew the presence of God and to recognize that he alone is worthy of our worship.[24] (Tom Schwanda)

We must resist the well-intentioned, but quite erroneous, teaching of some evangelists that Christians should stress evangelism over all other pursuits in the Kingdom—including worship. John Wesley seemed to emphasize evangelism while overlooking the importance of worship in the following quote:

The church has nothing to do but to save souls; therefore spend and be spent in this work. It is not your business to speak so many times, but to save souls as you can; to bring as many sinners as you possibly can to repentance.[25]

While we must engage in evangelism with all earnestness, I find it an egregious matter that any church leader would encourage us to pursue evangelism ahead of worship. To say that we have "nothing to do but to save souls" is much too extreme.

The truth is that worship and the presence of God must be the first and greatest quest of our lives. Only then will all other worthy pursuits and ministries be fully and powerfully experienced in our lives.

I close with LaMar Boschman's view on this matter:

Evangelism is a very important part of the mission of the church, but it is not the most important. Worship is. The church is first a worshiping community before it is anything else. . . It is the believer's utmost priority and highest occupation.[26] ✍

Chapter Twenty

RELEASING PROPHETIC WORSHIP THROUGH THE ARTS

Religion is the everlasting dialogue between humanity and God.
Art is its soliloquy.
Franz Werfel

≋

The Lord is calling the worshiping Church to take her place as a leader in many areas, but most specifically, in the artistic world. Those who stand before the King of Kings in worship must surely be the ones best able to declare His splendor in the most creative and excellent manner imaginable.

> Art is a collaboration between God and the artist, and the less the artist does the better.[1] (Gide)

> Worship is a rehearsal of God's saving acts in history. Art and beauty may serve it, but must never dominate.[2] (Hoon)

As much as we must admire and enjoy great artistic achievements and talents, man's creations must never be elevated above God. It is possible to place art above the Lord and let it usurp the place of our deepest worship.

Even Michelangelo repented of this fault as he wrote:

> . . . And where we all must haste to render up account
> Of every act committed—both ill and good.
> Wherefore I now can see, that by that love
> Which rendered Art my idol and my lord,
> I greatly erred.
> Vain are the loves of mortal man,
> And error lurks within his ev'ry thought.
> Lighthouses of my life, where are ye?
> When towards a twofold death I now draw nigh?
> One death well-known, the other threat'ning loud.
> Once-worshipped Art cannot now bring peace
> To him whose soul strives to that love divine,
> Whose arms shall raise him from the Cross to Heaven.[3]

Sadly, it is also possible to lose respect for God's gift of the arts and to settle for a lack of excellence in the kingdom of God. As Allen and Borror state below, many believers are not able to gain a correct perspective of their art form:

> . . . some Christians seem to believe that to be artistic is somehow unspiritual. They seem intentionally to avoid artistic pursuit and excellence so they will not fall into a possible trap of placing the art above God. We will see as we continue our thinking that true biblical spirituality and true artistic integrity are not mutually exclusive.[4]

Over the centuries various Protestant churches have wrongly feared the arts and misunderstood this great gift from the Lord. The arts were primarily imparted to us as a tool for greater worship. Writer Paul Hoon comments on the Church's rejection of the arts:

> Human nature was misread, our rationality was overestimated, and our imaginative and sensuous life was underestimated. The human mind was mainly seen as a continuously working "idol factory"—in Calvin's famous phrase—and the inescapability of symbols was not understood. The relation of the divine to the natural was distorted, and spirit was opposed to matter in an unbiblical dualism. . . . the shock of the human

predicament in which art could teach liturgy was prud-ishly declined.[5]

Andrew Wilson Dickson takes us a little further and calls for our creativity to become a truthful reflection of God's character and creativity:

> God has revealed himself in the way that humankind can best understand: through his son Jesus. But there is still much to be learnt about him through human cre-ativity, which is at its most truthful when it reflects God's own creative nature.[6]

The Lord is the consummate artist. He is a sculptor and potter who made His own clay and a painter who created all the colors (Gen. 1–2; Jer. 18:1–6); a musician who formed every sound and gave us ears to hear with, a dancer, and singer (Zeph. 3:17; Rev. 1:10); a poet (Job 38–41); a writer who has written the greatest best-seller of all time—the Bible (2 Tim. 3:16); a story teller and actor (Jesus used parables in the Gospels to convey mysteries–Hos. 12:10, Amp.); an architect (Ps. 90:2; Is. 44:24); a worker of needle and thread—He has woven a garment of light for Himself (Ps. 104:2), and has provided a golden wedding garment for His Bride (Ps. 45:9, 13–14); a creator of culinary delights (Ex. 16:31; Num. 11:7–8; Pss. 34:8; 119:103; Song 2:3); and a perfumer (Ps. 45:8; Song 1:3; 3:6; 5:1; 5:13). In all of these, He is without compare. There is none who can match His artistry, excellence, and genius.

The Shulamite sums it up in the Song of Solomon:

> . . . yes, he is altogether lovely—the whole of him delights and is precious. . . (Song 5:16, Amp.)

Other writers and artists are hard pressed to find the words to describe His brilliance and expertise as an artist:

> Christ was the greatest of all artists.[7] (Vincent Van Gogh)

> God is the perfect poet, Who in His person acts His own creations.[8] (Robert Browning)

> God is the supreme artist. He loves to have things beau-tiful. Look at the sunset and the flowers and the snow-

capped mountains and the stars. They are beautiful
because they have come from God. God loves to have
things beautiful in church, too.[9] (Baldwin)

Music strikes in me a profound contemplation of the
first Composer.[10] (Thomas Browne)

Although every art form is appropriate for use as an expression
of worship, some art forms are an easier idiom to apply in a public setting. These include: music, song, drama, dance, mime, poetry, and sewing and handiwork as used in banner making. (I have
seen other forms of art—such as sculpting, painting, stained glass
work, and architecture— skillfully used as instruments of worship,
even prophetically, but for ease of writing and giving examples, I
will refer to those previously listed.)

There appear to be three foundational reasons given in
Scripture for the Lord's use of His art and creation:

1. To reveal His glory and nature to all mankind: "The heavens
declare the glory of God; and the firmament shows His handiwork." (Ps. 19:1)

2. To communicate with His people and show us His ways and
thoughts: Gen. 1–2.

3. To give and receive pleasure: ". . . for You created all things, and
by Your will they exist and were created." (Rev. 4:11)

These three reasons for artistic expression must also apply to us.

THE FIRST REASON FOR ART—TO REVEAL THE GLORY AND NATURE OF GOD

The first and primary use for all art is to show the glory and
nature of God.

Good painting is nothing but a copy of the perfections
of God.[11] (Michelangelo)

True anointing in any art form will uncover something of God's
character and nature that we have never quite seen before. The
worship arena is the foremost place for all art, for the true meas-

ure of an artist's skill is in his or her ability to uncover and reveal the glory and nature of God.

For example, a banner has the potential to be more than a colorful decoration in the sanctuary—it is a point of faith. A skilled banner maker is able to draw us to God, time and again in worship, through handiwork that shows us something of the glory of God.

The first and primary use for all art is to show the glory and nature of God.

British writer and composer, Andrew Wilson-Dickson concurs somewhat with this assessment. He says that music can be judged as true or false according to the accuracy with which it reflects the nature of God's creation.[12] He goes on to quote the poet, Ezra Pound:

> Bad art is inaccurate art. It is art that makes false reports. . . If an artist falsifies his report as to the nature of. . . god. . . of good and evil. . . of the force with which he believes or disbelieves this, that or the other . . . if the artist falsifies his reports on these matters . . . then that artist lies. By good art I mean art that bears true witness, I mean art that is most precise. . .[13]

Any excellent artist should be able to communicate to one or more of man's five senses something of the glory of God. But it requires the prophetic anointing to fully accomplish this.

> . . . the artistic abilities of Paul were not to draw attention to the artist. They were to bring men and women to a personal knowledge of the power and glory of God.[14] (Sammy Tippit)

When Moses was commanded by God to make a tabernacle that would show forth His glory, he was instructed to call upon skillful artists of all kinds to craft the beauty and splendor that was due Him. Four chapters in Exodus (25–28) are used by the Lord to describe the elaborate and artistic beauty of the tabernacle that was to be constructed.

Likewise, when David built the tabernacle on Mount Zion, he consecrated it with skillful music, song, and dance (1 Chron.

15–16). His most skillful musicians were left before the ark to offer prophetic praises to the Lord day and night. Solomon called for workmen and artisans by the thousands to build a magnificent temple that would show forth the glory of the Lord (2 Chron. 2–4).

Similarly, all artists in this day should devote their talent to the description of God's unsearchable glories and manifest presence. I say "unsearchable," because all eternity will not afford us the time needed to complete the description of His wonders, even if crafted by the most exceptional artists of every sort.

Giorgio Vasari (1511-1574), an artist recognized as the first historian of art, says this of Michelangelo's statue *Moses*:

> . . . you seem, while you gaze upon it, [the marble statue of Moses], to wish to demand from him [Michelangelo] the veil wherewith to cover that face, so resplendent and so dazzling it appears to you, and so well has Michelagnolo [*sic*] expressed the divinity that God infused in that most holy countenance. In addition, there are draperies carved out and finished with most beautiful curves of the borders; while the arms with their muscles, and the hands with their bones and nerves, are carried to such a pitch of beauty and perfection, and the legs, knees, and feet are covered with buskins so beautifully fashioned, and every part of the work is so finished, that Moses may be called now more than ever the friend of God, seeing that he has deigned to assemble together and prepare his body for the Resurrection before that of any other, by the hands of Michelagnolo.[15]

Michelangelo used his rare genius to show us the glory of God lying beyond the figure he carved out of stone. Christian artists are those who have rivers of living water coming from their innermost beings (John 7:38). With a talent dedicated to God and the glory of God flowing like a river from our lives, Christian artists should be those who blaze the trail of distinction, beauty, and excellence above all other artists.

It is quite exciting to attend a worship service where the Lord uses His people to unfold something of His glory. In the summer of 1997, Morning Star Church, based in the Chicago area, invited a harpist from the Chicago symphony to join us in some special meetings.

During the worship, the Lord began to speak of the new day that was coming to the Church. The harpist (a Chinese woman) stood in front of her harp and began to slowly beat the bass strings with the palm of her hand. It sounded like the chiming of a gong or a clock—the Lord was declaring the hour of His glory over the nations. Some flute players joined in by playing unusual sounds on their instruments—somewhat like folk music. We were playing the sounds of the Chinese people. The congregation lifted their voices in intercession for China and for other nations as the evening progressed.

Such prophetic clarity is needed in all Christian artists today. To prophesy with instruments, dance, or song requires more than artistic ability. Church must not become a place for "jam sessions." Rather, it is the setting for the most profound unfolding of God's character and purposes.

Art, in a prophetic sense, makes a highway to God Himself.

THE SECOND REASON FOR ART—COMMUNICATION BETWEEN GOD AND HIS PEOPLE

The second use of all art is to promote and enhance communication between God and His people. It is the role of every artist to declare the heart cries and needs of the people before God. Likewise, the artist must "speak" for God and communicate His thoughts and ways to the people.

Again, the worship service and our daily devotional lives are the principal places for such artistic expression. Art connects mankind with each other and with God. It enables us to pour God's thoughts into the hearts of men.

Every emotion known to man has been expressed at some time through various art forms. When we look at all that He has created, the sheer magnificence of His handiwork speaks to us of His awesome power, unfathomable greatness, and infinite mercy.

Art connects mankind with each other and with God.

My husband, Michael, is an excellent singer of prophetic songs. I have seen him bear the burdens of hurting people before the throne of God when they were unable to verbalize the prayers themselves. As a prophet, he was able to "hear" their sorrows and sing a song of comfort and deliverance from the heart of God

THE THIRD REASON FOR ART—GOD CREATES FOR PLEASURE

God was and is creative for the sake of His pleasure—the third reason for art. He has given us this enjoyment with creativity also.

There is nothing wrong with the concept of art as entertainment. After creating a most spectacular and remarkable universe, the Lord stood back and said, "It is good!" He took pleasure in His handiwork.

We too can delight in the multitudes of exquisite things that are crafted by God and man. Such joy is a gift from God. Unfortunately, most artists (including Christian artists) see no more use for their skills than this. Art becomes an end in itself, and the highest goal of an artist, merely to achieve excellence.

As worshipers, the first two reasons for art must always be considered or we will fall into the trap of limiting our art to a worldly concept of performance, entertainment, and accompaniment. Too many churches have music programs that are founded on these limited principles.

The church organist or choir member, for example, should not view his or her role as providing entertainment for the people as they enter and exit the church, or mere accompaniment for the congregation as they sing. There is a higher calling upon these artists to declare the very manifest presence of God and His work among His people.

God did not give us art as an end in itself. The art forms and talents of man are not the goal or the end of our achievement—God's glory is.

Art, in a prophetic sense, makes a highway to God Himself. Our goal is His presence, not the excellence of our skill. Therefore, even children can function prophetically as able ministers in God's presence, if they have hearts that are dedicated to God and sensitive to His prophetic anointing.

This does not mean that we should abandon all pursuit of excellence and professionalism in our various artistic ministries—quite the contrary. I believe that Christian artists should strive to offer God nothing short of their best.

I am grateful for the churches that have made room for the very best of music, art, sculpture, and architecture over the centuries. Handel, Bach, Michelangelo and countless others were primarily church artists. Their talents spilled over from the church into the world so that millions could come to appreciate and cherish their exquisite handiwork.

> After creating a most spectacular and
> remarkable universe, the Lord stood
> back and said, "It is good!" He took
> pleasure in his handiwork.

Many churches today include accomplished artists on staff and in their services. I am regularly blessed by the outstanding singers and musicians who minister on Reverend Robert Schuller's Crystal Cathedral television broadcasts, and the pursuit of excellence in the arts at such churches as Living Waters Fellowship in Pasadena, California, and Bishop Earl Paulk's Chapel Hill Harvester Church in Atlanta, Georgia.

Esteemed composer, David Holsinger, is on staff as the Composer-in-residence at Shady Grove Church in Grand Prairie, Texas. His pastor, Olen Griffing, has it in his heart to do all that he can to ensure that Mr. Holsinger reaches the pinnacle of his artistic abilities as a church musician as well as a composer of symphonic band music.[16] Shady Grove Church is all the richer for having a composer and musician of this caliber "in residence."

Our emphasis should not be focused on the art form and the skill with which it is ministered, but the presence of God and His work in the earth. Art must never become the primary object of our attention in worship. It is not an end in itself, no matter how exceptional it is. Perfect performance will never be the primary goal of the prophetic artist. Rather, he will always set his eyes upon the ultimate goal of uncovering and declaring the glory of God.

Perfect performance will never be the
primary goal of the prophetic artist.
Rather, he will always set his eyes upon
the ultimate goal of uncovering and
declaring the glory of God.

While artists need to renew their vision and commitment to
worship, churches must also reassess their theology on this matter
of how we view all the arts in the light of our faith in Christ. I really appreciate Robert Webber's perspective on the role of art in the
Church today, and in worship:

> One of the great problems within the evangelical cul-
> ture is a repudiation of the arts in general, and more
> specifically the failure to employ the arts in worship.
> This disdain toward the arts is deeply rooted in a view
> that consigns material things to the devil. The pietistic
> and fundamentalist backgrounds of modern evangeli-
> calism are addicted to this erroneous view, a dualism
> that sets the material against the spiritual. . . . the visi-
> ble arts as well as theater, the dance, color, and tangible
> symbols have historically had a functional role in wor-
> ship.[17]

It is time for the worshiping Church to pursue excellence in all
the arts for the purpose of proclaiming and revealing the glory of
God in the earth. God is in the process of restoring and redeeming
art to its intended place as a prophetic tool of His glorious plan.
Let us shout with the Psalmists and the Prophet:

> Make a joyful shout to God, all the earth! Sing out the
> honor of His name; make His praise glorious. (Ps.
> 66:1–2)

> Let them praise His name in chorus and choir and with
> the [single or group] dance, let them sing praises to
> Him with the tambourine and lyre! For the Lord takes
> pleasure in His people; He will beautify the humble
> with salvation and adorn the wretched with victory. Let
> the saints be joyful in the glory and beauty [which God
> confers upon them] . . . (Ps. 149:3–5, Amp.)

"The glory of Lebanon shall come to you, the cypress, the pine, and the box tree together, to beautify the place of My sanctuary; and I will make the place of my feet glorious . . . " (Is. 60:13)

Chapter Twenty-One

RECOGNIZING THE PROPHETIC SOUND IN MUSIC

Music is a principal means of glorifying our merciful Creator.
Henry Peacham

T he style of our musical expressions in worship must reflect what God is doing, not merely that to which we have become accustomed. Tradition has long dictated artistic style and has greeted every degree of change with reluctance and skepticism. Each generation has had to fight for their music to be heard in the church, while the previous generations faithfully cling to the musical styles of their own teenage years. Some even continue the endless debate that attempts to confer God's blessing or Satan's inspiration on various art forms—particularly music.

> As far back as Pope Gregory, the Roman Catholic Church tried to "canonize" music. There are still orders of the Church which wholeheartedly subscribe to the Gregorian chant. . . Other attempts have been made to canonize music. . . History indicates that the body which canonizes musical form and style begins to fossilize right there. The very nature of music that has brought the church much good, demands that it will continue to develop and change. Sometimes we wish it would stop, but it will not.[1]

It seems the end result for every generation is that the worship music and styles of our young people are always soundly condemned and censured, and the prophetic people who attempt to bridge the gap stylistically are silenced. No wonder the Church lags behind the world by about ten to fifteen years in all areas of artistic expression.

There are only a few things the Bible has to say about the style of worship music. According to the book of Psalms, the two most common stylistic recommendations are that music should be: *joyful* (Pss. 5:11; 27:6; 32:11; 35:9; 40:16; 63:5; 66:1; 67:4; 68:3; 81:1; 95:1–2; 98:4, 6; 100:1; 149:5) and *loud* (Pss. 32:11; 33:3; 47:1; 98:4; 150:5). Perhaps an ageless innocence is captured in the simplicity and naiveté of music that is loud and joyous. Certainly every generation is able to comply with such an unmistakable bidding.

> The style of our musical expressions in worship must reflect what God is doing, not merely that to which we have become accustomed.

If we are to embrace prophetic worship, we must get ready for some dramatic changes in the styles of music we are prepared to include in the worship services. The issue of style, in itself, has the potential to bridge the gap between the generations within the Church, open the presence of God and the spirit of revival to the youth of our communities, and extend healing and reconciliation to the diverse ethnic groups within our society.

It is possible to include several styles of music in a service without compromising the flow of worship. Traditional hymns can blend quite well with contemporary and culturally unique worship music.

God is always desiring to come among us in His manifest presence. The Spirit of God is always longing to bring us into more and more truth so that we would be changed into His likeness. This changing is a process over time.

Hopefully, the Bride of Christ today is living more fully in the grace and knowledge of Christ than she did a decade or a century ago. We must learn how to expect and embrace change.

To worship is to be changed.[2] (Graham Kendrick)

You cannot step twice into the same river, for other waters are continually flowing on.[3] (Heraclitus)

Each move of God in the earth will birth songs and artistic expressions that reflect and trumpet the voice of God among us. True prophetic artists will be able to pick up the new sounds, styles, and messages of God and reinforce His summons to the Church through the arts. When determining the style of our worship music, we should not be consumed with our own national, denominational, and generational preferences. We must make room for the voice of the Lord to exceed each of these. As Norm Frederick has said:

There is no generation gap in the finishing generation.[4]

There has been an age-old debate in the secular world as to whether art should be a reflection of society or a statement concerning where society is going. A similar debate is needed in the Church, where artists have lingered years behind current trends, "cutting edge" expressions, and the voice of God.

This debate relates primarily to prophetic worship. We need to continually consider the voice of God and the direction in which He is intending the Church to go.

Consider this question in the light of your church's music and songs: Do we only sing of what He has done in the past or are our songs, at times, a prophetic reflection of what He is revealing of Himself today?

The skillful worship leader should be able to incorporate songs and musical styles that reflect God's present message without rejecting the rich volume of hymns and songs held dear by his or her congregation.

I believe it quite possible that some secular artists have, at times, tapped into a type of prophetic flow that has enabled them to express their art in a way that seems to be "cutting edge." Many of these have lived and worked in the forefront of our society.

Examples of this from my generation were the Beatles, Bob Dylan, and Elvis Presley, who brought a new sound and message with their music. The impact of their music permeated all of society and remains today as a foundation for those who have followed them.

The song, *Yesterday*, written by Beatle, Paul McCartney, has been recorded by over 2200 different artists. McCartney, billed as the most successful song writer of all time, received this song in a dream[5]

How much more should anointed Christian artists mark their work with excellence to impact the Church and the world in which we live! We must become a reflection of all that Christ has done over the centuries and also give voice to His present work and future glory in the earth.

THE PROBLEM WITH TRADITION

Churches that are bound by tradition will be content with the same songs, year after year, for their understanding of God will not change. They will also be remiss in incorporating other art forms in worship.

I am not advocating that we relinquish all the outstanding Christian music of the past centuries and give ourselves over to a youthful "free-for-all" in the worship service. There are hymns, for example, that contain timeless melodies and lyrics of unsurpassed depth and beauty.

However, I am calling for us to listen with a new and prophetic sensitivity to the music of all generations and all nations. Those songs and hymns that reinforce what God is saying in the church must remain, but let us not suppress the voice of God as He draws us on, through the sounds of the next generation.

We must also become open to other art forms in worship, such as dance, drama and mime. There remains no good reason for ignoring these cultural and artistic expressions that have already proven themselves to be such powerful tools in the prophetic worship of so many churches today. ✎

Chapter Twenty-Two

THE MATURITY OF
WORSHIPERS

Worship is a vital key to personal change.
It is the very essence of maturation.
Worship is not simply human activity,
but rather an encounter with a living God.
Sam Sasser

≈

Worship is one of the most exposing things we can ever
engage in as humans. To truly worship, we must pour
out our hearts before the Lord with vulnerability, honesty, and transparency.

But this is an act of spiritual maturity. Immature Christians will
be more comfortable with the same routine in worship week by
week, where they know what is going to happen from beginning
to end, and little is required of them.

The Holy Spirit has been calling out to the Church in these days.
His cry is that we would grow up and begin to experience greater
degrees of victory over every enemy, greater intimacy with Christ,
death to self, and service to one another than we ever have before.
This maturity is not just for church leaders, but the entire Body of
Christ, from the youngest to the oldest.

Mature Christian must read the Bible rather than seek blessings;
find God in prayer rather than through the prophets; lay hold of
God rather than always wanting hands laid on them; pursue His
presence rather than preachers; and follow the Lord's will rather
than their own wanderings.

Modern Christians have long been obsessed with how their Churches should meet their needs. Surely our first priority must be to please the Lord. Anointings and blessings can be received when others pray for us, but there is a greater place of anointing and blessing that awaits those who would lay down their lives and pursue God's presence with all their hearts. This anointing is only obtained through prayer and death to self.

Although we are servants and sons of God, we are also His Bride. It is time for us to act like a bride and not children who must have everything done for us. It is the bride who must make *herself* ready.

THE ROYAL BRIDE PREPARES HERSELF

Most leaders seem to agree that we are in the final hours of the Church Age here on earth. Exactly how many months or years will pass before Christ's return is uncertain, but the reality of His soon coming seems to be near.

One of the signs of His return will be the maturity and promotion of the Church to the position of His Bride. Although we are servants and sons of God, we are also His Bride. It is time for us to act like a bride and not children who must have everything done for us. It is the bride who must make *herself* ready:

> Let us be glad and rejoice and give Him glory, for the marriage of the Lamb has come, and His wife **has made herself ready.** (Rev. 19:7)

The Church must become an Esther Church, clothed in royal robes and found standing in the inner court of the King's palace (Es. 5:1–3). Esther knew that she lived a life of destiny—that she was in the kingdom *for such a time as this* (Es. 4:14). It takes a certain maturity in the Church in order to adopt this understanding of our destiny. The Lord wants His Church-Bride back. He is waiting for us to appear before Him in our royal apparel. Garments of self must be peeled off and we must be clothed with Christ and His nature (Col. 3:8–14).

Recall how Ruth prepared herself for Boaz (Ruth 3:3–8). She washed, anointed, and clothed *herself* then laid down at his feet. At midnight (the beginning of the new day), Boaz stirred himself and found a woman lying at his feet.

I would like to suggest that Ruth here represents the Church, who waits for her Kinsman-Redeemer (Christ) to recognize her. We must not expect others to wash, anoint, and clothe us. It is time for each of us to pay the price for our own washing, anointing, and clothing. Christ has provided a way for us to be formed into His likeness while we wait before Him as a mature woman who is ready for her Boaz.

Worship is one of the most exposing things we can ever engage in as humans.

THE BRIDE AND THE BRIDEGROOM

The Bride of Christ will know His voice, know how to respond to Him appropriately in worship, look and act like a mature woman, die to self, and be ready for greater depths of intimacy.

We only need to read the Song of Solomon to see the extent of God's purposes for us as those who profess to love Him. He has every intention of drawing the Church—which seems more like a giggling girl right now than a mature woman—into the most intimate of all relationships: marriage. We will rule with Him throughout eternity as those who have overcome and entered into a bridal relationship with Him:

> To Him who overcomes I will grant to sit with Me on
> My throne . . . (Rev. 3:21a)

The song of the Bride and the Bridegroom constitutes one of the great themes of worship today. More and more worship songs are being written that express this particular aspect of our encounter with God. But the Lord is calling us to push past merely sentimental or "soppy" feelings to the full maturity of bridal love.

Personally, I love the song by David Ruis called *True Love*, though it does take a certain level of spiritual maturity to experience the relationship described here in the public setting:

Jesus, I need to know true love,
Deeper than the love found on earth.
Take me into the King's chamber,
Cause my love to mature.

My heart, my flesh yearn for you, Lord.
To love You is all I can do.
You have become my sole passion,
Cause my love to be true.

Let me know the kisses of your mouth,
Let me feel your embrace.
Let me smell the fragrance of your touch,
Let me see your lovely face.
Take me away with you,
Even so, Lord, come.
I love you, Lord,
I love you more than life.
I love you, Lord,
I love you more than life.[1]

THE NATION THAT IS BORN IN A DAY

The prophet Isaiah asks us this question:

> . . . shall the earth be made to give birth in one day? Or
> shall a nation be born at once? (Is. 66:8)

Although the Church has been around for nearly two thousand years, on the day of her glory in the earth, it will appear as if she has just been born. *We are* this nation that is going to be born in these last days.

The Church that will arise will be mature and powerful—a nation that has been gathered from all the nations of the earth. Were we able to glimpse this glorious Church today, I do not believe we would even recognize ourselves, since we have lived as an immature and powerless people for so long.

In these days, we must not attempt to interpret the role of the Church according to what has taken place in church history, but we must look at the Church and her role in the earth according to what is about to take place in her future.

Our wholeness and maturity are a work of grace, but it is up to us to allow the Holy Spirit to weave great changes within our hearts. We have much to learn as we adorn ourselves in the robes and jewels He has provided.

ENCOUNTERING GOD

Because worship must include an encounter with an awesome and holy God—Who has more and more of Himself to show His people—we need prophetic worship to provoke the whole congregation to continued death, change, spiritual growth and maturity. Prophetic worship is not possible unless the congregation is committed to such advancement. Otherwise worship will remain a ritual rather than an encounter.

How easily God's people run from Him when He appears, or when worship does not go our way! We are more comfortable with the way things *are*, according to our traditions, rather than intelligently seeking the way things *should be*, according to God's standards.

An encounter with God is crucial to the worship experience. Every believer must come to the worship service with the expectation that the Lord will meet them personally. Paul speaks of this when he says:

> But **we all**, with open face, beholding as in a mirror the glory of the Lord, are being transformed into the same image from glory to glory, just as by the Spirit of the Lord. (2 Cor. 3:18)

Terry Wardle says this of 2 Cor. 3:18:

> People often do not encounter God in worship. This problem is by far the most devastating. Sunday after Sunday, people leave church without sensing the presence of God in worship. The entire experience becomes an exercise in human effort. Where and when this is true, people leave the service much as they entered. They are unchanged, uninspired, and unprepared to serve Christ in the marketplace of daily living.[2]

The "beholding" is for all of us, but the costly aspect of this is that the sight of God in worship so often involves the sight of self—and the sight of ourselves in the light of His glory and holiness can truly be devastating.

When we behold Him we have the opportunity to glimpse something of ourselves that we may never have seen or understood before—or been willing to face. But if we face the truth steadfastly, not turning away, we will find Him again—standing at the end of all our ugliness and failures, ready to redeem and restore every dark and broken place within. The final outcome of this holy encounter is that we are changed from glory to glory.

The sight of ourselves in the light of His glory and holiness can truly be devastating.

Despite the magnitude of this glorious transformation that is offered to us, change is still difficult and often frightening. Only with the knowledge and experience of His grace can this become a joy, and only when we are prepared to go on into maturity will we willingly offer ourselves for this most difficult course.

This is not to say that prophetic worship leaves a congregation in a place of insecurity and uncertainty—quite the opposite. There is nothing more secure than to have our eyes fixed upon the Almighty as we rest under His shadow.

Physical maturity is not necessarily related to spiritual maturity. For six years I had the privilege of leading the weekly chapel services for kindergarten to sixth grade students at the Shady Grove Christian Academy. These young people became skilled in ministering prophetically in many settings. They learned to sing prophetic songs, pray for the sick, receive words of knowledge and prophesy.

When a wind of revival blew through Shady Grove Church in the Spring of 1994, it was the children who first received God's outpouring. Many were "caught up" into heaven in visions; some began to quote scriptures they had never learned. They waited upon the Lord for hours in worship and intercession, saw miraculous answers to prayer and allowed the Lord to convict them of sin and hypocrisies.

These events should give us all pause for thought, for they reveal a crushing fact: *It is not our youthfulness, inexperience or lack of Bible knowledge that preempts the work of God in our lives, but our stubborn resistance and hard-heartedness to His Spirit.*

May each of us be as bold as these children as we encounter the Lord Almighty.

A PASTORAL DILEMMA

Former American President, Calvin Coolidge has said:

> It is only when men begin to worship that they begin to grow.[3]

Every pastor is faced with the responsibility of bringing his or her congregation to the place of maturity in worship. We have probably all experienced services where immature believers have "prophesied" crazy things or the expressions of worship have been inappropriate in some way.

For fear of these things, some pastors may be tempted to curb the opportunities for participation by the congregation, restricting all worship expressions and exercise of the spiritual gifts to the religious "professionals."

> . . . many believers have accepted the power of God in theory but have rejected it in practice. Fearing wild fire, congregations have opted for no fire at all.[4] (Terry Waddle)

It is sad that so many pastors are content for their flocks to remain in the spiritual shallows of worship. Perhaps it just seems easier for everyone if the worship team presents a pleasant, professional (and short) program of songs, rather than cracking the door to that mysterious chamber called "prophetic worship."

However, with regular teaching and practical training, God's people can quickly come to a place of proficiency and confidence in all aspects of prophetic worship and functioning in His presence. The Lord has not intended the things of His presence to be an unsolvable puzzle. Rather, He invites us all into the joy and simplicity of personal and corporate communion.

The path of developing into a mature congregation, able to move in prophetic worship is founded on the issue of training. In order for the saints to be adequately equipped to minister effectively and prophetically in worship (Eph. 4:11–12), the following needs to occur:

- Time needs to be given to regular training in worship. The pastor has the responsibility of finding and releasing every believer in his or her spiritual giftings.

- Opportunities must be opened up in every service for the people to actively participate in worship.

- We must make provision for believers to make mistakes from time to time without "shaming" them into non-participation.

- Experienced leaders must occasionally step aside and allow others to lead and exercise their giftings. People will rise only to the level of their leaders' expectations.

- Loving and constructive correction and encouragement must be given to those who minister in any capacity during the service.

Olen Griffing, Senior Pastor of Shady Grove Church, shows wisdom in how he encourages participation by all members of the congregation in the prophetic flow of the worship service.

A microphone is placed near the front of the congregational seating, where all are invited to contribute to the service what they feel the Lord has given them. However, each one must first consult with one of the pastors stationed there as to the content of their message and the best time to give it. Then, at the appropriate time in the service, they are invited to share their scripture, testimony, song, prophecy, or whatever.

This method would be quite easy for any church to adapt so as to make a place in the midst of the corporate worship for congregational participation. If someone makes a mistake (and, undoubtedly, there will be mistakes), this also becomes part of the maturing process, that we might all learn together, receive the appropriate correction and go on (Rev. 3:19).

Our standard for maturity must be measured by this scripture, which I have used previously:

> How is it then, brethren? Whenever you come together, each of you has a psalm, has a teaching, has a tongue, has a revelation, has an interpretation. Let all things be done for edification. (1 Cor. 14:26)

Every pastor should ask himself or herself if they have a good number of men, women, youth and children who are able to edify the congregation on a regular basis. If not—and if the same small group of people do all the speaking or singing—then it might be time for some training to take place for the whole congregation.

Every pastor is faced with this choice:

Should I do all the work myself—preaching, prophesying, controlling the worship service, organizing the music ministry, doing the announcements, and so on?

Or, should I invest my time in training each member of the church to serve the Body and flow maturely, correctly and deeply in prophetic worship?

My conclusion—voiced with great sadness—is that most pastors today seem to have chosen the former route, either doing everything themselves or giving over control of their services entirely to a group of paid professionals.

Every pastor is faced with the responsibility of bringing his or her congregation to the place of maturity in worship.

THE WORSHIP TEAM MUST ALSO COME TO MATURITY

The price for maturity must also be paid by the worship leader(s), the singers, musicians, dancers, and any other worship artists. Prophetic worship is not possible unless these ministers become students of the presence of God as well as of their craft.

These must also learn to embrace the prophetic anointing that comes with the artistic gifting and yield to the full cost of prophetic responsibility. There is so much more to being an able minister of the presence of God than just having an ability in music and the arts. It costs our time and effort to develop any artistic skill, but it costs our lives if we want to be adept at communing with God and ministering His voice or song prophetically in the midst of the congregation (Ex. 20:19).

In the Hebraic tradition, all worship ministers, from the reign of King David on, were trained in the prophetic realm. Young men and women were trained under their fathers to prophesy both in song and with their instruments. Thus, they were able to minister prophetically at the command of the King (1 Chron. 25:1–8).

It appears that there was no such thing as a temple musician who was not skilled in both music and the prophetic realm. This should serve as an example to those of us who would minister in worship.

> All worship ministers from the reign of King David on, were trained in the prophetic realm.

The maturity we all need in worship is born out of our private place of devotion to God. The place of His presence must be created in our hearts. It is a place of daily and continual communion.

> We are mobile temples of worship.[5] (LaMar Boschman)

Even as I speak of the price of maturity, I do not want us to lose sight of the simplicity of loving and serving Jesus. We do not have to be "perfect" in order to worship the Lord or lead others in worship. Isaiah was not confronted with his faults until he saw the Lord. He repented and consecrated himself to the Lord only after he saw the King (Is. 6:1–5).

> It is the simplicity and purity of devotion to Christ that must be the springboard for everything that we do.[6] (Dutch Sheets)

Our Christian maturity must not be gauged by our artistic abilities or our public displays of worship skills, but by the depth and reality of our personal relationship with the Lord. Our Christianity is expressed more truly in our every day lives than it is in our public performances. We must begin to see ourselves as living temples of His presence and ministers of His glory in the earth.

Come on Church—grow up!

Chapter Twenty-Three

BEGINNING THE CORPORATE JOURNEY

A church breathes through its worship system!
The vitality of a local church is linked to its devotion.
Earnest Gentile

≈

This statement will come as a revelation to many Christians today: *There is a difference between our personal worship experience with the Lord and our corporate worship experience.*

In our personal worship experience with the Lord, the communication is one-to-One. He speaks to us and deals with us on an individual level. When we gather for corporate worship, however, we need to understand that we are going in before the Lord as a group—a family.

We need the other members of the Body of Christ as much as our physical bodies need every one of their many parts. His glory is seen, His voice is heard through our brothers and sisters. They become His hands moving in ministry among us.

In corporate worship no one should hold to a personal agenda and remain as a separate entity—worshiping in his own way. For we are a "spiritual house" made up of "living stones" (1 Pet. 2:4–5); *one* Church made up of *many* dynamic individuals.

Richard Foster encourages a submission one to another as we gather corporately:

> The language of the gathered fellowship is not "I," but
> "we." There is a submission to the ways of God. There
> is a submission to one another in the Christian fellow-

ship. There is a desire for God's life to rise up in the group, not just within the individual.[1]

I wholeheartedly agree with Graham Kendrick as he bemoans the fact that the Church has fostered individuality within its community rather than a sense of covenant commitment and corporate worship:

> . . . worship has become tailored to individuality rather than community, and instead we have diplomatically learned to avoid anything that might upset the status quo of separation. We sit in rows facing the front of the building and stare at each other's heads as if to watch a performance or a show . . .[2]

CORPORATE WORSHIP AND THE PROPHETIC ANOINTING

Because of the relationship of commitment and covenant that we have with our brothers and sisters, our encounter with God should be strengthened whenever we meet together. When we encourage one another to participate in worship, the Holy Spirit delights in drawing upon each individual, as a master conductor directs a symphony.

Each person must function in their gifting in order for congregational worship to achieve its goal, for the Spirit desires to take us on a corporate journey into the knowledge of Him.

> . . . worship generally reaches higher levels of expression when a body of believers is worshipping together.[3]
> (Judson Cornwall)

The Lord stands in the midst of the whole congregation (Ps. 82:1) and calls for us to relate to Him and respond to Him as one. Observe the following examples where we see the Lord treating a body of people as if they were one man, where we see God's call upon us to become one and flow in worship as a unified people (there are many more examples, throughout the entire history of Israel and the Church, than can be listed here):

- The children of Israel went through the wilderness together as one group, not individual tribes. They were delivered (Ex. 12, 14); blessed (Gen. 12:3); fed (Ex.

16:10–36); visited by God (Ex. 19–20); and punished (Joshua 7) as one.

- The Book of Psalms calls for unified praise and worship from the whole congregation: Pss. 47:1; 67:3; 97:6; 106:48; 107:32; 111:1; 149:1

- In Paul's instructions on congregational worship (1 Cor. 11–14), he calls for us to consider ourselves as one congregation, with each one taking part in the service (1 Cor. 14:26)

- Ultimately, we are part of the innumerable company of heavenly hosts (Rev. 5:11–14). Our worship is never meant to stand alone. We participate in an extraordinary and continuous worship service before the throne of God. Surely our worship should be appropriate for the great King.

Please bear in mind, I am not saying that all worship is *exclusively* a congregational journey, since we may have individual experiences and receive individual blessings during corporate worship. Often, the Lord ministers in a dramatic way to individuals during a service.

Our focus, however, must include a much broader perspective. Wherever the Lord takes us in worship, we must go there together, and not hang back because of our own preferences or perspectives.

Because of the relationship of commitment and covenant that we have with our brothers and sisters, our encounter with God should be strengthened whenever we meet together.

Many Christians seem to become offended with worship leaders who ask for congregational participation and response, such as the clapping or lifting of hands. Some will fold their arms and demand the right to worship in their own way.

If we allow this attitude to continue and grow, the congregation will soon become just an assembly of individuals, experiencing God (or not) in different ways and on different levels throughout the service. They will cease to function and see themselves as parts of a whole.

Although this situation is quite prevalent today, I do not believe it is God's best for His people. Corporate worship with true prophetic anointing becomes difficult to achieve, only when our rebellious human nature stands in the way, not because of any barriers God has raised. We are a people who insist on having things our own way. The rights of individuals reign supreme in our Western world.

> A sense of community is sometimes difficult in our Western society with our democratic mentality and spirit of individualism.[4] (LaMar Boschman)

For example, in our personal devotional time with the Lord, He might be dealing with us about things in our lives that need to be changed, or we might be enduring a time of sadness or struggle. But when we join our congregation for worship, these intensely personal experiences need to be put aside, lest they hinder us from entering in to the fullness of His presence and working.

To some extent we will always be affected in corporate worship by our personal walk with the Lord and the things that happen to us on a daily basis, since worship springs from our personal relationship with Him (1 Pet. 2:4–5). However, there comes a point where we need to lay our personalities and individual lives aside and enter into worship as one with our brothers and sisters. (This a delicate matter, between our hearts and the Holy Spirit, so we do not need to become legalistic about it.)

It is always amazing to me to look out on a congregation—no matter what its size—and see how the Lord has molded everyone together. There are often folk from many different socio-economic, ethnic, generational, and intellectual groups, all joined together as one congregation.

We might not even choose one another as friends in another setting, but as Christians, the Lord has made us brothers and sisters. What joy it is to see unity grow within a body and the corporate prophetic anointing function as it should between every member!

I refer to corporate worship as a "journey into God" because the Lord actually invites us to enter His presence and "go" somewhere with Him.

For example, He might speak to the congregation prophetically through one person that He is our Shepherd—just one of the many wonders of His name. The musicians may then be inspired to play the sounds of the Shepherd using various instruments—perhaps a flute or a violin. Someone might step to the front and share a scripture revealing the heart of the Shepherd—possibly Psalm 23, Isaiah 40:11, John 10:11–16, Hebrews 13:20; 1 Peter 2:25 or 1 Peter 5:4. A singer might follow with a song based on one of these scriptures, including further revelation she has received from knowing Him as the Shepherd in his/her own life.

The "journey" continues as a dancer or mime depicts the way a shepherd puts oil on the heads of sheep who have been butting heads and fighting. A pastor may then invite those in the body who need healing or forgiveness from their brothers or sisters to come to the front for prayer.

What joy it is to see unity grow within a body and the corporate prophetic anointing function as it should between every member.

By the end of such a service, every member of the congregation can feel as if they have contributed to the overall understanding or revelation of God as He speaks to His people. Each believer should leave the service strengthened, with more of God in his/her heart. The effects of such an encounter must ring in our hearts forever.

PERSONAL DEVOTION

In emphasizing corporate worship, I do not mean to diminish the need for a growing depth of personal worship and relationship with God. Individual devotion enhances corporate worship, and our corporate worship encourages us in our personal relationship with God. We do not just worship on Sundays, but must become worshipers every day of our lives, and in every situation in which we find ourselves.

Our individual communion with the Lord should also strengthen our brothers and sisters. The stronger we are in our daily walk with Christ, the more we will be able to build up the rest of the Church and those who do not know Christ.

Any extreme is wrong. Forsaking the Church community and corporate worship is dangerous for any believer, while a lack of personal devotion to God will ultimately produce spiritual death.

Our public worship must always flow out of our personal devotion, but when we gather corporately, we must make those adjustments that are necessary to flow in unity.

The ideal in worship is that we see ourselves as a group of people who are on a journey into God. Each one is important and each one—from the youngest to the oldest—has a vital part to play.

The Lord often draws from the wealth of our personal communion with Him to speak into the corporate worship service.

> . . . as they (the early Christians) met, they were gathered into a unity of spirit that transcended their individualism. In contrast to the religions of the East, the Christian faith has strongly emphasized corporate worship.[5] (Richard Foster)

> Social religion is perfected when private religion is purified.[6] (A. W. Tozer)

Our public worship must always flow out of our personal devotion.

Perhaps we need to reassess the purpose and functioning of the Church where worship is concerned. We are to be a worshiping community rather than a place where individuals come for private rituals. The success of corporate worship depends upon the authentic devotion of individuals and their ability to grow together as a sincere worshiping community.

> Unless there are people who are responding to the love of God as revealed in Christ and so are worshipping Him, the Church is not very important.[7] (Eugene Carson Blake)

Chapter Twenty-Four

HEARING THE VOICE OF GOD IN WORSHIP

*We don't ever need to be afraid of the voice of God
unless we have already decided to disobey Him.*
Anonymous

✍

I t is not possible to have prophetic worship without hearing the
Voice of God. His voice is sweet, and—for those who have
taken time to know Him—it is easily heard. "My sheep hear
my voice, and I know them, and they follow me" (John 10:27).

God's voice must be obeyed (Ex. 19:5; 23:22; Deut. 13:4) especially in worship. Every prompting and whisper of the Lord in
worship leads us into the knowledge of God. His voice is able to
be heard through the gifts of the Spirit; the gentle, inward entreat-
ing of the Lord in our hearts; through a song; the sound of an
instrument; the distinct use of dance and all other art forms that
reveal His character; the preaching of the Word; the smile of a
child; the beauty all around us; the hug of a friend, and in so many
other ways.

It is not possible to have prophetic
worship without hearing
the Voice of God.

Hearing the voice of God through these many ways is part of
what we describe as *an encounter with God*. Prophetic worship is
dependent upon such an encounter, upon hearing and knowing His
voice. I wonder, on how many occasions does God desire to speak

to us, but our ears are deaf and our eyes dull to His prophetic presence?

> God often visits us, but most of the time we are not at home.[1] (Anon.)

One reason that we fail to hear God's voice is that we often do not recognize it. The following scriptures describe the variety of sounds that God's voice makes, from the sound of thunder and great rushing waters to a gentle whisper. His voice is described as being *powerful* and *full of majesty;* it is able to divide flames and defeat the enemy (the Assyrian). It is also interesting to note the context where His audible voice is heard by His people—such as the voice of God that came from the fire. As you read these scriptures, consider the volume and quality of God's voice:

> And they heard the sound [voice–KJV] of the LORD God walking in the garden . . . (Gen. 3:8)

> And when the blast of the trumpet sounded long and became louder and louder, Moses spoke, and God answered him by a voice [with thunder–NASV]. (Exod. 19:19)

> And the LORD spoke to you out of the midst of the fire. You heard the sound of the words, but saw no form; you only heard a voice. (Deut. 4:12)

> Deut. 5:22, 24–26 speak of the apparent possibility of a man being killed just by hearing God's voice.

> The LORD thundered from heaven, and the Most High uttered His voice [. . . the voice of the Most High resounded–NIV]. (2 Sam. 22:14)

> . . . and after the earthquake a fire, but the LORD was not in the fire; and after the fire a still small voice [gentle stillness–AMP; gentle blowing–NASV; gentle whisper–NIV]. (1 Kgs. 19:12)

> God thunders marvelously [wondrously– NASV] with his voice. . . (Job 37:5; see also Job 40:9; Ps. 18:13)

The voice of the LORD is over the waters; the God of glory thunders; the LORD is over many waters, the voice of the LORD is powerful; the voice of the LORD is full of majesty. The voice of the LORD breaks the cedars, yes, the LORD splinters the cedars of Lebanon. . . . The voice of the LORD divides the flames of fire [splits and flashes forth forked lightning–Amp.; hews out flames of fire–NASV; strikes with flashes of lightning–NIV]. The voice of the LORD shakes the wilderness [makes the wilderness tremble–Amp.; shakes the desert–NIV]; . . . The voice of the LORD makes the deer give birth, and strips the forests bare . . . (Ps. 29:3–9)

The LORD will cause His glorious voice [voice of authority –NASV; majestic voice–NIV] to be heard . . . For through the voice of the LORD Assyria will be beaten down [stricken with dismay and terror–Amp.; terrified–NASV; will shatter Assyria–NIV]. . . . (Isa. 30:30–31)

. . . The LORD will roar from on high, and utter His voice from His holy habitation [thunder from His holy dwelling–NIV]; He will roar mightily against His fold. He will give a shout, as those who tread the grapes . . . (Jer. 25:30) [The tumult will resound to the ends of the earth . . . –NIV (v. 31)]

. . . His voice was like the sound of many waters . . . [the roar of rushing waters–NIV]. (Ezek. 43:2)

The LORD also will roar [thunder–Amp.] from Zion, and utter His voice from Jerusalem; the heavens and earth will shake . . . (Joel 3:16; see also Amos 1:2)

For the Lord Himself will descend from heaven with a shout . . . [loud cry of summons– Amp.; loud command–NIV] (1 Ths. 4:16)

... I heard behind me a loud voice, as of a trumpet, [a great voice like the calling of a war trumpet–Amp.] saying, "I am the Alpha and Omega ... " (Rev. 1:10)

GOD'S VOICE IS HEARD IN MANY DIFFERENT WAYS

There are nearly one thousand references in Scripture referring to God speaking in some way to His people. I have listed some of the aspects of His audible voice above. It is clear from Scripture that God spoke often to His people and His prophets by way of an audible voice (for example, see: 1 Sam. 3:4, 6, 10; 1 Kgs. 8:15; Ezek. 37:3).

I have listed below some of the other ways that God speaks to us (only a few scriptures for each of these have been given, though a considerable number of additional examples can be found for many of these):

- Through angels—Gen. 31:11; Luke 1:19; Acts 8:26
- Through dreams—Gen. 31:11, 24; 1 Sam. 28:6
- Through visions—Gen. 46:2; Hab. 2:2; Acts 18:9
- Through a face to face encounter—Ex. 33:11
- Through the Urim—Num. 27:21; 1 Sam. 28:6
- Mouth to mouth—Num. 12:8
- Through a donkey—Num. 22:28
- Through His prophets—1 Sam. 9:9; 28:6; 2 Kgs. 3:11; 2 Kgs. 21:10; Matt. 1:22; 2:15; 3:3; 1 Cor. 14:3-5; Heb. 1:1; James 5:10
- Through the Spirit of the Lord—2 Sam. 23:2
- Out of a whirlwind—Job 38:1; Job 40:6
- Through the Word—Ps. 119:24; Jer. 30:2; 2 Tim. 2:15; 4:2; Heb. 4:12
- Through wise counsel—Prov. 1:5; 11:14; 19:21; Acts 20:27
- Through a heavenly voice—Jn. 12:28; Acts 10:13, 15
- Through tongues, interpretation, prophecy and other gifts of the Holy Spirit—Acts 2:11; 19:6; 1 Cor. 12:8; 14:3-5, 22-31
- Through preaching—Acts 4:29, 31; Rom. 16:25; Titus 1:3

- Through parables and mysteries—Mk. 4:33; Lk. 8:11; 1 Cor. 2:7
- Through creation—Rom. 1:20

Strangely enough, some Christians apparently live out their entire lives content with only the reports of what others have studied, heard and learned about the Lord over the centuries. Some believers seem to be satisfied with reading His written Word, and claim to never hear personally from the Lord. Surely it is impossible to read the Word of God and not hear His voice throughout!

In prophetic worship we depend upon the voice of God; we find that there is more and more to be found in Him. Paul calls us to behold the Lord and all His glory. The resulting transformation into the likeness and image of God is the reward and purpose of worship.

Traditionally, we have accepted God's voice and instructions from the past. The Word of God has been our basis for hearing the voice of God. In prophetic worship we must also learn to be open to the present voice of God as He is seen and heard among His people. What better place is there to receive His instructions for today and the future than in worship?

In prophetic worship we must learn to be open to the present voice of God as He is seen and heard among His people.

THE PROGRESSION OF THE VOICE OF GOD IN WORSHIP

Olen Griffing has described these different phases of communication with the Lord in Worship:[2]

- Man to Man
- Man to God
- God to Man
- Man to the world

Man to Man: The first phase in worship is a place of gathering. As we enter into the presence of God, we need to be in one accord. The worship leader should choose songs that gather the people and

unite their hearts. This gathering experience often takes place nat-
urally before the service begins. Time can be given for the congregation to fellowship with and greet one another. Some churches
make a place for such fellowship at the beginning of the service.

It might be noted that true worship will always unite a congregation in ways that nothing else can. Once we have experienced
His presence together, there comes a unity that time and interper-
sonal difficulties can scarcely mar.

Many churches include corporate prayer at the beginning of a
service. This does not necessarily detract from fellowship. We can
allow both to occur.

True worship will always unite a congregation in ways that nothing else can.

Man to God: The second phase is setting our attention upon the
Lord. It is here that our priestly ministry to the Lord begins. He
must always be the main focus of our worship, the central theme
of our songs and our chief goal.

We must never allow other things to tempt us to forsake this
focusing upon the Lord and ministering to Him. Otherwise we will
lose sight of the whole object of our worship. We need to arrest
ourselves when we find that we have turned the primary focus to
our needs and our desire to have the Lord bless us in worship. It is
true that the Lord will bless us and meet all our needs, but He must
always remain the principal focus of our praise and worship.

During this phase of the service there needs to be a sense of
ascension in our songs and communication with the Lord. Worship
leaders can compile their song list according to theme and key sig-
natures in such a way that we "lift" the congregation before the
throne of God. Lead the people to His face so that they can commune with Him. It is advisable here to include songs that involve
the people in ministering to the Lord.

The crucial point at this stage of the worship is to bring the congregation into a place of speaking or singing *to* God. Our responsibility is to minister to Him. Do not be too quick to move on. Stay
as long as the Holy Spirit holds you.

It is in this place of praise that the Lord comes to inhabit our
songs and "uncover," or show Himself to us (Ps. 22:3). It is impor-

tant for us to develop a healthy appetite for praise and thanksgiving. The Psalmist's cry, "For the LORD *is* great and greatly to be praised. . . " (1 Chron. 16:25) is repeated for a purpose (Pss. 48:1; 96:4; 145:3).

He is worthy of more than our perfunctory offerings of praise and worship. Our God is King of heaven and earth. He is worthy of our most extravagant and excellent praises.

God to Man: This leads into the third phase of worship where we wait upon the Lord for His response and His voice. Most of us have more difficulty with this place in worship than any other, as it takes a prophetic and listening heart to hear His voice, and the death of self to truly enter in.

Sadly, I would have to conclude that there are few churches today that make room for the voice of God in their services. Many no longer believe that God speaks today in the church setting. Still others lack sufficient maturity to be able to recognize or minister His voice in the prophetic context.

I am sure that many Christians would be absolutely shocked if God showed up in any way in their services. God would upset many an "apple cart" if He spoke in some churches. I am convinced that, though many Christians may like *the idea* of "God," they do not really feel comfortable with Him hanging around in person, since He is so systematically programmed out of most church services.

> The Lord must always be the main focus
> of our worship—the central theme of
> our songs and our chief goal.

We must believe that the Lord manifests Himself to His people. It is this manifest presence of the Lord that sets us apart from all the other religions on earth. Our God is real and present with us at all times, and He "shows" us His face in our midst.

> Man's spirit and God's Spirit are never more uniquely
> blended than when we are in worship. . . for worship is
> a love experience which, for one moment, blends two
> as though they are one.[3] (Judson Cornwall)

The children of Israel were invited to commune with the Lord as priests, and they eagerly accepted this honorable national office (Ex. 19:5–9). But it was at the very moment when God spoke to His people and displayed His awesome presence that they ran from Him and asked Moses to speak for Him instead.

They were not prepared to pay the price that was required of all who would desire to speak face to face with a holy God. Speaking with Him meant that they would die. Then they said to Moses, "You speak with us, and we will hear; but let not God speak with us lest we die" (Ex. 20:18–19).

Unfortunately, many of us are still running from God today. We say to our pastors, "You pay the price to go and talk with God, then come and tell us what He says and we will listen to you. But don't let God speak with us or we will die."

We must believe that the Lord manifests Himself to His people. It is this manifest presence of the Lord that sets us apart from all the other religions on earth.

Every believer has been invited to commune with God as a priest, but the price remains the same—death. The death to self we experience is not the death of this world, but is the price for intimate fellowship.

Because of God's grace we are invited to boldly draw near to Him (Heb. 4:16) with the understanding that He has a plan and purpose for every encounter with His people. Only those who have taken time to know Him will recognize His voice in the midst of all that assaults our ears in these days.

The flow of this conversation with the Lord should have a theme and definite subject. We must allow the Lord to impart knowledge of Himself and His thoughts concerning our personal lives. He has so much to say, but we have crowded out His voice in our worship. Consider carefully what He is saying and be cautious in the meeting place of God with His people.

As with any conversation, we must be very careful not to interrupt Him with our well-intentioned, but often unsuitable words. When we worship there is communion between God and His people. His thoughts and ways become ours. He uncovers Himself and His likeness is formed within us.

It is during, and following this time of worship, that we are most likely to see the gifts of the Spirit flowing in the service. Many times, the Lord will use the atmosphere of worship to speak to His people through the nine gifts.

Many congregations skip this phase of communion with the Lord altogether, or they dominate the conversation with prayers of petition and statements concerning their own needs. I encourage you to take the time, here, to wait upon the Lord and tune your ear to the sound of His voice.

> If you would have God hear you when you pray, you must hear Him when He speaks.[4] (Brooks)

Man to the world: In the fourth phase of worship, we go from communion with the Lord to becoming living witnesses of His excellence. In the book of Acts, the boldness of Christians who had been face to face with the Lord caused unbelievers to recognize Christ in them (Acts 4:13).

Worship is not intended to keep us away from the world, but to propel us into becoming dynamic examples of the holiness, power, grace, and love of God. Worship was never intended to become a separate experience from the wider community of fellow human beings. Whatever God shows us of Himself must now be modeled in our lives.

Worship takes us out from the walls of
our churches as more able ministers of
God's glory.

Prophetic worship is not for the few who come to our services, but it signals a time of blessing for all the earth. When we commune with the Lord, we gain His heart for the lost, His love for the nations, and His perspective for every situation. Worship takes us out from the walls of our churches as more able ministers of God's glory.

Hopefully, a new day of supernatural evangelism awaits the world as the Church learns how to enter the most supernatural and life-changing encounter known to man: "prophetic worship."

> I look upon the world as my parish.[5] (John Wesley)

TUNE YOUR EAR TO THE VOICE OF GOD

We live in an age of media. There are so many words and opinions coming at us from so many different sources. Let us still our hearts and tune our ears to the voice of God. Allow Him to break in upon your news, TV, radio, movies, e-mail, cyberspace, newspapers, magazines and advertising billboards and fill your life with His voice and perspective.

The voice of the Lord, powerful and full of majesty, is able to break the cedars, divide the flames of fire, shake the wilderness and cause the deer to give birth (Ps. 29). Surely, if we would allow His voice to be heard in our churches, we would see the evidence of his transforming power on a regular basis. I adjure you to let the mighty voice of the Lord be heard in your worship. ✍

Chapter Twenty-Five

THE CONCLUSION OF THE MATTER

Christian worship is the most momentous,
the most urgent, the most glorious action that can
take place in human life.
Karl Barth

≈

I f the things I have said here about prophetic worship are true and theologically correct, then they must be able to stand up under the test of all denominations, generations, people groups, and personalities.

In other words what I have said must be applicable to any church. It must be able to work within the framework of any liturgy or service that is Bible-based. It must be simple enough for children to participate in, and profound enough for the seeker to run after forever. It must be able to apply within any culture that is willing to submit to Christ, and no individual should feel excluded because of his or her personality.

In order for prophetic worship to flow in every church and in the lives of all believers, every one of us needs to be willing and brave enough to face God in the most honest way, at the deepest level. When He reveals Himself to us, we *will* be shaken to the core—we will be ruined for ordinary things forever. Self will be forced out of our hearts again and again, and will suffer a glorious death.

God's kingdom and the concept of relationship with Him must surely make sense to all mankind at some deep level of our being, since His foremost priority in creating us was to enjoy intimacy with us in worship. Ernest Gentile puts it this way:

Every religion finds its highest expression in worship.[1]

When He reveals Himself to us, we will be shaken to the core—we will be ruined for ordinary things forever.

The main question is: do we make sense to Him? Are there areas of our belief systems and lifestyles that must change in order to welcome His manifest and prophetic presence?

We will never be able to fully grasp the extent of God's desire for us. Since the creation of man, the Lord has been forming, wooing, and waiting for His people to delight in His presence and have intimate fellowship with Him. The passionate song He sings over us must resound to every corner of our hearts until we are conquered by love and devoted to His Kingdom forever:

My dove in the clefts of the rock, in the hiding places on the mountainside, show me your face, let me hear your voice; for your voice is sweet, and your face is lovely. (Song 2:14, NIV)

I will betroth you to Me forever; yes, I will betroth you to Me in righteousness and justice, in lovingkindness and mercy; I will betroth you to Me in faithfulness, and you shall know the LORD. (Hosea 2:19–20)

May each of us respond to Him with renewed vision for prophetic worship, which is the only way to know Him in extravagant intimacy.

IS IT TIME TO MAKE CHANGES?

For many, the entrance into prophetic worship will involve great changes in the way they have approached the Lord and related to Him in the past. Change is very difficult and unsettling for every one of us. It is always much easier to maintain the status quo.

I entreat the Church: *Regardless of your denomination or tradition, will you prayerfully consider making gentle and appropriate changes to your worship based on the principles outlined in the previous chapters?*

Even though change is difficult, we must press through. Those in opposition may be strong and quite persuasive—men have programmed God out of their lives and religious services since the beginning of time.

Let God have His way with you. He desires to break in upon us, fill our hungry hearts with His presence and transform us by His glory.

Several writers remind us of the difficulty we all endure when faced with change:

> People can cry much easier than they can change.[2]
> (James Baldwin)

> When you're through changing, you're through.[3]
> (Bruce Barton)

> It is hard to be told that one is not worshipping properly. Nobody likes to hear that; however, the Spirit of God wants to adjust us so that He can break into our churches in all His fullness.[4] (Ernest Gentile)

THE LORD CALLS US TO INTIMATE WORSHIP

We also need to give time to the place of private devotion. Richard Foster speaks of "the sanctuary of the heart," meaning that a place of inner devotion must be set aside for personal and intimate communion with the Lord. Our corporate expressions of worship are an extension of private worship. If any congregation has ardent and faithful worshipers in attendance, their corporate worship will have a greater chance of being vital and prophetic.

I believe that the worship I have described in this book is Biblical and ultimately fulfilling for every man, woman, and child regardless of denomination and culture. Such worship must be born out of a deep reverence and fear of God and a respect for the traditions and integrity of every Church and nation. In the final analysis, the Psalmist asks a most pertinent question:

Who may ascend into the hill of the LORD? Or who may stand in his holy place? He who has clean hands and a pure heart, who has not lifted up his soul to an idol. (Ps. 24:3–4)

In the end it all comes down to the purity of our love, passion and devotion to Christ, our Lord and King. Our worship of Him is induced by His passion for us.

In the Song of Solomon, the Bride pleads with her Lord that He wear her on His heart and hand as a sign of His devotion to her. The love between Christ and His Church is a holy love which is described here as a fire:

Wear me as a seal close to your heart, wear me like a ring upon your hand; Love burns like a blazing fire; a most vehement flame (Song of Solomon 8:6, compilation of various translations)

Songwriter Mimi Ribble has written a song which expresses my final prayer for the Church in these days—that we allow the flame of our devotion to be exposed to the winds of the Holy Spirit, grow within our hearts, and draw us to new depths in worship:

KEEPER OF THE FLAME

Keeper of the flame,
the flame within my heart.
The flame of my desire to know You
and worship You more.
Blow upon the embers,
let the flame grow brighter
'til all I do honors You,
O Keeper of the Flame.[5]

The New Testament responds to this cry: "Let us therefore come boldly to the throne of grace . . ." (Heb. 4:16a).

Teach men how to seek God—When they encounter Him, they will worship.[6] (Anon.)

All has been heard.
The end of the matter is,
Fear God—know that He is,

revere and worship
Him—and keep His
commandments;
for this is the whole of man
[the full original purpose of His creation,
the object of God's providence,
the root of character,
the foundation of all happiness,
the adjustment to all inharmonious circumstances
and conditions under the sun],
and the whole duty for every man.
(Eccl.12:13, Amp.)

THE LAST MOVEMENT

Bonnie Wilks[7]

Skilled hands that sculpt and paint
rest in quiet stillness
light dancing feet repose
patiently poised
strings and gleaming brass
woods and drums mute
arrested without sound
worshippers anticipating
the last queue
waiting in silver silence
holy silence
to worship Earth's last Movement
We linger in sacred communion
holy tryst of Groom and bride
attentive with constant
dove's eyes and hearts
enraptured by the
Movements of our great Conductor

Our clay hearts long to pour out gold
our clay hearts burst with treasure
to lavish each illumined gift
redemption's perfect offering
upon our gentle Lamb conquering Warrior
the great Conductor

All of life's Movements of worship
through ages of history have brought
those who worship to this
unfolding mystery
great end-time finale of worship

Dazzled in a prism of crystal silence
we wait we weep we strain
to perceive
the theme of the last Movement

we'll offer
before the King returns triumphant

Oh we've lifted the songs of harvest
and we've danced the Lamb's and King's
melodies
the Bride's songs about golden streets
how we've marched as onward battling
soldiers
and painted great classics
we have written poetry's praises
and poured our laud
in majestic strains and wonderment
upon our King
in purple in red in gold
we've woven Earth and Heaven together
in celestial tapestries of worship
we've sung His anthems aloud
melded His mysteries in hushed
and holy stained-glass whispers

We've trekked the land and crossed the sea
beautiful feet published
the Good News now
every tongue and tribe as one
yields to worship the last Movement

Now as we wait
our hearts beat wildly
our breath expires in short pants
to extol with ribboned banners
colors trailing tambourines
sounds and voices and horns
flutes and drums
silken dancers spinning
chiseled marbled forms
and pens with parchment paper
we want to move the Movement
to express
to honor Him through

this last Movement
for all that we are in Him
for all that He is in us

How we shine the prophets' promises
the Bridegroom's glory spotless
as a sparkling bride prepared
white linen dipped in blood

In unison at last
the silence consumed like our flesh
by daily death
we worship the last Movement
as silver purified
as one clear sound
with strings and toes and pens
and hearts and voices and minstrels
we worship in great global throng
resounding the last pure Movement

Over and over we
extol the message
that one old song etched
with blood upon our hearts

The old story
Love's sweet suffering
Sacrifice's bleeding
and Resurrection's light
of tribes and nations
gathered to say
thank you
to gaze upon Jesus' face
touch His pierced hands and feet
lean into His scarred side

That old, old story
will ring out
the theme of Earth's
last Movement

and through eternal ages
we'll offer our worship
the joy of that same story
only sweeter than the time before

As worshippers of every nation
we'll never tire of
that old old story
the one etched in blood upon our hearts
Earth's last Movement of worship
and Heaven's only song.

NOTES

CHAPTER 1

1. Tom Schwanda, *The Complete Library of Christian Worship*, Volume Two, p. 401.
2. Judson Cornwall, *Meeting God*, p. 154.
3. Ralph W. Neighour, Jr., *The Worship of God*, p. 10.
4. John W. Stevenson, *The 2nd Flood—The Discipline of Worship*, p. 22.
5. Bob Sorge, *Exploring Worship*. p. 126.
6. Ibid., p. 125.
7. Ibid., p. 125.
8. Ibid., p. 142.
9. Ronald F. Youngblood, General Editor, *Nelson's New Illustrated Dictionary*, p. 1033.
10. Robert Morris—Elder/Pastor at Shady Grove Church, Grand Prairie, Texas. These notes on the five types of prophecy are taken from Pastor Morris' teaching on prophecy and are not necessarily direct quotes.
11. Robert E. Webber, *The Complete Library of Christian Worship*. Volume Two, p. 346.
12. A. W. Tozer, *The Pursuit of God*, p. 36.
13. Ibid., p. 33.
14. Ibid., pp. 34–35.
15. William Nicholls, *Jacob's Ladder: The Meaning of Worship* (Richmond: John Knox Press, 1958), p. 9. Quoted in: Ralph W. Neighour, Jr, *The Worship of God*, p. 209.
16. David Peterson, *Engaging With God—A Biblical Theology of Worship*, pp. 17–18.

CHAPTER 2

1. Tom Schwanda, *The Complete Library of Christian Worship*, Vol. Two, p. 402.
2. Michael Coleman, President, Integrity Incorporated. Jacket notes from CD, *Because We Believe*, ©1997, Hosanna! Music.
3. Paul Sarchet-Waller, *Praise and Worship*, p. 15.
4. Ralph P. Martin, *The Worship of God*, p. 6.
5. Ibid., p. 20.
6. *Life Application Bible*, notes on 1 Chron. 16:25, p 696. *Life Application Bible. New King James Version*, 1993, Tyndale House Publishers, Wheaton, IL.
7. Random House, *Webster's Dictionary*. p. 762.
8. *The Oxford English Dictionary*, Vol. 12, V–Z, Oxford: Clarendon Press, 1933, pp. 320–321.
9. Judson Cornwall, *Elements Of Worship*, p. 1.
10. Sally Morgenthaler, *Worship Evangelism*, p. 48.
11. Ralph P. Martin, *The Worship of God*, p. 29.
12. Sammy Tippit, *Worthy of Worship*, p. 13.
13. David Peterson, *Engaging With God—A Biblical Theology of Worship*, p. 70.
14. Sally Morgenthaler, *Worship Evangelism*, p. 46.
15. Gerrit Gustafson, *The Complete Library of Christian Worship*, Vol. Two, p. 311.
16. Sammy Tippit, *Worthy of Worship*, p. 97–98.
17. Ernest Gentile, *Worship God*, p. 240.
18. Paul Sarchet-Waller, *Praise and Worship*, p. 8.
19. Bob Sorge, *Exploring Worship*, p. 1.
20. Terry Law, *The Power of Praise and Worship*, p. 121.
21. David Peterson, *Engaging With God—A Biblical Theology of Worship*, p. 26.
22. Gerhard Tersteegen.
23. Judson Cornwall, *Elements of Worship*, p. 45.
24. Ibid., p. 47.
25. LaMar Boschman, *A Heart of Worship*, p. 25.
26. On pages 124–132, I give examples from Scripture of many who have received a revelation of the Lord.
27. Judson Cornwall, *Meeting God*, p. 15.

CHAPTER 3

1. J. Daane, *The International Standard Bible Encyclopedia*, Vol. Four, pp. 826–827.
2. Robert E. Webber, *The Complete Library of Christian Worship*, Vol.Two, p. 291.
3. G. Thomas Halbrooks, *The Complete Library of Christian Worship*, Vol. Two, p. 293.
4. Henry Jauhianinen, *The Complete Library of Christian Worship*, Vol. Two, p. 338.
5. LaMar Boschman, *A Heart of Worship*, p. 52.
6. Sally Morgenthaler, *Worship Evangelism*, p. 49.
7. Henry Jauhianinen, *The Complete Library of Christian Worship*, Vol.Two, p. 337.
8. Richard Foster, *Celebration of Discipline*, pp. 158–159.
9. Kevin Conner, *The Tabernacle of David*, p. 103.
10. This paragraph is based on the author's notes of a sermon preached by Pastor Olen Griffing entitled, "The Praise Life of Jesus."
11. Richard Foster, *Celebration of Discipline*, p. 170.
12. Mark Horst, *The Complete Library of Christian Worship*. Vol. Two, p. 297.
13. In his book, *Celebration of Discipline*, p. 158, Richard Foster explains the term "Shekinah" as follows: "'Shekinah' means the glory or the radiance of God dwelling in the midst of His people. It denotes the immediate Presence of God as opposed to a God who is abstract or aloof."
14. Richard Foster, *Celebration of Discipline*, p. 158.
15. Thomas Carlyle
16. Charles H. Spurgeon, *Evening by Evening*, p. 28.
17. Ibid., p. 29.
18. Henry Jauhianinen, *The Complete Library of Christian Worship*, Vol. Two, p. 338.
19. Gerrit Gustafson, *The Complete Library of Christian Worship*, Vol. Two, pp. 310–312.
20. Gregory Wilde, *The Complete Library of Christian Worship*, Vol. Two, p. 276
21. G. W. Bromiley, *The International Standard Bible Encyclopedia*, Vol. Three, p. 596.

22. A. W. Tozer, *The Pursuit of God*, p. 58.
23. Judson Cornwall, *Meeting God*, p. 149.
24. From the Greek word, *epiklesis*, the "calling down" of the Holy Spirit during the eucharistic prayer to make Christ present in the Eucharist—in the elements of bread and wine and in the gathered community of worshipers.
25. Gregory Wilde, *The Complete Library of Christian Worship*, Vol. Two, p. 278.

CHAPTER 4

1. Andrew Wilson-Dickson, *The Story of Christian Music*, p. 11.
2. David Peterson, *Engaging With God—A Biblical Theology of Worship*, p. 56.
3. Ernest B. Gentile, *Worship God*, p. 241.
4. Terry Law, *The Power of Praise and Worship*, p. 135.
5. Ernest Gentile, *Worship God*, p. 243.
6. Ernest Gentile, *Worship God*, p. 242.
7. Ronald B. Allen, *Lord of Song*, p. 150
8. Andrew Hill, *Enter His Courts With Praise!*, p.6
9. Carroll E. Simcox
10. Francis J. Hall
11. Richard C. Leonard, *The Complete Library of Christian Worship*, Volume One, p.21

SECTION 2 INTRODUCTION

1. Herbert Lockyer, *All the 3s of the Bible*, p. 20.
2. Ibid., p. 25.

CHAPTER 5

1. Michael Marshall, *The Complete Library of Christian Worship*, Volume Two, p. 375.
2. Robert E. Webber, *The Complete Library of Christian Worship*, Volume Two, p. 374.
3. Graham Kendrick, *Worship*, pp. 183–184.

CHAPTER 6

1. Charles H. Spurgeon, *Evening by Evening*, p. 54.
2. A. W. Tozer, *The Pursuit of God*, p. 41.
3. These three points originated in a sermon preached by Olen Griffing, Senior Pastor of Shady Grove Church in Grand Prairie, Texas.
4. *The Abingdon Bible Commentary*, p. 1197.

CHAPTER 7

1. Charles H. Spurgeon, *Evening by Evening*, p. 12.
2. Judson Cornwall, *Elements of Worship*, p. 45.
3. Herbert Lockyer, *All the 3s of the Bible*, p. 51f.
4. W. E. Vine, *An Expository Dictionary of New Testament Words*, pp. 64–65. Each of the definitions for the Greek words in this row come from Vine's dictionary.
5. F. W. Danker, *The International Standard Bible Encyclopedia*, (Eerdmans), Volume Three, p. 382.
6. Adam Clarke, *The New Testament of our Lord and Saviour Jesus Christ*, pp. 326–327.
7. Sammy Tippit, *Worthy of Worship*, pp. 69–70.
8. Charles Spurgeon, *Evening By Evening*, p. 241.
9. Dr. David Blomgren, *Restoring Praise and Worship to the Church — An Anthology of Articles*, p. 129–130. This article is entitled, "The Prophetic Spirit in Worship."
10. In 1997 Gary Thomas painted a selected wall of the Assembly of God Church in Manteca, California. Gary regularly paints during worship services at the annual International Worship Symposium in Pasadena, California.

CHAPTER 8

1. Judson Cornwall, *Meeting God*, p. 155.
2. E. F. Harrison, *The International Standard Bible Encyclopedia*, Vol. Two, p. 479.
3. Adam Clarke, *The New Testament of our Lord and Saviour Jesus Christ*, p. 326.

4. Richard C. Leonard, *The Complete Library of Christian Worship*, Volume One, p. 72.
5. Charles H. Spurgeon, *The Treasury of David*, Volume One, pp. 318–319.
6. I heard this through the teaching of Charlotte Baker. She insists, however, that Paul Wilbur (formerly from Israel's Hope) told her this truth.
7. Merrill F. Unger, *Unger's Bible Dictionary*, p. 409.
8. Charles H. Spurgeon, *Evening By Evening*, p. 237.
9. LaMar Boschman, *Pathways*—LaMar Boschman Ministries newsletter, June 1998, Vol. One, Number One.
10. Robert E. Webber, *The Complete Library of Christian Worship*, Volume Two, p. 373.
11. Richard Foster, *Celebration of Discipline*, p. 160.
12. Ibid., p. 158.
13. Richard C. Leonard, *The Complete Library of Christian Worship*, Volume One, p. 71.
14. C. H. Spurgeon, *The Treasury of David*, Volume One, p. 160.

CHAPTER 9

1. John Dryden, source unknown
2. Sally Morgenthaler, *Worship Evangelism*, p. 47.
3. George MacDonald.
4. John W. Stevenson, *The 2nd Flood—The Discipline of Worship*, p. 46.
5. Richard Foster, *Celebration of Discipline*, p. 173.
6. W.E Vine, Merrill F. Unger, William White, Jr., *Vine's Complete Expository Dictionary of Old and New Testament Words*, p. 639.
7. Random House Webster's Dictionary, p. 415.
8. William Morris—Editor in Chief, *Young Students Intermediate Dictionary*, p. 455.
9. John Milton
10. Richard Foster, *Celebration of Discipline*, p. 173.
11. A. W. Tozer, *The Pursuit of God*, p. 94.
12. *The Jerome Biblical Commentary*, p. 279.
13. Richard Foster, *Celebration of Discipline*, p. 173.
14. A. W. Tozer, *The Pursuit of God*, p. 36.

15. Terry Law, *The power of Praise and Worship*, p. 136.

CHAPTER 10

1. St. John of Damascus lived during the years of c. 700–c. 760. This was the most frequently quoted definition of God used during the Middle Ages.
2. Bernard of Clairvaux 1090-1153.
3. Alan W. Watts.
4. Eugene H. Peterson, *The Message*, p. 423.
5. Ralph P. Martin, *The Worship of God*, p. 210. The information from this chart was first taken from the writing of Stephen S. Smalley—"The Christ-Christian Relationship in Paul and John," in *Pauline Studies*. (Grand Rapids: Wm. B. Eerdmans; Exeter: Paternoster Press, 1980), pp. 95–105 (p. 98).
6. A. W. Tozer, *The Pursuit of God*, p. 14.
7. Eugene H. Peterson, *The Message*, p. 373.
8. Judson Cornwall, *Let Us Worship*, p. 137.

CHAPTER 11

1. Judson Cornwall, *Let Us Worship*, p. 96.
2. A. W. Tozer, *The Pursuit of God*, p. 17.
3. Richard Foster, *Celebration of Discipline*, p. 158.
4. Adam Clarke, *The New Testament of our Lord and Saviour Jesus Christ*, p. 326.
5. Madame Guyon, *Experiencing the Depths of Jesus Christ*, p. 96–97.
6. E. F. Harrison, *The International Standard Bible Encyclopedia*, Vol. Two, p. 481.
7. Matthew Henry, *The Bethany Parallel Commentary on the Old Testament*, p. 1828.
8. Sammy Tippit, *Worthy of Worship*, p. 9.
9. Words and music by Paul Baloche, © 1997 Integrity's Hosanna! Music/ASCAP.
10. Robert E. Webber, *The Complete Library of Christian Worship*, Volume Two, p. 343.

CHAPTER 12

1. Jack Hayford, *Worship His Majesty,* p. 24.
2. Sammy Tippit, *Worthy of Worship,* p. 64.
3. Jaroslav Pelikan.
4. Matsuo Basho.
5. Ambrose Bierce, *The Devil's Dictionary.*
6. Andrew Hill, *Enter His Courts With Praise!* p. 52. The first sentence of this quote comes from C. D. Erickson, *Participating in Worship: History, Theory and Practice.* Richmond, VA: Westminster/John Knox, 1988, p. 16.
7. Paul Waitman Hoon, *The Complete Library of Christian Worship,* Volume Two, p. 403.

CHAPTER 13

1. Sammy Tippit, *Worthy of Worship,* p. 43.
2. Matthew Henry, *The Bethany Parallel Commentary on the New Testament,* p. 526.
3. Ibid., p. 526.
4. Ibid.
5. Adam Clarke, *The Bethany Parallel Commentary on the New Testament,* p. 526.
6. A. W. Tozer, *The Pursuit of God,* p. 33.
7. Richard Foster, *Celebration of Discipline,* p. 165.
8. LaMar Boschman, *A Heart of Worship,* p. 26.
9. Richard Foster, *Celebration of Discipline,* p. 158–159.
10. Ronald Allen and Gordon Borror, *Worship—Rediscovering the Missing Jewel,* p. 39.
11. Judson Cornwall, *Elements of Worship,* p. 45.
12. Matthew Henry, *The Bethany Parallel Commentary on the New Testament,* p. 526.
13. Graham Kendrick, *Worship,* p. 18.

CHAPTER 14

1. Richard Foster, *Celebration of Discipline,* p. 165.
2. Ronald Allen and Gordon Borror, *Worship—Rediscovering the Missing Jewel,* p. 42.
3. Sally Morgenthaler, *Worship Evangelism,* p. 67.

CHAPTER 15

1. Tom Schwanda, *The Complete Library of Christian Worship,* Volume Two, p. 401.
2. Robert Webber, quoted in: *Worship Evangelism,* by Sally Morgenthaler, p. 49, from Robert Webber, *Worship is a Verb,* Waco: Word, 1985. p. 12.
3. Robert Webber, *Worship Old and New,* p.127–128.
4. Tom Schwanda, *The Complete Library of Christian Worship,* Volume Two, p. 400.
5. Ralph P. Martin, *The Worship of God,* p. 228.
6. Jack Hayford, *Worship His Majesty,* p. 89.
7. Sammy Tippit, *Worthy of Worship,* p. 96—97.
8. Judson Cornwall, *Elements of Worship,* p. 109.
9. Andrew E. Hill, *Enter His Courts With Praise!* p. 110.
10. Tenney was speaking at a workshop on Friday May 8th, entitled *Touching the Face of God: Changing the Face of Your City.*

CHAPTER 16

1. Anonymous quote by an Employment Counselor.
2. W. E. Vine, Merrill F. Unger, William White, Jr., *Vine's Complete Expository Dictionary of Old and New Testament Words,* pp. 542–543.
3. Andrew E. Hill, *Enter His Courts With Praise!* p. 106.
4. A. W. Tozer, quoted in *Worthy of Worship,* by Sammy Tippit, p. 18.
5. A. W. Tozer. quoted in *Who said that?* p. 459, by George Sweeting. Taken from Tozer's pamphlet: *Worship: The Missing Jewel of Evangelism.*
6. Ladislaus Boros
7. Hubert Van Zeller
8. Andrew E. Hill, *Enter His Courts With Praise!* p. 102.
9. Charlotte Baker—speaking at the Shady Grove Church Worship Conference in 1997.
10. Andrew Hill, *Enter His Courts With Praise!* p. 103.
11. Ibid., p. 96.

CHAPTER 17

1. Edgar Watson Howe.
2. Robert Webber, *The Complete Library of Christian Worship*, Volume Two, p. 344.
3. Notes on worship by Dr. Sam Sasser.
4. Bob Sorge, *Restoring Praise and Worship to the Church—An Anthology of Articles*, p. 35. This article is entitled, *The Full Purpose of Worship.*
5. Ronald B. Allen, *Lord of Song*, p. 151.

CHAPTER 18

1. A. W. Tozer, *The Pursuit of God*, p.35.
2. Sally Morgenthaler, *Worship Evangelism*, p. 17.
3. Ibid., p. 36.
4. Henry Jauhianinen, *The Complete Library of Christian Worship*, Volume Two, pp. 337–338.
5. Judson Cornwall, *Let Us Worship*, p. 116.
6. Judson Cornwall, *Elements of Worship*, p. 47.
7. Ronald Allen and Gordon Borror, *Worship— Rediscovering the Missing Jewel*, p. 75.
8. Ernest Gentile, *Restoring Praise and Worship to the Church—An Anthology of Articles*, p. 21. This article is entitled, *Worship—Are We Making Any Mistakes?*
9. Robert E. Webber, *The Complete Library of Christian Worship*, Volume Two, pp. 344–345.
10. Ibid., p. 347.
11. Richard Foster, *Celebration of Discipline*, p. 169.
12. Paul Sarchet-Waller, *Praise and Worship*, p. 68.
13. LaMar Boschman, *A Heart of Worship*, p. 55.
14. Ralph P. Martin, *The Worship of God*, p. 216.
15. Graham Kendrick, *Worship*, p. 17–18.
16. Terry Howard Wardle, *The Complete Library of Christian Worship*, Volume Two, p. 405.
17. Paul Hanson, *The Complete Library of Christian Worship*, Volume Two, p. 361.
18. Sally Morgenthaler, *Worship Evangelism*, p. 50.

CHAPTER 19

1. Tom Schwanda, *The Complete Library of Christian Worship*, Volume Two, p. 399.
2. Gerrit Gustafson, *The Complete Library of Christian Worship*, Volume Four, Book One, p. 181.
3. Ibid., p. 183.
4. Kent Henry, *The Complete Library of Christian Worship*, Volume Two, p. 351.
5. Judson Cornwall, *Elements of Worship*, p. 108.
6. John Haggai, quoted in *Who Said That?*, George Sweeting, p. 325.
7. James Strong *Strong's Exhaustive Concordance*, (Appendix: Dictionary of the Hebrew Bible) p. 107.
8. Sosene Le'au offers an interesting and helpful list of the strengths of various people groups in his 1997 book, *Called to Honor Him*, p. 97–99.
9. I attended a Promise keepers Worship Summit in Denver, Colorado in March 11–12, 1997 with Dr. Roberta King, Dr. Appianda Arthur, Sosene Le'au and other ministers in the area of worship, where they gave a report on their work in several nations.
10. Sosene Le'au, *Called to Honor Him*, p. 29–30.
11. This thought was originally put to me by Rebecca Walden, my assistant. We have had many delightful hours of discussion on this matter.
12. See pp. 122–124 for an explanation of the numinous aspect of God's presence.
13. Kent Henry, *The Complete Library of Christian Worship*, Volume Two, p. 352.
14. Dutch Sheets, *Intercessory Prayer*, p. 116.
15. Ernest B. Gentile, *Worship God*, p. 24.
16. Oswald Chambers, quoted in *Who Said That?*, George Sweeting, p. 325.
17. Henry Martyn, quoted in *Who Said That?*, George Sweeting, p. 325.
18. Anton E. Armstrong, *The Complete Library of Christian Worship*, Volume Four, Book One, p. 180-181.
19. See pp 67–71.
20. Kent Henry, *The Complete Library of Christian Worship*,

Volume Two, p. 351.

21. Robert E. Webber, *The Complete Library of Christian Worship,* Volume Two, p. 399.

22. Sally Morgenthaler, *Worship Evangelism* , p. 39.

23. Ibid., p. 41.

24. Tom Schwanda, *The Complete Library of Christian Worship,* Volume Two, p. 402.

25. John Wesley—source unknown

26. LaMar Boschman, *A Heart of Worship,* p. 31.

CHAPTER 20

1. André Gide.

2. Paul Waitman Hoon, *The Complete Library of Christian Worship,* Volume Two, p. 402.

3. Michelangelo, quoted in *The Great Masters,* Vasarai, Giorgio, p.301–302.

4. Ronald Allen and Gordon Borror, *Worship—Rediscovering the Missing Jewel,* p. 22.

5. Paul Waitman Hoon, *The Complete Library of Christian Worship,* Volume Two, p. 402.

6. Andrew Wilson-Dickson, *The Story of Christian Music,* p. 11.

7. Vincent Van Gogh in c. 1880, quoted in Uhde, *Vincent Van Gogh,* 1947.

8. Robert Browning, *Paracelsus,* 1835.

9. John S. Baldwin.

10. Thomas Browne.

11. Michelangelo Buonarroti, quoted in *Holland De Pintura Antigua,* (16th C).

12. Andrew Wilson-Dickson, *The Story of Christian Music,* p. 12.

13. Ibid., p. 12. Quoting from T.S. Eliot, *The Literary essays of Ezra Pound,* London,1960, pages 43 and 45.

14. Sammy Tippit, *Worthy of Worship,* p. 96.

15. Giorgio Vasari, *The Great Masters,* p. 235–236.

16. Dr. David Holsinger's music is published by TRN Music, P.O. Box 1076 Ruidoso, NM 88345. At the time of this writing, Holsinger has six volumes of his symphonic wind music recorded by Mark Custom Recording,

Clarence, NY, including (to my utter delight) a short piece entitled *A Jolly Walk in Hibbertland,* a "national anthem" in honor of my husband and myself. Thank you, David!

17. Robert Webber, *The Complete Library of Christian Worship,* Volume Two, p. 348.

CHAPTER 21

1. Source unknown.
2. Graham Kendrick, *Worship,* p. 174.
3. Heraclitus, quoted in: *Who Said That?,* George Sweeting, p. 79.
4. Norm Frederick, Elder/Pastor at Shady Grove Church, Grand Prairie, Texas, Feb. 24, 1998.
5. Paul McCartney speaking to Oprah Winfrey—*Oprah Winfrey Show,* December 19, 1997.

CHAPTER 22

1. Words and music by David Ruis, © 1994 Mercy/Vineyard Publishing.
2. Terry Howard Wardle, *The Complete Library of Christian Worship,* Volume Two, p. 405.
3. Calvin Coolidge, quoted in: *12,000 Religious Quotations,* p. 479.
4. Terry Howard Wardle, *The Complete Library of Christian Worship,* Volume Two, p. 406.
5. LaMar Boschman, *A Heart of Worship,* p. 18.
6. Dutch Sheets, *Intercessory Prayer,* p. 143.

CHAPTER 23

1. Richard Foster, *Celebration of Discipline,* p. 171.
2. Graham Kendrick, *Worship,* p. 44–45.
3. Judson Cornwall, *Elements of Worship,* p. 111.
4. LaMar Boschman, *A Heart of Worship,* p. 164.
5. Richard Foster, *Celebration of Discipline,* p. 163.
6. A. W. Tozer, *The Pursuit of God,* p. 87-88.
7. Eugene Carson Blake

CHAPTER 24

1. Anonymous.
2. Pastor of Shady Grove Church in Grand Prairie, Texas. These four phases were first spoken of by Ralph W. Neighbour, Jr. in relationship to cell ministry. Pastor Griffing applies them to worship.
3. Judson Cornwall, *Elements of Worship*, p. 119.
4. Thomas Benton Brooks.
5. John Wesley, *Journal*—June 11, 1739.

CHAPTER 25

1. Ernest Gentile, *Worship God*, p. 22.
2. James Baldwin, quoted in: *Who Said That?*, George Sweeting, p. 79.
3. Bruce Barton, quoted in: *Who Said That?*, George Sweeting, p. 80.
4. Ernest Gentile, *Restoring Praise and Worship to the Church—An Anthology of Articles*, p. 20–21. This article is entitled, *Worship—Are We Making Any Mistakes?*
5. Words and Music by Mimi Ribble, © 1991 Mastersong Music.
6. Anonymous.
7. Bonnie Wilks and her husband, Wayne, are the directors of the Messianic Jewish Bible Institute in the Ukraine as well as being elders at Shady Grove Church in Grand Prairie, Texas. Bonnie shares my vision of seeing all the Arts restored to worship. Her poem makes a fitting end to this book. Thank you, Bonnie.

BIBLIOGRAPHY

The Abingdon Bible Commentary. New York, NY, and Nashville, TN: The Abingdon Press, Inc., 1929.

Allen, Ronald, *Lord of Song,* Portland, OR: Multnomah Press, 1982.

Allen, Ronald and Gordon Borror, *Worship; Rediscovering the Missing Jewel,* Portland, OR: Multnomah Press, 1982.

Alsobrook, David, *True Worship,* Paducah, KY: Anointed Bible Study Fellowship, Inc., 1983.

Baker, Dr. E. Charlotte, *On Eagle's Wings,* Seattle, WA, 1979.

_____, *The Eye of the Needle and Other Prophetic Parables,* Hagerstown, MD: Parable Publications, 1997.

Barclay, William, *The Letters to the Philippians, Colossians and Thessalonians,* Philadelphia, PA: The Westminster Press, 1975.

Bartlett, John, *Bartlett's Familiar Quotations,* 15th ed., Little, Boston, MS: Brown and Company, 1980.

Bay, William, *The Beauty of Worship,* Pacific, MO: Mel Bay Publications, 1984.

Bellinger, W. H. Jr., *Psalms: Reading and Studying the Book of Praises,* Peabody, MA: Hendrickson Publishers, Inc., 1990.

Billheimer, Paul E. *Destined for the Throne,* Ft. Washington, Pa: Christian Literature Crusade, 1975.

Blomgren, David K., Douglas Christoffel, and Dean Smith, *Restoring Praise and Worship to the Church—An Anthology of Articles,* Shippensburg, PA: Revival Press, 1989.

Blomgren, David K., *The Song of the Lord*, Portland, OR: Bible Temple Publications, 1978.

Bonner, Mickey, *Brokenness, the Forgotten Factor of Prayer*, Houston, TX: Mickey Bonner Evangelistic Association, 1994.

Boschman, LaMar, *A Heart of Worship*. Orlando, FL: Creation House, 1994.

————, *The Prophetic Song*, Bedford, TX: Revival Press, 1986.

————, *The Rebirth of Music*, Shippensburg, PA: Destiny Image Publication, 1986.

Bromiley, Geoffrey W., General Editor, *The International Standard Bible Encyclopedia*, Volumes One—Four, Grand Rapids, MI: William B. Eerdmans Publishing Company, 1986.

Buttrick, George Arthur, *The Interpreter's Dictionary of the Bible. An Illustrated Encyclopedia*, Nashville, TN: Abingdon Press, 1986.

Clarke, Adam, *The New Testament of our Lord and Saviour Jesus Christ*, Volume Five, Nashville, TN: Abingdon, from text written C. 1624.

Conner, Kevin J., *The Tabernacle of David*, Portland, OR: Bible Temple Publishing, 1976.

Cornill, Carl Heinrich, *Music in the Old Testament*, Chicago, Chicago, IL: The Open Court Publishing Company, 1909.

Cornwall, Judson, *David Worshiped a Living God*, Shippensburg, PA: Revival Press, 1989.

————, *David Worshiped With a Fervent Faith*, Shippensburg, PA: Revival Press, 1993.

————, *Elements of Worship*, South Plainfield, NJ, Bridge Publishing, Inc., 1985.

————, *Let Us Draw Near*, Plainfield, NJ: Logos International, 1977.

————, *Let Us Praise*, Plainfield, NJ: Logos International, 1973

_____, *Let Us Worship,* South Plainfield, NJ: Bridge Publishing, 1983.

_____, *Meeting God,* Altamonte Springs, FL: Creation House, 1987.

_____, *Worship as David Lived It,* Shippensburg, PA: Revival Press, 1990.

_____, *Worship as Jesus Taught It,* Tulsa, OK: Victory House Publishers, 1987.

Craigie, Peter C., *Word Biblical Commentary,* Waco, TX: Word Books, 1983.

Foster, Glen, *Victory Liberty Jubilee,* Dubuque, IA: Kendall/Hunt Publishing, 1989.

Foster, Richard J., and James Bryan Smith, editors, *Devotional Classics,* San Francisco, CA: Harper, 1993.

Foster, Richard J., *Celebration of Discipline,* revised edition, San Francisco, CA: Harper, 1988.

_____, *Prayer. Finding the Heart's True Home,* San Francisco, CA: Harper, 1992.

Garmo, John, *Lifestyle Worship,* Nashville, TN: Thomas Nelson Publishers, 1993.

Gesenius, William, *Gesenius' Hebrew and Chaldee Lexicon to the Old Testament Scriptures,* trans. by Samuel P. Tregelles, Grand Rapids, IA: Eerdmans, 1976.

Grauman, Helen G., *Music in My Bible,* Mountain View, CA: Pacific Press Publishing Association, 1956.

Guyon, Jeanne, *Experiencing the Depths of Jesus Christ,* Goleta, CA: Christian Books, 1983.

Hayford, Jack W., *Moments with Majesty,* Portland, OR: Multnomah Press, 1990.

_____, *Worship His Majesty,* Waco, TX: Word Books, 1987.

Henry, Matthew, *Commentary on the Whole Bible,* 4th ed., USA: Hendrickson Publishers, 1985.

_____, Jamieson/Fausset/Brown, and Adam Clarke, *The Bethany Parallel Commentary on the New Testament*, Minneapolis, MN: Bethany House Publishers, 1983.

_____, *The Bethany Parallel Commentary on the Old Testament*, Minneapolis, MN: Bethany House Publishers, 1985.

Hibbert, Mike, and Vivien Hibbert, *Music Ministry*, Christchurch, New Zealand, 1982.

Hill, Andrew E., *Enter His Courts With Praise!*, Grand Rapids, MI: Baker Books, 1985.

Jacobs, Cindy, *The Voice of God*, Ventura, CA: Regal Books, 1995.

The Jerome Biblical Commentary, Englewood Cliffs, NJ: Prentice-Hall Inc., 1968.

Joyner, Rick, *The Harvest*. Volume Two, Charlotte, NC: Morning Star Publications, 1994.

Kempis, Thomas à, *Of the Imitation of Christ*, Springdale, PA: Whitaker House, 1981.

Kendrick, Graham, *Learning to Worship as a Way of Life*, Minneapolis, MN: Bethany House Publications, 1984.

_____, *Worship*, Sussex, Great Britain: Kingsway Publications Ltd., 1984.

Kraeuter, Tom, *Developing an Effective Worship Ministry*, Hillsboro, MO: Training Resources, 1993.

Law, Terry, *The Power of Praise and Worship*, Tulsa, OK: Victory House Publishers, 1985.

Lockyer, Herbert, *All the 3s of the Bible*, Grand Rapids, MI: Fleming H. Revell, 1973.

Le'au, Sosene, *Called to Honor Him*. Tampa, FL: Culture Com Press, Inc., 1997.

Martin, Ralph P., *The Worship of God*, Grand Rapids, MI: Eerdmans, 1982.

_____, *Worship in the Early Church*, Grand Rapids, MI: Eerdmans, 1974.

Morris, William, Editor in Chief, *Young Students Intermediate Dictionary*, Middletown, CT: Field Publications, 1973.

Morgenthaler, Sally, *Worship Evangelism*, Grand Rapids, MI: Zondervan Publishing House, 1995.

Nelson, Alan E., *Broken in the Right Places. How God Tames the Soul*, Nashville, TN: Thomas Nelson Publishers, 1994.

Newport, John P., *Nineteenth Century Devotional Thought*, Nashville, TN: Broadman Press, 1981.

Peterson, David, *Engaging With God—A Biblical Theology of Worship*, Grand Rapids, MI: Wm. B. Eerdmans Publishing Co., 1992.

Peterson, Eugene, H., *The Message*, Colorado Springs, CO: Alive Communications, 1993.

Pettis, Ashley, *Music: Now and Then*, New York, NY: Coleman-Ross Company, Inc., 1955.

Roberts, Debby, *Rejoice: A Biblical Study of the Dance*, Little Rock, AR: Revival Press, 1982.

Sarchet-Waller, Paul, *Praise and Worship*, Hong Kong: Elim Full Gospel Publications, 1986.

Sendry, Mildred, and Alfred N., *David's Harp*, New York, NY: Philosophical Library, 1969.

Sendry, Alfred, *Music in Ancient Israel*, New York, NY: Philosophical Library, 1969.

Simcox, Carroll E., *A Treasury of Quotations on Christian Themes*, New York, NY: The Seabury Press, 1975.

Sheets, Dutch, *Intercessory Prayer,* Ventura, CA: Regal Books, 1996.

Sorge, Bob, *Exploring Worship: A Practical guide to Praise and Worship,* New Wilmington, PA: Son-Rise Publication, 1987.

Spurgeon, Charles H., *Evening by Evening,* Pittsburgh, PA: Whitaker House, 1984.

_____, *The Treasury of David,* Vols. 1 & 2. MI: Byron Center, Associated Publishers and Authors, Inc., reprinted 1970.

Stevenson, John W., *The 2nd Flood,* Shippensburg, PA: Destiny Image Publishers, 1990.

Strong, James, *The Exhaustive Concordance of the Bible,* Grand Rapids, MI: Baker Book House, 1980.

_____, *The New Strong's Complete Dictionary of Bible Words,* Nashville, TN: Thomas Nelson Publishers, 1996.

Tame, David, *The Secret Power of Music,* New York, NY: Destiny Books, 1984.

Tenney, Merrill C., *The Zondervan Pictorial Encyclopedia of the Bible,* Grand Rapids, MI: Zondervan Corporation, 1976.

Tippit, Sammy, *Worthy of Worship,* Chicago, IL: The Moody Bible Institute, 1989.

Tomkins, Iverna, *If It Please the King,* Decatur, GA: Iverna Tomkins Ministry, no date.

_____, *The Ravished Heart,* Decatur, GA: Iverna Tomkins Ministry, no date.

Tozer, A. W., *The Pursuit of God,* Camp Hill, PA: Christian Publications, 1993.

_____, *Signposts,* Compiled by Harry Verploegh, Wheaton, IL: Victor Books, 1988.

Truscott, Graham, *The Power of His Presence,* Burbank, CA: World Map, 1972.

Unger, Merrill F., *Unger's Bible Dictionary,* Chicago, IL: Moody Press, 1966.

Vine, W. E., Merrill F. Unger, and William White, Jr., *Vine's Complete Expository Dictionary of Old and New Testament Words,* Nashville, TN: Thomas Nelson, Inc., 1985.

Vine, W. E., *An Expository Dictionary of New Testament Words,* Westwood, NJ: Fleming H. Revell Co., 1940.

Vasarai, Giorgio, *The Great Masters,* Translated by Gaston Du C. de Vere, edited by Michael Sonino, Hong Kong: Hugh Lauter Levin Associates, Inc. 1986.

Venolia, Jan, *Write Right!,* third edition, Berkeley, CA: Ten Speed Press, 1995

Wilson-Dickson, *The Story of Christian Music,* original ed., Oxford, England: Lion Publishing, 1992. This ed., Minneapolis, MN: Fortress Press, 1996.

Webber, Robert E., ed., *The Complete Library of Christian Worship,* Volumes One to Seven, Nashville, TN: Star Song Publishing Group, 1993.

_____, *Worship Old and New,* Grand Rapids, MI: Zondervan Publishing Co., 1982.

Wiersbe, Warren W., *Classic Sermons on Worship,* Grand Rapids, MI: Hendrickson Publishers, Inc., 1988.

Wiley, Lulu Rumsey, *Bible Music,* New York, NY: The Paebar Company, 1945.

Yancey, Philip, *Reality and the Vision,* Dallas, TX: Word Publishing, 1990.

ABOUT THE AUTHOR

꒰ꔷ

VIVIEN HIBBERT, originally from New Zealand, began full-time ministry in 1977 as a teacher of praise and worship. In addition to her teaching skills, God has given her a unique ability to lead Christians—from every culture and every denominational background—into a deeper experience of worship and of the presence of God.

For more than twenty-five years she has traveled to many nations ministering in churches and conferences as well as on television and radio, in prisons, hospitals, schools, and missions/youth training centers.

Over the past several years, Vivien has produced a variety of teaching tapes, worship tapes and a practical manual on praise and worship—entitled *Music Ministry*—which is often used in her seminars. She is a faculty member of the International Worship Symposium, the International Worship Leaders' Institute, which sponsors annual worship conferences throughout the world, and has consulted with Promise Keepers in developing a strategy for cross-cultural worship. Vivien is also a frequent instructor with Youth With A Mission D.T.S. and Schools of Worship world-wide.

Though Vivien served for a number of years as a Minister of Worship at Shady Grove Church—a long-time center for the worship renewal movement—God has opened the door to establish *The Worship Arts Conservatory*, (www.worshiparts.org) an online school for worship artists, where singers, instrumentalists, dancers and artists of every kind may be trained to use their talents and giftings in worship. It is her goal to mentor and equip students to become vessels for releasing the power and presence of God into the earth.

In addition to her duties at *The Worship Arts Conservatory*, Vivien continues to travel and minister internationally and throughout the USA. Vivien and her family currently reside in Northern California.

www.vivienhibbert.org
www.worshiparts.org

THE WORSHIP ARTS CONSERVATORY

WWW.WORSHIPARTS.ORG

The Worship Arts Conservatory was commissioned in 1999 as an on-line school to aid worship ministers and Christian artists in the pursuit of a deeper knowledge of God while learning to use their art for His glory. We draw our expert faculty from local churches as well as from internationally renowned ministries to provide the specific training needed.

Founder and President Vivien Hibbert brings over twenty-five years of practical experience in the field of Worship Arts to our program and her leadership ensures that both our mission and values are articulated and transmitted to all constituencies.

Our current program offerings include our Associate of Worship Arts (A.W.A.) degree program and the Independent Study program. Course titles include: Worship Leading; Theology of the Psalms; Engaging Youth in Worship; Biblical Basis for Art; Fine Arts Vision & Administration; Prophetic Song; Prophetic Worship; Foundations for Leadership; Ministry Ethics; Theology of Worship; and many others.*

If you are interested in learning more about The Worship Arts Conservatory please email or write to:

The Worship Arts Conservatory
P.O. Box 2317
Woodland, CA 95776-2317

info@worshiparts.org

Visit our bookstore for Vivien Hibbert's book, *Praise Him*, her instrumental CD, *Shepherd's Suite*, and a variety of Native American flutes: www.worshiparts.org/html/wacshop.html

*Course Chart, Syllabi and Catalogue information is available online at www.worshiparts.org

INTRODUCING VIVIEN HIBBERT'S LATEST WORK:

PRAISE HIM

*This book is an excellent resource that will
expand your personal devotional and praise life!*

Vivien Hibbert, in her compellingly sweet and simple treatise, **Praise Him**, calls all Believers to live lives of praise in the midst of every trial and circumstance, during good times and bad. May your heart join the praise song of Charles Spurgeon: *Among all the joys of earth, and I shall not depreciate them, there is no joy comparable to that of praise...the purest and most exhilarating joy is the delight of glorifying God!*

Hibbert's latest book is a devotional look at all the reasons, places, ways and occasions to praise the Lord. It is her hope that **Praise Him** will become an excellent resource for worship leaders, songwriters, poets, prophetic artists of every kind, and worshipers from any denomination.

Let this book draw you ever nearer to the One who is worthy of all praise and adoration, extending the boundaries of your life to include songs of praise that are tested and proven by the immeasurable love, grace and mercy of our Lord.

If you are interested in learning more about *Praise Him* please email or write to:

The Worship Arts Conservatory
P.O. Box 2317
Woodland, CA 95776-2317
info@worshiparts.org

Visit our bookstore for Vivien Hibbert's book, *Praise Him*, her instrumental CD, *Shepherd's Suite*, and a variety of Native American flutes: www.worshiparts.org/html/wacshop.html